A Cord of Three Strands

A Cord of Three Strands

A New Approach to Parent Engagement in Schools

Soo Hong

Harvard Education Press
Cambridge, Massachusetts

Library of Congress Control Number 2010942136

Paperback ISBN 978-1-934742-54-9
Library Edition ISBN 978-1-934742-82-2

Published by Harvard Education Press,
an imprint of the Harvard Education Publishing Group

Harvard Education Press
8 Story Street
Cambridge, MA 02138

Cover Design: Sarah Henderson

The typefaces used in this book are Bembo and Scala Sans.

7478547

To Edwin
For the love and hope that makes all things possible

To Lauren and Christopher
For teaching me the joy and meaning of parenting

CONTENTS

ACKNOWLEDGMENTS

Behind every book is a story that shapes its inception. This book is bound together by the many students and their families who have shaped the teacher I have become. They are the families who have welcomed me into their homes; shared their hopes, dreams, and concerns for their children with me; challenged me to do better; and essentially entrusted their children in my care. My early ideas about families and schools were profoundly shaped by their willingness to get to know me and to share themselves and their families with me.

This book has been shaped and influenced by the dedication of numerous groups and individuals. Without the generous support of the Harvard University Achievement Gap Initiative, David Rockefeller Center for Latin American Studies, the Spencer Foundation Research Training Grant, and the Harvard Graduate School of Education, the extensive travel and data collection for this multiyear project would not have been possible. This study was also part of a larger research project, the Community Organizing and School Reform Project, led by Mark Warren and Karen Mapp of Harvard University. Generous funders from that project allowed me to pursue this research project more fully: Ford Foundation, Charles Stewart Mott Foundation, Edward W. Hazen Foundation, Spencer Foundation, the Carnegie Corporation of New York, and the Center for American Political Studies at Harvard University.

While this book is rooted in practical purposes, it is also a product of intellectual inquiry and conversation that was nourished and supported by key mentors. Mark Warren, Sara Lawrence-Lightfoot, and Richard Elmore were discerning readers, enthusiastic supporters, and generous contributors to a constantly evolving discussion on parent engagement. Their insight and questions have shaped every part of this project.

From the beginning of this research journey, Mark Warren has been a constant source of support, encouragement, and inspiration. Over the years, he has been a masterful mentor, taking every opportunity to support my ideas, push my thinking, and nurture my development as a budding researcher. As I seek to strike the ever-challenging balances between work and family, research and teaching, and scholarship and practice, he has been a model. He has taught me that these elements are not conflicting binaries but complementary forces. In nurturing one force, we develop the other. In many ways, his mentoring has shaped the researcher-teacher, mother-student, and scholar-practitioner that I am today. I am grateful to him for the joy, pleasure, growth, and satisfaction that have defined my research journey.

Research is often a solitary endeavor, and we must sometimes find ways to connect our work to other projects and voices. Over the past three years, I have been part of a research community—a doctoral research seminar on education organizing—that has strengthened my emerging analysis and provided me with the collegial support and collaboration of like-minded researchers. Led by Mark Warren and Karen Mapp, the seminar has been an invaluable opportunity for me to understand the work of the Logan Square Neighborhood Association (LSNA) within the context of other similar successful groups around the country. Generous funding from this project allowed me to collect data for another year of the project, adding depth and richness to the narrative. Conversations and discussions with past and present doctoral students in the group—Keith Catone, Roy Cervantes, Tiffany Cheng, Connie Chung, Sarah Dryden-Peterson, Cynthia Gordon, Ann Ishimaru, Zenub Kakli, Paul Kuttner, Sky Marietta, Meredith Mira, Thomas Nikundiwe, Soojin Oh, Carolyn Rubin, Kenneth Russell, Dulari Tahbildar, Amanda Taylor, Mara Tieken, Kerry Venegas, Anita Wadwha, and Helen Westmoreland—have not only shaped the development of my own ideas but also made me feel part of a community that is collectively concerned about organizing, social justice, and community transformation. I am especially thankful to Mark and Karen for their leadership throughout the project and their sharing with me the individual opportunities to question, discuss, and write.

These opportunities strengthened my analysis and led me to the findings I present in this book.

I thank my gracious editor, Caroline Chauncey, for her insightful wisdom in shaping the final form of the book. She brought clarity to a process and product that sometimes seemed to defy resolution. Ashley Paquin provided razor-sharp research assistance in the last leg of the project. I also thank Paul Kuttner of Kuttner Designs for providing visual images that make concepts come alive. Maria Isabel Hernandez and Maria Tagle provided excellent assistance in translating and transcribing the Spanish-language portions of the data collection; their work gave voice to many parents who may have otherwise been overlooked.

Throughout every step of this research project, colleagues and friends have given me feedback on this book—by questioning my assumptions, affirming the findings, and providing critical perspectives that shaped the direction of the book. I am indebted to their commitment to this project and the time and attention they have given to the best interests of this book. I thank them immensely: Barbara Beatty, Joanna Brown, Ilene Carver, Sarah Dryden-Peterson, Anne Henderson, Karen Mapp, Priya Nalkur, and Carolyn Rubin.

Years ago, when I learned about LSNA, I was moved by its stories of change, empowerment, and hope. Throughout my experience as a teacher, I never encountered the work of community organizing groups involved in education, yet I remained steadfastly committed to schools as sites for social change. Upon learning about LSNA's work with parents, I, like many other groups and individuals across the country who encounter its story, felt inspired and compelled to learn more. I thank Nancy Aardema, LSNA's executive director, Joanna Brown, LSNA's lead education organizer, as well as the team of education organizers and parent leaders who welcomed me to the school sites and introduced me to the countless parents, students, teachers, and other individuals who form the collective voice in this book. In particular, I am grateful to Leticia Barrera, Bridget Murphy, Ofelia Sanchez, and Reynalda Covarrubias. I have been profoundly touched and inspired by the organization's clear vision and remarkable success. Across the organization and across the school sites, I have been met with a willingness to share the triumphs, struggles, and questions that are deeply embedded in this kind of community work. In particular, I am indebted to those parents, organizers, and school staff at Funston Elementary School who taught me, in more intimate detail, how truly powerful and inspiring parents can be.

This is a book about families, and quite fittingly, this project has been a family endeavor. My daughter Lauren, born during the early planning stages of this project, opened my eyes to the world of parenting. Each encounter in the field was shaped by my newfound role as mother. My son Christopher, whose first smile, first laugh, first crawl, and first sounds became defining moments and rays of light during the writing, sustained me through a time of thinking, writing, rethinking, and rewriting. While my children have been and continue to be a source of inspiration and joy—fueling my personal and professional endeavors—my mother, Young Hong, is the solid rock and foundation who made this all possible. My brother Warren, who often plays the multiple roles of friend, confidant, and ardent supporter, has provided me with rich conversation and discussion that always leads me to think and dream bigger. And with Erin, I look forward to many more conversations about our twin interests in youth and families.

In many ways, this was also a journey in faith. For a project that spanned five years of planning, travel, fieldwork, and writing, I often had to believe in something that was not yet formed or realized. Before the words were written and the pages complete, I had the enduring faith of two who never wavered in their confidence in me. My husband, Edwin, by celebrating every achievement and accomplishment along the way, lifted my spirits and carried me through a long, sometimes lonely journey. His love for me, his enthusiasm for my work, and his discerning questions were a constant source of inspiration, encouragement, and rich discussion. Waiting at every airline gate, listening during every midnight call from Chicago, poring over every written word, he was steadfast in his faith that this story was one worth telling and one that he, too, committed himself to. In doing so, he carries on a role originally fulfilled by my late father, Choon Hong, my first and enduring supporter and a constant source of inspiration and encouragement. From my earliest memories of accomplishment, he was there, waving the award energetically in his hands, framing the artwork on the wall, writing a note to congratulate, and tucking my prize essays into his briefcase. This book is a story that celebrates parents like him—a tireless advocate for the deep connections between schools, communities, and families, an immigrant who found ways to cherish the past and embrace the future, an educator focused on the broader definitions of education, and a father finding ways to navigate the worlds of school and community.

FOREWORD

Among the problems contributing to the failure of so many urban schools are not only an unjust political economy, but an educational culture that too often disrespects children, parents, and communities. In Newark's Marcy School, the site of long-term observations recorded in my 1997 book *Ghetto Schooling*, district policies and educator behavior belittled students and parents—and a wary distance characterized school-community relationships. *Ghetto Schooling* offered a number of strategies for improving the political economy in order to increase economic and educational opportunities in Newark. At that time, however, the means to change the school culture—to provide concrete suggestions for how we might alter educators' habits of mind and action long in the making—were not available. With the publication of *A Cord of Three Strands*, Soo Hong at last offers us a remedy.

Hong's book draws on the work involved in a Chicago community's twenty-year effort to improve education in the local schools. During a time when the attempt to improve educational achievement has typically taken the form of school closure, student displacement, and the shift of control to private financial backers, this community in Chicago—and the organizing group representing it—discovered that a powerful tool for increasing achievement was improvement in the school culture. They found that to energize students and teachers fully to the education process it was necessary to engage parents and other members of the community as *partners*. In the Logan Square neighborhood that the book describes, parents and families were ultimately welcomed into the schools not only as volunteers, but as engaged equals—and ultimately as partners in creating change. With parents and other community members fully engaged in daily life in the school, the interactions, the expectations, the attitudes, and the mores guiding educator and student behavior changed over time from disaffection and disregard to a culture marked by care, respect, and trust. As the school culture became more nurturing, student academic achievement grew. This book, as the author states, "is a call to action for practitioners, policy makers, and researchers alike—to recast a new vision for parent and community engagement in schools."

At the core of the work to improve the culture in these Chicago neighborhood schools was the Parent Mentor program. Begun in 1995, the program has prepared more than one thousand parents across eight schools to work in classrooms with teachers. The program has a leadership-development component, which serves as a foundation for parent engagement as community and school leaders. Fifty-six of the parents have entered the Grow Your Own Teachers preparation program, and this program has become the model for a statewide initiative that has launched similar programs across Illinois. The Parent Mentor program and the Grow Your Own Teachers program are both well-known in community organizing reform circles. What Hong vitally contributes is an in-depth examination of how these programs worked to change the school culture. Most parents in the community's schools were immigrants, often with very little formal education, and thus were unprepared to take leadership in local affairs in the United States. Hong documents how the parents and the schools built a culture that supported both parent and student growth.

One of the important characteristics of *A Cord of Three Strands* is its multilayered ethnographic methodology. Hong insists, and rightly so, that schools are embedded in a number of systems—districts, neighborhoods, cities, political economies, and cultures of various constituent groups. To fully understand schools, then, we need to study this embeddedness. Hong achieves this by extending traditional ethnography to incorporate the different levels.

In accord with her systems approach, Hong characterizes the development of parent engagement as an ecological process involving three stages. The first, *induction*, comes about as parents are introduced to the complex world of schools and as educators come to understand and value the histories, narratives, and assets parents bring. *Integration*, the second stage, occurs as parents develop an identity as part of the school collective, working together with educators and students for positive changes. And the third phase, *investment*, emerges when leaders surface from among the parent group and begin to see themselves as central figures and leaders in a school.

Clearly, processes that successfully promote the development of low-income, urban parents of color as equal partners in the school their children attend are very rare. What generated the appreciation of these parents and the assets they presented, and what encouraged a collective sense of working for change in the schools Hong describes, was largely a result of the long-term work of community organizing, particularly by the group on which she focuses, the Logan Square Neighborhood Association (LSNA).

We are accustomed to thinking about community organizing for school reform as involving protest, public conflict, and confrontation with district leaders. What characterized LSNA's approach, however, was that its activity went beyond protestation. While public protest is—and was, in this case—necessary to obtain the attention of politicians and administrators, it is the cooperation that follows that can create and sustain change. LSNA worked closely with both educator and parent groups. For example, organizers held weekly training sessions within schools and monthly training sessions across schools in the community to encourage the development of a rich social network where, as Hong states, "parents could find support, develop a greater awareness about the school community, and maintain ties of friendship and collegiality that draw them into the school community in more lasting ways."

I have long argued that it is unlikely that significant improvement in urban schools can be sustained without increased opportunities in the political economy for both student graduates and families. Hong demonstrates in this important book that significant change in schools may be dependent upon change that is *cultural* as well.

Jean Anyon, PhD
Professor of social and educational policy
Doctoral Program in Urban Education
Graduate Center, City University of New York

INTRODUCTION

Jade is a documentary filmmaker. In recent years, she has begun working with school districts and teachers to support the educational use of documentary films in the classroom.[1] As a workshop trainer, she often finds herself in the reception area of schools—a busy hub of activity where the phone rings, overhead announcements are made, teachers come to collect their mail or messages, and students walk into and out of a principal's office. She recalls the very first time she visited a school to give a workshop. She entered the main office, where the receptionist was currently occupied. Jade stood by a counter as the receptionist moved about the room organizing paperwork. After a few minutes and without any eye contact or greeting from the receptionist, Jade noticed a sign-in sheet and promptly signed herself in to follow what she gathered might have been the formal procedure for the reception area. To her dismay, she stood waiting for another five minutes for a response or reception, after which point she finally interrupted the receptionist for her attention. Indeed, it was now almost time for her workshop. Upon introducing herself and the nature of her visit to the receptionist after this period of idle waiting, the receptionist quickly excused the delayed response by saying, "I'm sorry, I thought you were a parent."

Jade's story is not unusual. Across the country, stories speak to the fractured or distant relationship between schools and communities. In Jade's example, we see a school that has become accustomed to brushing parents aside and turning instead to the "real" business of running schools—keeping schedules, filing the proper paperwork, submitting grades—in effect, managing the bureaucracy of schools. In this environment, a parent's interaction with the school is minimal, likely reduced to the daily rituals of dropping off and picking up children in the schoolyard. When parents are discouraged (or, in some cases, barred) from entering main offices or front hallways, this often indicates a broader school culture that keeps parents and families at a distance that feels safe and comfortable to school staff and administrators.

Then there are schools like McAuliffe Elementary School on Chicago's Northwest Side. *Sophia* is a mother of two children who attend the school. When her son first started school, her encounters with McAuliffe were limited to dropping him off and picking him up each day. She was not familiar with the school, and other mothers told her stories of negative encounters with school staff. The general sentiment was that parents were not welcome inside the school. As a result, Sophia never spent time inside her son's school. However, over time, through the arrival of a new principal and the development of new school-based programs and activities for parents, the climate has changed. She describes a main office where the receptionists often know the parents by name, where the principal's door is almost always open, and where parents move freely in and out as they go about their activities in the school. In fact, when I first visited McAuliffe one afternoon, I was greeted by a woman working in the main office. To see if she could assist me, I asked if she was the school receptionist, to which she replied, "No, I'm a parent, but I'm pretty sure I can help you. What do you need?"

Stories like these speak to the wide variety in how relationships between schools and families are negotiated. The experiences of parents and community members like Jade and Sophia capture the necessity in creating a movement for change in schools and communities, particularly in low-income communities of color, where issues of race, class, culture, and power influence the dynamics between families and schools. How do we begin to mend the relationship between schools and families? By examining the experiences of parents like Sophia— how they navigate the institution of school, manage relationships with school staff, and define their experiences in schools—we can better understand how schools and communities must change to become places that work productively and in partnership with parents. But the experiences of Jade and Sophia underscore the persistent pattern of distrust and distance that frames the interactions between many schools and families.

In my own early years as a teacher in a diverse, urban school, while I felt increasingly confident in my abilities to develop curriculum and manage classrooms, I felt inadequately prepared to interact with families. I had an overwhelming impulse to reach out to families in the traditional ways I had experienced and seen growing up in U.S. schools—through open houses, parent-teacher conferences, and classroom volunteers. These strategies turned up a few wonderful parents who would support me in and out of the classroom—preparing materials for the next day, displaying student work in the classroom, and helping to coordinate and plan local field trips. But I wondered about the rest of the parents—those who spoke languages other than English, those who never returned my calls, those who were seldom present in the school. My own inability to think outside the box when reaching parents surprised and concerned me. Even as a novice classroom teacher, I could see that to reach my students successfully in the classroom and to build their success as individual learners, I had to make connections that were more meaningful to their lives outside my classroom. It mattered when *Terry's* family became homeless, when *Mark's* father struggled with alcoholism, when my students came to school hungry, and when parents had not completed high school. Indeed, it was my responsibility to find better ways to interact with parents. I began including my students in my conferences with their parents and using the conversation as an opportunity to hear and listen rather than to tell and report. I visited their homes if parents could not come to the school, went to libraries and churches in the community with my students and their families, and included their family narratives and experiences in our classroom learning. Over the years, as I built relationships with families and came to understand their experiences, I added to and revised my repertoire of strategies to engage families.

Admittedly, my strategies and ideas were not perfect, and over the course of different teaching assignments, my years as a graduate student and researcher, and now as a parent, these ideas have evolved. During my years as a teacher, I sought the ideas and wisdom of those around me within the school—fellow teachers, a guidance counselor, a librarian, a social worker, the principal. Through these conversations,

I learned the most from individuals who had personal connections to the community. From *May*, a white teacher who lived in the school's neighborhood; *Jean*, an African American librarian who was closely connected to many of the families of color within the school; and *Amelia*, the Latina social worker who visited the homes of Spanish-speaking families who were struggling with family and school issues, I learned immensely about the importance of meaningful ties to families and the broader community.[2] For the vast majority of teachers, however, these meaningful ties did not exist, and it often left me wondering what schools were to do when they were not equipped with the resources to reach out to families.

This book is founded on that premise—that schools have much to learn about the families and communities they serve and that they stand to gain clarity and greater understanding from those individuals and groups that are closely connected to the lives and experiences of those communities. This book is the story of one community's quest to change the very nature of relationships between families and schools. In the midst of a school reform era that seeks to make drastic changes, build new schools, rebuild failing ones, and radically turn around existing practices, this book is a call to action for practitioners, policy makers, and researchers alike—to recast a new vision for parent and community engagement in schools. In response to the strong pull of tradition and the vital need for community expertise, I chose to explore the role of one community organizing group, the Logan Square Neighborhood Association (LSNA), and its efforts to identify new ways to engage families and schools.

WHY COMMUNITY ORGANIZING?

For the schools and teachers that, like me, have struggled to move beyond the more traditional school-family relationship, community organizing groups can offer compelling narratives for school and community transformation. By their very nature, community organizing efforts seek to build a constituency of individuals who develop common goals in demanding change, holding institutions or officials accountable. These efforts seek to put an end to long histories of problematic practices that have become institutionalized. The persistent inequality in urban schools and the lack of shared power and authority among families and schools demand a school-reform approach that will seek to radically transform the nature of relationships between schools and communities. While many parents may struggle individually when facing issues with schools, through community organizing, they can be connected to other parents with similar experiences and band together to make their voices heard.

The confrontational side of community organizing is certainly the more familiar image to most. While these tactics can be useful in demanding the kinds of changes desired, a mere emphasis on these popularized images—sit-ins, rallies, public protests—fails to realize an equally important aspect of community organizing. These public displays are often acts of resistance to the oppressive nature of institutions and individuals that perpetuate inequality in cities and towns across the country. And while the public eye may often only see the glossy pictures of conflict and confrontation shared across media outlets, the careful and patient work of relationship building and leadership development often forms the basis for any campaign. Understanding both dimensions of community organizing—relationships and power—will be fundamental to realizing the contributions of the field as it undergoes recent growth. Estimates from 2009 project that over five hundred organizing groups are working on public education issues in urban areas alone.[3]

The expert attention to relationship building and power will be especially valuable to challenges in building parent and community engagement. While schools may be limited in their understanding of family and community experiences, community organizing groups are intimately connected to the individuals and groups they work with. Staffed by organizers who may have shared language, cultures, and experiences with the community, organizing groups are well equipped to communicate with parents and develop a clear sense of parents' perspectives and the situations that affect families. By working on broad-based community issues such as affordable housing, immigration reform, health care, and safety, these groups bring a much-needed holistic view to educational issues. As one parent organizer in Chicago put it, "Life doesn't happen in these neat arrangements and categories. Whether I have a job, fear being evicted from my home, feel unsafe on my street—that will shape how my child shows up at school."

THE LOGAN SQUARE NEIGHBORHOOD ASSOCIATION

Through an exploration of community organizing efforts that build parent participation and leadership, this book seeks to address the challenges schools face in building family engagement. By examining a successful case, we can begin to identify the processes that may be fundamental to building effective forms of parent engagement.

When I first came upon the work of the Logan Square Neighborhood Association (LSNA), I was struck by the organization's ability to do what seemed impossible in other places. In schools that had struggled to meet the needs of immigrant, low-income students who often were not fluent in English, parents had begun to become forceful advocates for much-needed changes. In communities that had struggled with animosity, distrust, and misunderstanding between families and schools, parents were working together with school staff to identify common goals and support students. In those communities that would be commonly labeled as hard to reach, parents were present at school functions, worked alongside teachers in classrooms, and were tutoring students in the hallway. What could we learn from this organizing group? Could an exploration of its practices lead us toward some fresh new understanding about parent engagement?

This is precisely the question that this book seeks to answer. This book presents a rare, in-depth account of LSNA's success as an exemplary model in driving educational change at the community and state levels.[4] Based in Chicago's Northwest Side community of Logan Square, LSNA has, for almost two decades, been involved in building parent participation and leadership in local schools. At the core of its work in schools is the Parent Mentor program. Started in 1995, the program has trained over thirteen hundred parents across eight schools to work in classrooms with teachers and to support student learning.

Every parent mentor devotes more than one hundred hours each year to a teacher's classroom, building connections with teachers and students. Using a model for leadership development, the program serves as a first step for parent participation in schools and for long-term engagement as parent leaders. From this, LSNA created five school-based community learning centers that offer programming for adults (e.g., General Educational Development [GED] and English as a second language [ESL] classes) and children (homework support, folk dancing, and book clubs) after school four days each week. The community centers are staffed and coordinated by parent leaders. Parents have also gone on to work in the AmeriCorps-sponsored Parent Tutor program, where parents work individually with students who need additional academic support. And parents who develop an interest and passion for teaching can enroll in a bilingual teaching degree program organized by LSNA. The Grow Your Own Teachers program was the model for a statewide initiative that has launched similar programs across Illinois. Fifty-six LSNA parents are enrolled in this degree program, and five candidates have already become teachers. These remarkable accomplishments have served as the basis for local and state initiatives. LSNA's work has generated national discussions on community organizing for school reform, helped launch a community schools initiative in Chicago, and been the subject of numerous research projects and reports.[5]

In fact, within Chicago and across the country, other school and community groups have sought out LSNA's education work, in particular, its Parent Mentor program, as a potential model. Various cities and towns that struggle to engage families in schools and seek to explore nontraditional strategies for developing parent participation have looked toward LSNA's example. While many education organizing efforts and campaigns promote broad-based policy changes at the state or district level, LSNA's work with parents seeks to change the culture of individual schools and classrooms. Changes in school culture are some of the most challenging to promote, because they require a change in beliefs and attitudes of individuals and often require the slow and patient work of building trust, relationships, and understanding. LSNA's work offers rare insight into these home-and-school relationships and offers solutions to communities beyond Chicago that also struggle with similar issues.

A LAYERED ETHNOGRAPHY

In its work with parents, LSNA underscores the importance of process. How do parents enter their relationships with schools? And how do they work within schools and together with school staff to create the necessary changes in home-and-school relationships? Through the yearlong Parent Mentor program, parents are given the opportunity to understand schools more clearly and to develop new and evolving ways of participating in schools. Through this experience, schools themselves—their staff and culture—can adapt and change as parents redefine their relationship with schools.

This process of change that was prompted by the Parent Mentor program became central to my study. To understand the experiences, beliefs, and narratives that drive this change, I structured the study as a multiyear ethnography. Over four years, I developed relationships with parents, community organizers, and school staff in the Logan Square neighborhood—interviewing parents, attending training sessions and leadership workshops, visiting classrooms, meeting with organizers, and walking the school hallways with parent mentors. Because the Parent Mentor program often serves as a first step for many parents who later become involved in other school and community campaigns, I also explored LSNA's many related programs and activities, such as the community learning centers, the Literacy Ambassadors program, and the statewide Grow Your Own Teachers program.

In addition to this broad view of LSNA's work across various schools and across the community, I chose one school and its group of parent mentors as a focal point of the study. This allowed me to explore the experiences of one group of parents as they began their involvement in schools, became connected to others in the school community, and understood the impact of their participation. Because parents often reflected on their personal and familial journeys and experiences throughout participation in the program, I designed this aspect of the

8

study with more care and attention to the relationships I would build with parents. From this group of parents, I chose four newly involved parent mentors whom I would follow more closely throughout the year. I interviewed these parents regularly throughout their first year of the program, observed them in their classrooms as parent mentors throughout the year, informally met with them and their families, and observed them as they participated in training sessions, workshops, and meetings. Unless otherwise stated, all quotations in the book come from interviews I conducted with these and other parents, with teachers, and with other people in the community between May 2006 and May 2010.

These multiple layers of analysis and inquiry provided a complex and rich portrait of parent participation as I began to view and understand parents' motivations, personal narratives, hopes, and goals in their journey toward parent engagement. In joining traditional ethnography and portraiture, I wanted to design a methodology that would bring attention to the relationships within the field, acknowledge my evolving relationship with participants in the study, and reflect the distinct layers of analysis. I have called this hybrid methodology *layered ethnography*. A more detailed explanation of this methodology can be found in the appendix, "A Layered Ethnography: At the Crossroads of Relationship, Theory, and Methodology."

PLAN OF THE BOOK

Chapter 1 explores the interactions between families and schools. By blending the work of scholars with the realities facing practitioners, I present the shortcomings of a more traditional model of parent involvement that we might normally see in schools. Then, I present an ecological perspective on parent engagement—a perspective shaped by the undeniable reality that schools are fundamentally shaped by families and communities. In chapter 2, we explore the narrative of LSNA and how and why the organization came to its ultimate interest in the intersection between school and community life. Through the perspectives of community organizers and parents, we also track the creation of the Parent Mentor program and the evolution of education organizing. The real-life experiences and narratives of parents are the foundation of this story. Chapter 3 provides an in-depth portrait of a group of parents who take us on a journey—to help us understand their motivations, experiences, and perspectives in the Parent Mentor program. Chapters 4, 5, and 6 examine the three key processes that will move us from a traditional to an ecological conception of parent engagement. In chapter 4, I recommend moving beyond the notion that parent engagement practices should be school centered or family centered, arguing instead for mutually engaging practices. Chapter 5 identifies the importance of relationship building, and chapter 6 discusses how schools can share power and leadership with parents. The conclusion finds that when schools and communities aim for the goals described in chapters 4, 5, and 6—mutual engagement, relationship building, and shared leadership and power—they can move toward an ecological conception of parent engagement and can transform schools, families, and communities. Finally, an appendix explains the methodology of research that I conducted for this book. I explore the theories of relationships that shape the design of this study and examine the central role that identity, relationships, and trust played in the research process.

1

CHALLENGING THE TRADITION

Revealing the Transformative Potential
of Parent Engagement

ON A CLEAR DAY IN APRIL, I am swept aside by an unwieldy group of fourth-graders who make their way through the school's back entrance and into the cavernous back hallway. They are the last group to enter the school building, and as they form an organized line that moves steadily up the staircase, I can hear the lingering noises of students as they move into classrooms, reach the tops of staircases, and start winding down to quiet for the start of a new school day. From my arrival at the school and as I make my way down to the new annex of the school building into a kindergarten classroom, I can feel the presence and visibility of parents in the school. Parents are in the schoolyard, lingering and talking as their children wave good-bye and join their classmates in the lines that move into the building. Parents nudge students back in line as the children become distracted by some activity on the playground. Parents patrol the sidewalks and streets surrounding the school, greeting students as they arrive and ensuring their safety from the streets to the school. Inside the school building, parents accompany students to their classrooms while greeting other parents and teachers in the hallway. These parents move swiftly through the hallways with a sense of familiarity with the space and its inhabitants. They speak in English and in Spanish, informally with children they know from the neighborhood, with authority to the students they usher down the hallways, and with collegiality toward the teachers they have come to know well.

This is a typical morning scene at Funston Elementary School, a school in Chicago I have come to know well. Parents are a visible and routine presence in the formal and informal spaces that make up the school. Later this morning, when I talk with *Gilberto*, a neighborhood resident who graduated from Funston years ago and whose four children currently attend the school, about this parental presence, he admits that it wasn't always this way:

> It used to be that you either saw families and neighborhood folks in the community and on your street or you saw teachers and principals at the school. If you told me years ago that we would see teachers in students' homes and parents in the school, I would have never believed you. It just didn't happen that way. Schools and families were just completely different worlds, and they didn't mix.

This sea change—from the isolation to the integration of families within schools—is the central concern of this book. The worlds of home and school are strangely distant in the earlier days of Gilberto's Logan Square neighborhood as well as in many present-day urban communities. However, through the collaborative efforts of parents, organizers, and school staff, families have become a visible presence in the same schools that have long struggled with parental presence and involvement. Over time, as I come to know Gilberto and other parents like him, I see his family at the school's Family Reading Night, his presence countless times at the school, his leadership in the community, and his participation with his daughter on an affordable-housing campaign. I experience some of his family's dinnertime conversations about their educational hopes and aspirations. These are his attempts to change the old culture of schools and community and to blur the boundaries between families and schools.

WORLDS APART: ENCOUNTERS BETWEEN FAMILIES AND SCHOOLS

During an earlier era at the school, everyone had his or her place in a community, Gilberto reflects. The teachers drove in from surrounding communities to teach, and they returned home to those communities at the end of the day. Children who played together on neighborhood streets were classmates at school. Parents and grandparents supervised their children in the neighborhood and dropped them off at the school door every morning. Parents knew the names of a child's teacher, but not much beyond that. In the school, there were certain events that invited families in, but for the most part, "they were in different worlds," says Gilberto. "It wasn't strange; it was simply the way it was."

The estrangement that Gilberto describes is not uncommon. Studies of school environments document the distance, tension, and antagonism between schools and families, particularly in low-income communities of color.[1] Schools and families are worlds apart—sometimes distant and estranged, often conflicting and adversarial.[2] There is great irony in this discontinuity between families and schools. Although both entities are engaged in the complementary tasks of educating and nurturing young people, they commonly find themselves in great conflict.[3] There is a presumption that parents and teachers would be natural allies, but some family-school interactions, particularly in low-income communities of color, suggest that the relationship is more adversarial. How and why does this conflict emerge?

This question can be answered in part by the very nature of parents' and teachers' roles and positions. They approach children in different ways. While teachers may approach children with a sense of formality and a focus on intellectual development, parents may view their children in more holistic and personal ways. These differing outlooks, by role and position alone, set parents and teachers on separate paths, which can ultimately end in conflict, distrust, and antagonism.[4] The relationships between teachers and parents are also shaped by their perceptions of one another. Both parents and teachers share a quiet and deeply personal desire to be seen and heard for their interactions with children, but often

instead feel misunderstood and underappreciated. This struggle for legit-
imacy, power, and appreciation creates tangible distrust between teachers
and parents and between families and schools, leading each party to approach the other defensively.[5] In an environment of distrust and misunderstanding, both teachers and parents fear criticism from one another;
in response, both groups often isolate themselves.[6]

Parents and teachers can also be haunted by past negative experiences. According to Willard Waller, parents remain in conflict with
teachers because mothers and fathers are haunted by early memories of
oppression and fear toward their own childhood teachers:

> The idealized conception tends to become a caricature, and an unpleas-
> ant and belittling caricature, because a real enmity exists between teacher
> and taught, and the memory transmutes the work of memory into irony.
> In accordance with this theory, each generation of teachers pays in turn
> for the sins of the generation that has gone before; it would require some
> decades of sensible and friendly teaching to remove the stigma from the
> occupation.[7]

Sara Lawrence-Lightfoot suggests that these "generational echoes"
are haunting to parents and teachers alike and are shaped by "their own
autobiographical stories and by the broader cultural and historical narratives that inform their identities, their values, and their sense of place in
the world."[8] Through an in-depth exploration of the relationships and interactions between teachers and parents, Lawrence-Lightfoot found that
each group's personal narratives and experiences with the other group
profoundly shaped the attitudes, perceptions, and actions of teachers and
parents alike. These formative encounters could be traced back to early
childhood interactions—from the circumstantial to the profound—that
made lasting impacts and where the wounds of injury remained fresh.
While these generational echoes are deep and penetrating (yet often
overlooked), their revelation is essential in building authentic dialogue
between parents and teachers.[9]

Ethnographic accounts such as Lawrence-Lightfoot's study of
parent-teacher interactions reveal the historical, personal, and socio-

cultural dimensions of family-school relationships. These studies explore the motivations, narratives, and experiences that shape existing relationships in schools and seek to find meaningful ways to challenge them. Authentic dialogue is critical, because when schools and families remain distant, estranged, or antagonistic, such attitudes can pose added tensions on children, who must navigate the dissonant worlds of home and school. In a classic urban study of Boston's Italian West End community, Herbert Gans found that parents often view schools as threatening, overpowering institutions that have negatively influenced their children with contradicting messages and values. Suspicious of schools that label and rank their children in ways that don't carry meaning in the community and that project differing values and priorities, parents feel that their children are being pulled away from the comfort and familiarity of their homes to the radically different structure and priorities of schools. From this perspective, for students to be successful in the larger society, they often have to leave the cohesive social networks of family and community for the complex world of work and industry.[10] Children are the ones who feel this tension between their families and their schools the most.

In a more recent study of Mexican-immigrant and Mexican American youth, Angela Valenzuela adds that schools develop "subtractive" practices and policies that demean the culture of youth and families, diminishing their net resources. In a three-year ethnography of a high school in Houston, Valenzuela found that the school's organization (e.g., English-only curriculum, a lack of Chicano staff) produced monolingual, English-speaking, ethnic-minority Mexican youth who neither identified with Mexican culture nor had the requisite skills to function successfully in mainstream U.S. culture. Through these practices, schools ultimately cripple students by eliminating the cultural assets the youth bring to schools. Valenzuela emphasizes the intentionality behind these schooling practices, which are undergirded by blatant forms of institutional racism.[11]

Valenzuela's study suggests that schools, in their totality, disinfect youth of their appearances, their language—their identities—during the process of educating them. While schools may believe that no harm is committed when there are no efforts at parent involvement, Valenzuela's study shows that by ignoring the cultural assets and experiences of students' families, schools actively cripple the children's growth and development. How do these observations play out in our schools today? How can schools be more engaging in their interactions with the community?

THE PROBLEMS AND POSSIBILITIES OF PARENT INVOLVEMENT

When David Pino became principal of McAuliffe Elementary School in Logan Square, he was perplexed by these very questions. The school had a history of keeping parents at a distance, and the few staff-parent exchanges that existed were rife with confrontation, distrust, and other forms of conflict. School had become a place that viewed parents in a negative light, treating them as adversaries rather than as allies. When he became principal, "changing the attitude towards parents—from one that challenges the very value they bring to one that seeks to involve them—was the primary concern." In his experience as a teacher and an administrator, David found that if parents were not actively engaged in schools, they were often ignored or treated negatively and with suspicion. Both approaches had dire consequences, he says:

> On the one hand, you might have a situation where there is a real negative interaction between the school and the families. This may come from a person's belief that the way parents are raising their children is harmful or shows that they lack education or don't care. Maybe a school is going to shut out these parents or claim that they are not worth working with. This is going to impact the children in a serious way. You are sending the message that their families don't have much to offer and are actively harmful. This is a big source of conflict.

Through an adversarial relationship with parents, schools perpetuate a belief that families have few resources or little expertise to offer and become places of subtractive schooling, as Valenzuela argues. These negative encounters and exchanges with a smaller group of parents can set the stage for interactions across the school community. In addition to these adversarial relationships, David believes that schools also ignore the presence of families:

> Then, you might ignore the parents in a school. Maybe you don't have a relationship with them yet, maybe you don't have time, or maybe you feel it could become negative. You might not think it's important to what you do. But when you ignore these families, you are sending a message to their children that you are not interested in their personal lives. You are saying that parents are not important or necessary in educating their children. That is a strong message that will create a barrier with the parents.

In this way, schools can send equally strong messages to families when educators fail to reach out to them. Schools take on the sole responsibility for educating children and make active decisions to leave parents out of the process. While this might be seen as a more passive and harmless exchange, the absence of a relationship or an interaction between families and schools is usually detrimental.

David's school scenarios represent two common ways that family-school interactions play out in urban and low-income communities. To be effective, parent engagement strategies must confront these school realities. In failing to do so, educators will continue to be puzzled by the parents who are hard to reach, and these schools will persist with the very strategies that keep these parents out of the picture. But what does parent involvement usually look like in schools?

What Does Parent Involvement Look Like?

Many schools have puzzled over the dilemma of parent-school interactions, but which current models have educators drawn from? Within the field of parent and community involvement, there has been wide support for models that describe effective practices within schools and families. One of the pioneers of this field, Joyce Epstein, at the Center on School, Family, and Community Partnerships at Johns Hopkins University, describes six key components of effective parent involvement. The framework includes parenting, communicating, volunteering, learning at home, decision making, and collaboration with the community. This model is based on an understanding that the spheres of family, school, and community overlap and are influenced by the history, developmental patterns, and changing experiences of the individuals and institutions within each sphere. One of the goals, according to this model, is to develop "school-like families and family-like schools."[12]

These activities often serve as the basis for popular images of parent involvement, where parents support schools in ways that encourage home-school communication and collaboration. As a novice teacher, I could rattle off a list of these parent practices, as they formed my early expectations of a parent's involvement in a child's education: parents could read my weekly newsletter; they could attend my open house, where I would show them how they could support their children at home; they could participate in parent-teacher conferences; they could volunteer in my classroom. Beyond the domain of my classroom, I expected that parents could be active in the PTA or even serve on a school committee that invited parent input. If my school could employ these strategies and drum up parent participation, then we were surely on a good path toward parent involvement. I began to realize, however, that although the school community was racially and socioeconomically diverse, the active group of parents was not. Parents who volunteered in the classroom, participated in PTA meetings, organized fund-raisers, and lobbied for changes in the school were almost always white or middle-class parents for whom these strategies seemed familiar and natural. What about the families that were not present? What about the families that were not fluent in the almost-exclusively-used English language at my school? What about the families we labeled hard to reach?

This is not an unusual scenario for urban schools today. As more middle-class and upper-middle-class and white families settle into urban neighborhoods that have traditionally served low-income families and communities of color, some school leaders have found that white middle-class families respond more favorably to traditional venues for parent participation. One school principal I met at a community engagement workshop puzzled over this phenomenon in his school: "With the influx of middle-class families at my school, I am realizing that some of the strategies we use are written for them. If you look at our events, it looks like we have more parent involvement, but really, we just have more middle-class parents who are responding to our use of the 'greatest hits' in parent involvement."

This school leader understands that while these activities may prove to be useful in some situations, steep barriers in many communities of color impede the rapid expansion of parent involvement.[13] These barriers often result from long-standing legacies of racism, deficit views (i.e., views that treat cultural differences as problems rather than mere variations), and a history of distrust and antagonism.[14]

One of the main problems with the more traditional approach or the "greatest hits" described by this principal is that the approach focuses on the *activities* of parent involvement, rather than its dynamic *process*.[15] Under this model, parents support the needs and wishes of schools through activities that are determined and initiated by teachers and school leaders.[16] As parents support schools in this activity-based, individualistic manner, they rarely find opportunities to connect meaningfully with school staff or fellow parents, reinforcing the distinct boundaries between schools and families.[17]

Additionally, this approach may place a premium on the culture of schools, which typically reflects white, middle-class values, and the burden of change squarely upon parents.[18] In this approach, schools—not communities—decide what constitutes good and acceptable parent involvement practices. Schools may design parent education programs that seek to change home-based practices and promote more synchrony between home and school, but the problem with many of these efforts is that students' families are viewed as problematic. As a result, these programs and workshops do little to encourage schools to change their practices.[19] When these practices are not accepted by parents, the schools may simply devise new activities or tinker with the timing of parent education programs or the format of the sessions. These changes affect the superficial qualities of school practices, but do not fundamentally alter how parents and school staff interact with each other.

As we have also learned from Gilberto and David, school-family relations can be entrenched in systems of distrust and isolation. In these communities, we need an approach that will fundamentally shift the scale and manner of parent participation in schools. How can we radically transform the relationship between parents and schools?

Confronting Power Through Community Organizing

The process of transformation is a central concern of this book, and community organizing efforts can offer valuable perspectives in understanding *how* change can be achieved. To be effective at transforming the home-school relationship, strategies to engage parents must address rigid school structures, unwavering institutional norms, and the deep-seated legacies of racism and social inequality that shape school dynamics and interactions. Any approach to involve parents in ways that will transform the culture of schools must require a radical rearrangement of power relations between schools and families.[20] However, many schools are ill equipped to acknowledge or analyze the lopsided power base that exists within the institution, and although parents often understand these unequal institutional arrangements, they do not have the power necessary to push for needed change.[21]

A growing number of community organizing groups have recently organized parents to improve the outcomes for students in underfunded, overcrowded, and poor-performing schools.[22] In contrast to traditional approaches to parent involvement, these efforts are led by parents and are overtly political—seeking to change the power relations that perpetuate educational inequities.[23] In 1996, Dennis Shirley examined the rise of the Alliance Schools network—a coalition of more than one hundred schools that had been organized to demand changes in low-income schools and communities. He calls for a rethinking of parent participation—from the more traditional concept of passive parent involvement to a more power-laden, context-specific, and leadership-centered idea of parent *engagement*.[24]

These early organizing efforts to reform schools began to shift the ways that low-income parents and parents of color would interact with schools.[25] As more recent studies show, community organizing efforts seek to develop a more permanent base of leaders with skills and resources to take on community issues. Rather than looking to schools for expertise or guidance, parents can become an independent base of leadership within the school. While school-based involvement is often individualized around each parent and the needs of the child, community-based involvement counters this trend by bringing people into relationships with one another, establishing a strong sense of community and collective power.[26] This approach focuses on relational power—the power to act collectively to produce systemic change.[27] With an explicit focus on power, community organizing intentionally builds parent power, unlike standard parent involvement approaches, which typically avoid issues of power and consign parents to support the status quo.

In addition to disrupting uneven power distribution, community organizing focuses on the slow, patient, and transformative work of relationship building. The building of relationships between teachers and parents, between district officials and organizers, and between different parents in a school can lead to greater trust and understanding and can pave the way for collaborative and collective action. Considering the broader benefits and opportunities from these relationships—a form of social capital—we can and should work intentionally to build relationships in schools. Studies of community organizing efforts focus on the development of social capital in local communities, but what can social capital offer to our understanding of parent engagement?[28] How do these relationships work?

When relationships are infused with opportunities that lead to greater understanding and critical analyses of school practices along with the resources that key networks carry, they provide benefits for those involved. In organizing, these relationships begin through conversations—during one-on-one meetings between an organizer and a parent, in house meetings where parents build points of connection with other parents, and in training sessions where a parent shares his or her stories of struggle and isolation with an understanding group of other parents. Through these important conversations, participants learn that relationships can be hindered by a lack of understanding, distrust, or individual fears and anxieties. By bringing people into conversation with each other, organizers attempt to encourage new points of connection and break down the barriers that keep individuals and groups at a distance. These conversations, in turn, reveal critical points of connection that often allow organizers to work together with individuals to effect change.[29]

As we seek clearer strategies for *how* we can build meaningful relationships between families and schools, the process-oriented field of community organizing has much to offer. Researchers have begun to identify the salience of strong relationships and attention to power in the transformative work of community organizing groups. In a national study of community organizing groups working on educational issues, Mark Warren, Karen Mapp, and the Community Organizing and School Reform Project examined the core processes and strategies that drove key successful school-reform efforts.[30] Through case studies of six community organizing groups (of which the current study of the Logan Square Neighborhood Association, or LSNA, was a part) around the nation, the researchers found that building relationships and building power were key processes in creating individual, institutional, and community transformation. These key processes were rooted in the history and tradition of community organizing, and each played a critical role in generating significant change in educational settings rife with challenges.[31]

This book seeks to expand our current definitions of parent involvement in ways that confront the divisions that exist in many school communities and that challenge the school-centered, middle-class framework dominating current practice. Through an in-depth examination of one community organizing group's attempts to build family and community engagement in schools, we consider the possibility of a new model of engagement that is rooted in the realities of power, inequality, and a desire for social change. David and Gilberto's stories represent the pressing challenges and concerns that face principals, teachers, parents, and community members in this Chicago neighborhood and beyond. In light of the struggles to effectively engage families in schools, how has this particular community responded?

A NEW MODEL: FAMILY, SCHOOL, AND COMMUNITY TRANSFORMATION THROUGH AN ECOLOGICAL MODEL OF PARENT ENGAGEMENT

Susanna is a parent mentor whose children attend a school in Logan Square. She understands how difficult it can be to build a sense of community in a school where different languages, cultures, and life experiences interact:

> If you think about it, the school is like a smaller version of the community. You have the families, and you have the people who don't live there but they work in the community, like the teachers. You have a mix of adults, children, Latinos, other groups. And every day, everyone is coming together in this same building, and we are trying to understand each other and find out how we can get along, right? And then, we have the same issues—some people, they are not getting along, they are poor, they are not speaking English, the races also have problems with the different groups. I just think it is some of the same going on from the school to the community. That is why the school is hard to bring together, just like it is hard in the community.

When Susanna began to work in the classroom as a parent mentor, she was struck by how much life outside school affects what happens in school. She found that students struggled with family tensions, neighborhood violence, and peer relations, and their struggles shaped the kinds of experiences they had throughout the school day. Because she lives in the community, she can understand and relate to her students, but she often finds that teachers cannot. Susanna feels that one of the greatest challenges that schools face is to understand how life outside schools and classrooms influences life inside. Although it is not uncommon for educators to consider schools and communities separately, we need an approach that acknowledges the complex, inseparable interaction of schools and communities—an ecological approach.

How is school life shaped by community forces? Urie Bronfenbrenner, in *The Ecology of Human Development*, urges us to understand human development through an ecological orientation that considers the individual as embedded within multiple spheres of influence. He describes the environments within which individuals interact as nested structures and argues that it is not only the immediate setting within which an individual resides that has influence but also the interaction between these multiple spheres of experience. The interconnectedness of individuals within and across settings shapes an individual's ability to learn, grow, and develop.[32] Understood through Susanna's reflections, a lack of connection occurs both in the school and in the broader community, and this disconnectedness will burden students in the school. The environments are hard to bring together. If learning environments for students are conceived of in this way, a child's ability to learn will be directly affected by classroom dynamics, communication between the home and school, the stresses of difficult family situations, and the persistent societal messages of success or failure. It is critical that we understand the interaction between environments. For children and adolescents, the most critical ecological transitions and intersecting connections are the interactions between home, school, and peer groups.

Schools, however, are not the only community institutions that shape young people. Extended families, religious institutions, peer groups, and other groups can also play a critical role in shaping a child's whole experience. Each group is formed by a distinct set of values, cultural norms, and pedagogy that shapes its interactions with students. As students move about these various environments, Lawrence Cremin says, they are shaped by the "knowledge, values, attitudes, skills, and sensibilities" of institutions that additionally seek to screen and interpret the teaching of other institutions.[33] Thus, schools are deeply embedded in communities. When students are defined primarily by their experiences within school culture and not by their experiences as family members, friends, neighbors, or churchgoers who belong to a host of institutions outside schools, schools fail to understand the multifaceted dimensions of a student's life and the various experiences they face in their daily lives that inevitably spill over into their lives as students.

Toward an Ecological View of Parent Engagement

While the aforementioned studies have primarily examined how school and community forces influence students, these ecological spheres of interaction also influence parents. How do their experiences in and out of schools spill over into their interactions with the school? Can we move beyond an understanding of parent engagement as a set of concrete activities isolated to the environment of schools and classrooms to a more holistic understanding of how and why parents become actively engaged in schools? Assuming that such a transformation is possible, we can take a more context-specific and process-oriented ecological view of parent engagement. Through an ecological view, we consider the multiple spaces within which parents may be involved (in support of children at home, in schools and classrooms, and within the broader community), the various groups and individuals they will connect with through their actions, and the stages of time and development across which parents will act. Rather than merely focusing on the types of activities that parents engage in, we consider parent engagement across many dimensions. The case for this model is further advanced in the chapters that follow, but for now, we can see a summary of the major differences between the traditional and ecological models in figure 1-1.[34]

As described earlier, under the more traditional models practiced by schools (the aforementioned "greatest hits" model), parent engagement is viewed primarily as a school-centered, activity-based, and individualistic enterprise. Programs and activities are primarily designed by school staff, who may or may not understand and value the experiences of families. Opportunities to interact with families, consequently, may not be planned in a manner that is amenable to the lives of families. By

FIGURE 1-1

Traditional versus ecological models of parent engagement

Traditional model	Ecological model
1. Centers on schools	1. Centers on parents
2. Promotes activities	2. Promotes engagement
3. Views parents as deficits	3. Views parents as assets
4. Limits participation	4. Broadens participation
5. Alters parenting practices	5. Transforms families, schools, and communities

focusing on these planned events and activities, parents may gain a limited view into school culture, but are relegated to view only those situations that have been planned and orchestrated by schools.

In contrast, with an ecological perspective on parent engagement, schools design processes for parent participation that actively *center around parents* rather than limiting them to roles in the periphery. From this central view, parents gain a broader perspective into the life and culture of schools. Instead of being confined to the narrow perspectives of planned activities, formal invitations, and other events, parents can navigate the multiple spaces and dimensions of schools. They have opportunities to be part of decision-making meetings where conversations and discussions unfold, to be part of everyday classroom interactions, and to build relationships with adults and children beyond their own child's classroom. In this way, parents have a *perspective-opening* experience where they come to understand and influence school culture.

But broader views and open perspectives are not enough. As Rudy Crew suggests, schools can benefit from "demand parents"—strong, organized groups of parents who see themselves as leaders and can share decision making with schools, in ways that can be challenging without being adversarial.[35] To do so, schools must no longer view parents from a deficit perspective, but must recognize the resources and assets that parents can be in their children's lives and in schools. By designing parent-engagement strategies that view *parents as assets*, we expect parents to become leaders, advocates, and decision makers in schools.

Consequently, the culture of schools becomes critical to parent engagement. Are parents welcome to participate and learn about schools, or are they kept at a distance, which protects the schools as sole authorities in their children's education? As Arne Duncan, then CEO of the Chicago Public Schools, explains, the kind of parent engagement that LSNA promises requires a change in school culture and a restructuring of the educational environment traditionally conceived: "I would argue that historically, we created an environment where not only weren't parents welcome, they were actively told not to come, and so again, we're talking about now trying to change that culture so that our schools are welcoming, that they're inviting parents in, and that schools are places where parents feel they want to come."[36]

If school practices are steeped in tradition, as Duncan presumes, and those traditions seek to undermine the development of relationships between families and schools, schools must find innovative solutions to confront those challenges.

Parents come to school engagement from a variety of experiences and backgrounds. Some parents may be newly involved, and some may be looking for more meaningful opportunities to exercise leadership. While some adults may be available during school hours, others are only available after school hours, or for shorter- or longer-term commitments. To develop parent engagement approaches that draw the widest net of parent participation, schools must offer a variety of programs and invitations that meet various parent needs and experiences.

What Kind of Change Is Necessary? A Multilayered Approach to Transformation

The burden of change cannot be placed on families alone, and the interactions that schools have with parents should work to transform at multiple levels. With meaningful and authentic forms of parent engagement, schools can be environments that change their beliefs and attitudes toward families, and communities can be more open and receptive to the institution of school. Consequently, parent engagement approaches should be designed in ways that work to *transform families, schools, and communities*. This stands in contrast to parent engagement efforts that focus on supporting the activities, events, and projects of schools; these efforts may be more connected to the material and organizational resources of the schools rather than the broader goals of transformative practice. A multilayered approach to transformation is central to this ecological model and is further explained later in this chapter.

We know change is sorely needed in our schools, but what kind of change do we want? Relationships of trust and understanding must replace deep-seated fears and anxieties. Change should be palpable throughout a school community. Whether families live in affluence or poverty, whether parents speak English or Vietnamese, whether parents stay at home with their children or work multiple jobs to support them, every child's family should have a chance at being reached. Every family should experience meaningful points of connection between home life and life in the classroom.

As explained above, reaching families across a broad spectrum of experiences in meaningful ways will require a fundamental shift in how schools interact with communities—a transformation that has to occur on multiple levels. Traditionally, educational institutions have believed that low levels of parent involvement in a school reflect a prevalence of families that are too busy to be responsive, don't care about their child's education, or don't understand how to support their children. These beliefs reflect deficit views of families, but also emphasize the family's responsibility for becoming more involved. As a response, schools adjust the format of their programs to nudge more families into participation. This singular focus on changing the behavior of families masks the equally important responsibilities that schools have to reform their own practices.

The multiple levels of parent engagement must approach the challenge from three fronts:

1. Bring *families* to a greater understanding of school culture.
2. Alter the culture of *schools*.
3. Transform the very *communities* that lie outside the school door.

Figure 1-2 illustrates the ecologically significant multiple dimensions of family, school, and community transformation discussed in this book. These multiple levels of transformation are confirmed by studies of other organizing efforts as well. In a study of six community organizing groups, Mark Warren, Karen Mapp, and the Community Organizing and School Reform Project found that the most significant school reform required transformation at three distinct levels: communities (the rural or urban neighborhoods that were part of the study), individuals (parents, young people, community leaders), and institutions (schools and school districts).[37] Through these successful, multilayered reform efforts, individuals are transformed and new leadership emerges. Similarly, through the collective efforts of parent leaders, schools can undergo a cultural shift in how school staff and administrators interact with families. While the larger study was focused on broader issues of school reform and not necessarily on parent engagement, these findings

FIGURE 1-2

Parent engagement that transforms at multiple levels

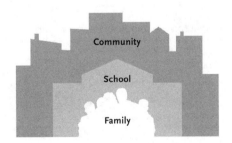

confirm that authentic transformation will require work at multiple levels. This premise certainly has the potential for broad applicability; this book, however, will focus on the specific processes around parent engagement in an effort to deepen our understanding of how this transformation can occur at the family, school, and community levels.

How Do We Get from Here to There? Three Core Processes in Building an Ecological View of Parent Engagement

To move toward an ecological approach to parent engagement, schools and communities must make radical shifts in values and beliefs and strive toward truly transformative practices. Three core processes guide the movement toward the ecological model: developing mutual forms of engagement, building relationships, and sharing leadership and power (figure 1-3). Through an examination of LSNA's organizing efforts and work with parents, we will understand how these core processes can transform parent engagement.

Whereas myriad parent programs are school-centered, that is, schools determine the kinds of activities that parents are engaged in, an ecological approach is *mutually engaging*. Viewing parent engagement approaches as school-centered or even family- or community-centered encourages a strict either–or approach. Either schools decide on programs, or families do. But strategies for parent engagement are proven more effective when families and schools design them together—in

FIGURE 1-3

Moving from a traditional to an ecological view of parent engagement

Mutual engagement
Authentic relationships
Shared leadership and power

Traditional model   **Ecological model**

conversation and collaboration.[38] A mutually engaging approach considers the interests and needs of schools in conjunction with the interests and needs of families.

To close the gap between schools and families, we must focus on the *relationships*, rather than the activities of parent engagement. While a school needs to engage parents in ways that are interesting and meaningful to them, this engagement also needs to encourage parental interaction with school staff and other parents. Through active relationships with others in the school, parents become more central figures in schools—establishing parental presence and an environment where parents are commonly seen in all corners of the school. They are in classrooms, serve on committees, and are frequently seen in hallways and in conversation with students and school staff. Schools have much to learn from the experiences and perspectives of families.

Parent engagement approaches should also take on the difficult task of *sharing leadership and power* with parents. This challenges the uneven power base that exists in many schools where parents are left out of decision making. By developing and exercising their leadership skills, parents can create opportunities to build power and advocate for children, and schools can learn to promote relational power—emphasizing the power to get things done collectively, rather than power over individuals.[39]

How did LSNA come to develop these three core processes? How did the experiences of organizers within the community shape the school-centered questions that resulted? Let us now turn to the organizational history of LSNA and its development of a central educational narrative.

2

A COMMUNITY RESPONDS

The Logan Square Neighborhood Association and the
Reinvention of School-Community Relationships

*Back in the days when I was young, this neighborhood was completely dif-
ferent. I was one of the few Latinos in the school, and I had to prove myself,
make people understand who I was, what my family was about. I thought it
was because we were the only Latinos back then, but even now, when there
are so many Latinos, I still feel as if my kids have to prove themselves, make
teachers understand who they are. All that time, I thought it was because we
were new, but now I realize it's because we were just different.*
      —*Elena*, parent and longtime resident of Logan Square

T O *ELENA*, LOGAN SQUARE IS HOME. She grew up in the neighborhood, went to school in the neighborhood, and now sends her
son to the very same school she attended as a child. But as we see
from her account, she has a complex relationship with her community. She has lived through and experienced some significant changes
in the neighborhood. A community that has struggled with issues of
diversity and broad-based participation, Logan Square has experienced
steady demographic changes that have shaped the neighborhood. From
the early 1960s through the 1970s, the neighborhood witnessed a period of increasing deindustrialization in the urban core and the ensu-
ing suburbanization of the metropolitan area. Working-class European
immigrant families fought to curb the deterioration that resulted from

the exodus of long-term residents and businesses. At the same time, the neighborhood experienced an influx of Latino families—primarily of Cuban and Puerto Rican descent—that began to view life in Logan Square as a symbol of social prosperity and achievement.[1] As neighborhoods across Chicago began to struggle with financial disinvestment, deindustrialization, and intense racial segregation, Logan Square, with its commercial development, community banks, access to public transportation, available housing stock, and proximity to the downtown area and O'Hare airport, began attracting middle-class professionals in the 1970s and was thus spared the intense community deterioration that occurred in many low-income Latino and African American neighborhoods.[2] In a city that has struggled historically with racial segregation, Logan Square remains one of the few Chicago neighborhoods that have maintained diversity in race, ethnicity, and class. However, Elena's experience shows that this increasing diversity has not come without its share of challenges.

When LSNA executive director Nancy Aardema first joined the organization in the mid-1980s, her early mission was to integrate the board of directors and the staff. With the increasing diversity of the neighborhood, she felt that the organization needed to reflect that diversity as well. LSNA was founded in the early 1960s by a group of local churches, businesses, and home owners to address their concerns about increasing deindustrialization. Decades later, LSNA's board and staff still primarily represented the European immigrant families that formed the early organization. Nancy recalls, "We knew that we wanted to represent the people and the community groups. Organizing often takes the form of helping people who don't have the money to be able to make change through people power. In our community, we knew that we had to be integrated because it was people of all races who needed to come together to impact social justice issues."

Demographic changes in Logan Square have continued into the present, shaping LSNA's interests and activity in the community as well. According to the 2000 Census reports, 65 percent of Logan Square residents were Latino; by 2005 Census estimates, that figure had increased to 71 percent. Although Puerto Rican families began the movement into Logan Square, immigrants from Mexico, Cuba, and Central America have more recently settled throughout the community. Of the 28,855 households in Logan Square, more than 12,000 were considered low-income, earning less than 80 percent of the city median, $38,625.[3] While Pilsen and Little Village are often cited as Chicago neighborhoods associated with the working poor, Logan Square is home to a greater share of limited-income households than those communities. Along with the challenging situations of poverty and persistent lack of economic opportunity came ensuing struggles with crime and violence. Through these rapid shifts, LSNA began to organize campaigns for safety, immigration reform, affordable housing, and community health.

In recent years, however, the future of low-income families has been more intensely threatened by a westward movement of gentrification across Chicago's northwest corridor. Upscale developments are displacing hundreds of low- and moderate-income families. The median sale price of housing rose from $235,000 in early 2001 to $325,000 by late 2004.[4] That has translated into vast changes in public school enrollments. Some schools face plummeting enrollment from Latino families that have been priced out of the neighborhood, and other schools face soaring enrollments from the influx of these displaced families. In response, LSNA has created broad-based redevelopment strategies and campaigns for affordable housing to prevent displacement and to support the needs of low-income families amid gentrification.

Throughout these campaigns, as organizers listened to the concerns of residents and other members, they became increasingly aware that for many families, strong communities meant strong schools.[5] From housing to unemployment to immigration reform to education, the issues were interconnected. When neighborhoods were plagued by violence, immigrant issues, and high rates of mobility among families, these factors hurt the daily operations of schools. Joanna Brown, LSNA's lead education organizer, describes the organization's belief that school and community interests are intricately connected: "We have seen the ways that schools can breathe life into communities. Schools are themselves representations of the larger community. If there are issues of poverty, violence, and a general feeling of anxiety or insecurity about your neighborhood, it is going to play out in schools and classrooms. We can't work on one—schools or communities—without the other."

With this growing awareness that improving schools would be central to improving communities, LSNA began to set its sights on organizing in schools, with the assistance of a sweeping change in Chicago school politics.

The Context of Chicago

Like many other Chicago community organizations that began to stake a claim in the city's educational issues, LSNA began its involvement in schools with Chicago's school reform legislation of 1988. Enacted a year after U.S. Secretary of Education William Bennett referred to Chicago's school system as the worst in the nation, the state law created local school councils (LSCs) that would serve as administrative bodies for each school.[6] According to some experts, this sweeping policy change in support of local control resulted from the civic capacity built over time in Chicago through a well-organized business community and a strong network of community-based organizations that were invested in local schools.[7] This civic capacity was built over the years, as schools became increasingly notorious for resisting change, as community groups insisted on openness, transparency, and community involvement, and public outcry concerning the school system's persistent failure began to mount.[8] The city's public institutions were also a target for increasing criticism against unfair and unequal access for disenfranchised African American communities. For a school system viewed by many as a fortress closed to parents and outside organizations and defined by sharp resistance to outside influences, the 1988 Chicago School Reform Act called for significant change.

LSCs are stacked heavily in support of parent and community members.[9] Each council is granted considerable decision-making authority and is charged with administrative tasks such as renewing and awarding four-year contracts to principals and approving the school's improvement plans and discretionary budget. LSNA, along with other Chicago community organizations, began its work in schools after passage of the Chicago School Reform Act. Early organizing efforts focused on recruiting and training new LSC members and attempting to build a broad base of community and parent participation. With the strong presence of community groups and a district-wide momentum toward local control, many organizations like LSNA became more deeply involved in school politics and governance. Today, local school councils of LSNA's partner schools consist of a variety of past and present LSNA members who, through their active engagement in schools, have sought leadership positions on the council. As members of a critical decision-making body with the school and with a vested interest in families, these parents often work to promote a community-based and family-centered school environment. In effect, the institutional arrangement of Chicago schools provides LSNA with a formal avenue for community participation in schools.

Shifting Gears: From Representation to Transformation

The central goal for LSNA's early work in schools, as was the case for many community organizations at the time, was to form strong LSCs that would function smoothly and encourage broad participation in the community. Parents and community members, for the first time, had a representative voice in schools. Through the work with LSCs, however, LSNA began to develop closer ties with parents and school staff and a greater understanding about the issues facing schools. It found that both parents and school administrators were concerned with school overcrowding. Principals were concerned with swelling school enrollment from the influx of Latino families, which placed added stress on already-challenging classroom situations; parents were distressed by increasing demands to bus their children to schools outside the neighborhood because of over-enrollment. Under the direction of LSNA's Education Committee, three groups—the LSCs, school principals, and other community members—joined together in a campaign to address school overcrowding. Nancy Aardema recalls that LSNA began to create a sense of trust with the groups it was partnering with:

> During this time, we began to create trust with the parents, with the administrators, with some of the teachers and some of the students . . . If you are a school during this time of school reform, you don't naturally have a sense of trust to groups that are working in the community. And

while we had worked with community members on other issues, we hadn't really shown parents a real vested interest or expertise in schools at that point. We knew that we couldn't just walk in and start making these changes. We knew that we would have to build trust to get there.

Through the collaboration with school leaders and councils, LSNA won an outcome that individual schools had failed to attain. According to lead education organizer Joanna Brown, "the principals had been struggling with the overcrowding issue for years and had been trying to get something done and couldn't get it done." By bringing principals and LSCs into a collective campaign and by taking on the public confrontation, LSNA generated momentum for a community project that would benefit schools and protect principals from an openly antagonistic role with the Board of Education. Amanda Rivera, who worked with LSNA as a teacher and principal during this time (and has since worked at Central Office and as assistant principal), recalls that until schools began working collaboratively with LSNA, they lacked collective knowledge of their individual efforts, not realizing that they were often struggling with the same issues and bureaucratic unresponsiveness:

What we realized was that as a school, we would go to the Board of Education, to Central Office, requesting assistance around overcrowding. They would say yes, but nothing happened, and then when LSNA came around, we started engaging with the schools within our community that were within a mile and a half away that we never talked to, and we found out that they were going to Central Office and asking for assistance with overcrowding and getting the same, "Oh, yes, yes, yes." But nothing was happening.

Through smaller, isolated efforts, school leaders realized that they failed to generate the power and momentum that was necessary to win significant change, but through the collective effort initiated by LSNA, schools began to realize their collective voice. Amanda explains:

So when LSNA came around, they were able to bring us together. And then we became a collective voice, a more unified and powerful voice.

So, then, when we started going to Central Office, then we were getting answers; we were getting meetings; we got a response. And we were able to get additions built onto our schools, and we were able to get a middle school built for the community, which I became the principal of . . . And it was, we were told, because we were the squeaky wheel, which was good for us, but unfortunate for other schools who didn't have the backing of an organizing group.

As a result, schools were able to attain much-needed resources through a collective process that joined the schools, for the first time, with other schools facing similar needs. Nancy believes that by working alongside rather than in opposition to school leaders, LSNA built relationships and trust with schools that would later prove to be instrumental: "The smart thing we did was that we brought the administrators to the table. We weren't confronting the principal. We were bringing the principal in to be part of the process, to say, 'I need more space.' It was far better for all of us to be at the table. Right then and there, we began building those relationships."

Compared with the tense, confrontational relationships between schools and community groups prior to the 1988 reform law, LSNA's approach signaled a new movement toward collaboration. Concretely, this collaboration resulted in the development of five new annexes and two middle schools over several years, subsequently demonstrating LSNA's power as a community organization. This partnership encouraged a willingness on the part of schools to work with LSNA and recognized the valuable assets LSNA could bring to schools, in turn paving the way for future school involvement.

What was more important, LSNA began to move beyond the parent and community representation that LSCs provided, toward efforts to radically transform schools. Organizers and parent leaders became exposed to the underbelly of the school system and began to collectively demand school reform plans that responded to the issues they identified with school staff. Schools were not functioning well for families and school staff, and this had a direct impact on the broader community. Through these early organizing efforts, LSNA reduced school overcrowding by winning campaigns to build needed annexes to school buildings, to build a new middle school, and to sharply reduce the busing of neighborhood children to schools beyond the community. For Amanda Rivera, who was then the first appointed principal of the newly constructed Ames Middle School, this meant that "schools could have the resources and state of mind to go about the business of educating children well. It was an utterly transformative experience."

As a result of these experiences, education became a prominent issue in LSNA's first Holistic Plan, a mission statement that charted a vision for the group's work and focused its efforts in a few domains. In its first Holistic Plan, written in 1995, LSNA resolved to achieve certain goals:

1. Develop schools as community centers because "the health of any community is dependent on the availability of common space for interaction, education, service provision, recreation, culture and arts."
2. Train parents to work in the classrooms of LSNA schools because "children learn better when their parents are actively involved in their education."
3. Support community-controlled education because the "health of any community is dependent on the quality of education provided to its residents."[10]

From this Holistic Plan, LSNA made a commitment that linked improved communities to improved schools. Upon adoption of the Holistic Plan, LSNA began to devise a strategy that would bring parents into schools and classrooms in meaningful ways. The strategy was shaped by conversations with parents and school principals, both of whom saw a need to bring families into schools, although no one had a clear understanding of how this could be done.

Starting from Scratch: Building New Forms of Parent Engagement Through the Parent Mentor Program

During one such conversation within LSNA's Education Committee, Sally Acker, then Funston School principal, shared a trend she noticed among the families she encountered daily at the school. The school's surrounding neighborhood, over the years, had become predominantly Latino, and many were Spanish-speaking immigrant families. She noticed that parents rarely came into the school building beyond the routines of dropping off and picking up children from school. She began to wonder how the school could encourage greater parent involvement, particularly for those parents who dropped their children off at school, only to turn around to go back home for the day. She began to discuss the need for greater parent involvement in schools, wondering if LSNA could be of help. Nancy Aardema recalls the principal's concern:

> [Sally Acker] felt like the issue was that parents only came to the school when there was a problem, or if they were the "good parents of the good kids" . . . She felt like we had to figure out a way as a community to get just the average parents, or the parents of the kids who were struggling into the school—not in a way that they felt like they were there to be told what was wrong, not in a way that put them at a disadvantage, or put them down—but she felt they should be in the school in a very real, continuous way.

The school struggled to reach parents beyond the "good parents of the good kids." The vast majority of parents were, in fact, hard to reach, by the school's estimation. Sally Acker reached out to LSNA organizers, hoping they could assist her with an issue that she and her staff had little experience or expertise in. Working on the idea that parent involvement should be more continuous and genuine, LSNA collaborated with another organization, Community Organizing and Family Issues (COFI), to create a training program that would become the basis for the emerging Parent Mentor program.

Meanwhile, at the Funston School, Amanda Rivera was the school's bilingual program coordinator, working with the school's families and trying to get a sense of their needs. She recalls that when Funston staff and LSNA began forming the ideas behind a parent involvement program, they were particularly concerned—just as Sally had been—with the parents who were retreating back to their homes after dropping children off at school. Many of these parents were immigrant mothers, isolated within their homes, leaving only to take their children to school. Sally believed that these mothers could use their time more productively by supporting the needs of the school. LSNA organizers set their goals on empowering and organizing parents within the school. Susan Adler Yanun, LSNA's New Communities program director who also organized the creation of the Parent Mentor program, recalls the importance of bringing parents to a more central role in schools:

> We had these wonderful parents who were just not a part of the daily life of schools. As an organization, we wanted to see families play more active roles in the school, but we needed to create a space and opportunity for parents to get there. The Parent Mentor program would help us build a core of parents who could navigate the school environment and offer their expertise and ultimately their leadership. They would bring incredible insight into the classrooms they would become a part of.

The Parent Mentor program brought mothers into classrooms, where they worked alongside teachers as community mentors, attending to the instructional goals of the classroom rather than the administrative tasks more typical of parent volunteers. To date, LSNA has trained over twelve hundred parent mentors across eight schools. For four days a week, two hours each morning, over the duration of a school year, parent mentors are committed to a classroom—reading to children in small groups, working with individual students, and supporting classroom activities. Each Friday morning, parent mentors in each school come together for training sessions as a cohort; they also meet monthly with LSNA's other cohorts. Parents are paid a $600 stipend after they complete one hundred hours. The reasons behind this payment are various: it counters the notion that the parents are merely serving the school, it encourages consistent participation, and it develops a sense of respect and recognition for their work. By bringing parents into schools in this way, LSNA sought to build a familiarity with schools and the broader community among immigrant parents. In doing so, the program also strived to encourage neighborhood schools to have a more open attitude toward families.

But to make parents essential to the life of a school environment where parents were once visibly and figuratively absent would require an institutional change—a fundamental shift in the school model. Teachers were unaccustomed to having parents in the school, particularly in their classrooms working with students. Amanda recalls that this was one of the greatest challenges in establishing the program: "You really felt that you were starting from scratch with no existing relationship to build upon." At the time, parents simply were not part of school classrooms and had no regular interactions with teachers. She remembers navigating those delicate relationships:

> For me it was very difficult, because I had to then meet with the teachers, and let them know that we were going to have parents in the school, but [the parents] were going to be placed in classrooms to assist them. And because this was so new, there was no prior practice of parents being engaged in the classroom in a significant way. So, I had to figure out, how do we change this paradigm, where there's this mistrust of parents in the school, in the classroom, and people feeling . . . 'I'm going to be spied upon and critiqued,' or feeling threatened by the parents in the classroom?

According to Amanda, parents rarely spent time in classrooms. The few interchanges that did exist between parents and teachers were often hostile and antagonistic, centered on disagreements concerning a child. This situation escalated feelings of mistrust, fear, and resentment, posing challenges to any program that sought to bring parents into classrooms. Amanda sensed that fear—among parents and teachers—was the overriding barrier to building these new relationships, so she designed a training program that would seek to dispel the myths, break down the sense of mistrust, and develop some common ground. She recalls the goals of the first training sessions:

> Little did the teachers realize that the parents felt just as fearful about going in the classroom, so we always did some team building at the beginning with the teachers and the parents, where we actually put

them together, and did activities—teachers and parents—to help them talk about their commonalities as human beings first, and they realized, "Oh, I'm a mother, and you're a mother, and these are some of my hobbies, or some of my interests, and these are some of my challenges," so just team-building activities like that.

These team-building activities, which created a sense of common purpose and shared experience among parents and teachers, were essential to the successful start of the Parent Mentor program. By developing these relationships intentionally, Amanda says, the program "began to build rapport and began to break down barriers before [parent mentors] actually were placed in the classroom." Building a sense of trust between teachers and parents would be critical to the success of the program, and beginning this relationship before the start of the program would ensure a smoother launch.

But understanding that many of these parents, especially immigrant parents who are also unfamiliar with U.S. schools, enter schools for the first time with fear and uncertainty, the training also focused on the personal goals and leadership development of parents. Encouraging parents to see themselves as leaders and role models to children, organizers called on parents to identify their own personal goals for the year. For many parents, the goals centered around education—such as obtaining a GED or taking English classes—or employment. Throughout the year, parents charted their progress in accomplishing their goal, with the added support of a parent mentor cohort. These training sessions introduced parents to broader community issues, and by focusing on leadership development and the explicit recognition of power and inequality, LSNA encouraged parents to view themselves as active agents for personal and community transformation.

Over time, the Parent Mentor program has become a springboard for new programs and initiatives that have provided added opportunities for parent and community engagement in schools. As parents become immersed in a training program that connects them to the school community and fosters a sense of leadership, they begin to alter the environment and encourage schools to view families in a different light. Despite the program's evolution and the host of initiatives that have

44

since developed from its existence, the Parent Mentor program remains the foundation of LSNA's work in schools and the community. As one organizer explains:

> The program is a stepping-stone for everything else. These parents go on to find full-time jobs outside, or they start working in the schools as tutors or paraprofessionals, serve on school committees, lead one of our programs, or become elected to the local school council. It's a little seed that gets planted that grows into a whole bunch of other things. As parent mentors, they build new skills of leadership and activism, and this becomes the base for their work as leaders in many of our other programs or in the school and community more broadly.

For these parents, engagement with the Parent Mentor program is a first step toward greater participation and leadership in the school and community. It is the beginning of a new conceptualization of parent engagement.

The varied narratives of parents drive the central themes of this book. But before we look at these central themes, we will follow a community of parents beginning their effort for engagement in one school setting. Their individual voices and experiences, as described in the next chapter—and throughout the book—help set the stage for the pressing call to action that shapes this book.

3

BUILDING COMMUNITY
WITHIN SCHOOLS

One School's Connection with Parents and Families

Fear is one common reason why parents don't want to be in the school. For me, I had to overcome my fear and find my place in the school, but that is hard to do without help and without others showing you it is possible.

—Ada Ayala, former parent mentor

THESE ARE THE WORDS of former parent mentor Ada Ayala as she recalls her own experience in the program years ago. Ada is a force of quiet strength—she radiates both soft sensibility and hard determination. A petite Puerto Rican woman, she is meticulously well dressed, polite, and pleasant and glows with a smile of genuine goodness and care. She walks the halls of Funston Elementary School with a sense of purpose and determination, meeting everyone—children and adults alike—with a warm smile and welcome greeting. This soft-spoken woman of few words has an unassuming presence but is also persistently determined in her efforts to make the school a welcome place for students and their families. On the playground, at the start of the day, she often chats with parents and keeps a watchful eye on the families who come and go with their children. At the end of each school day, as classroom teachers pack up their bags and as children move en masse out of the building, down the streets, and into their cars, Ada begins her day, opening the school's community learning center for an evening full of classes and activities for students and their families. Ada coordinates the Funston Elementary School's Community Learning Center in partnership with LSNA's larger network of school-based centers. After school Monday through Thursday, she visits classrooms, making sure teachers have the materials they need. She walks with students into their rooms for after-school programs, asking them about their day, inquiring about their parents. Walking the hallways, she waves into classrooms to parents she knows, and she takes notice of who comes and goes during the four busy evenings that the community learning center is open each week. Every evening, she is the visible leader of a school space that opens its doors to the parents and families of Funston students.

Things were not always this way for Ada. When she began sending her two young children to school, she spoke very little English and did not feel that the school was a place for parent activity. When she was approached by school staff to participate in the first run of the Parent Mentor program, Ada was surprised by the very idea: "How could they be asking me to be in the classroom working with a teacher? How could I be of help? I was a young mother, and I was new to the school, to everything. I didn't know anyone, I could hardly speak English, and I was nervous."

During that year, she recalls, she met other parents for the first time as they were trained to enter classrooms and work with teachers and students. The parent mentor cohort became a stable force within the school community and a source of support for Ada. They were bonded, in part, by a common purpose to support children in classrooms and, in part, by their own excitement to be involved in ways that would support their own children at home. Ada remembers this excitement vividly: "It was just what I needed. I loved coming to the first meeting. I didn't want to leave when the two hours were over and we had to go home . . . Then we all became connected to each other, many of us becoming friends. We began to see ourselves as a community, connected to each other."

Ada also remembers how much she gained and learned in the program. She struggled with English, and this often became a key barrier in helping her children with their homework. The Parent Mentor program exposed her to classrooms and gave her opportunities to strengthen her own English-language skills and, consequently, to overcome some of her own fears of communicating with others at school: "I was learning English and beginning to recognize words that I didn't know with my children, and that helped me get a bit more involved in the program. The program helps you overcome fear. Communication is better when you know the teacher and you know the principal and you know the other parents who have the same problem you have."

Ada believes that for many of the immigrant and Spanish-speaking families in Logan Square, LSNA offers a parent-participation model that addresses their fears and their unfamiliarity with schools. Her own fear of getting involved in schools stemmed, in large part, from her unfamiliarity with U.S. schools as well as her own lack of English-language fluency. Through her interactions with families, she finds that many parents hesitate to get involved in the school: "They are nervous and they hesitate to come into the school, and sometimes, I have to really talk with them to help them understand what we are trying to do. They are nervous, maybe because they're afraid, maybe because they don't know the language, maybe because they think that they're not going to overcome their fear."

Ada's story shows us that the personal experiences of parents and families matter when we discuss parental engagement strategies in schools. The particular culture and nature of a school matters, too. The families, interactions, classrooms, and immigrant lives of the Funston school community will inevitably shape how parents like Ada will experience the Parent Mentor program. With this in mind, let us look in depth at the parent experiences in one school, Funston Elementary School.

Funston is a story of change and evolution. The narrative of parent engagement has changed over the course of school leaders, across cohorts of parent mentors, and through a neighborhood's struggles with issues such as school safety, displacement, and crime. As a participant and observer during the 2006–2007 school year, I was witness to the development of a cohort of parent mentors, the experience of newly involved parents, and the cultural environment of the school. Through relationships with parents, school staff, and community members, I began to understand more clearly how particular family situations, classroom dynamics, individual relationships, and collective identities interact with the contextual influences of history, personal narratives, and community experience to paint a rich and multifaceted portrait of one school's connection with parents and families.[1]

This chapter will describe these changes at Funston—the individual and the collective, the personal and the professional, the adaptive and the resistant—produced in part by the Parent Mentor program, in part by the relationships among individuals in the school, and in part by the increased presence and voice of parents within schools. We will hear the narratives and experiences of two parent mentors, *Isabel* and *Graciela*, both women involved in Funston's Parent Mentor program for the first time, from their initial experiences to their final reflections at the end of the school year.[2]

Through these training sessions, the informal conversations that surround them, and the relationships built over time, I begin to see the Parent Mentor program less as a *program* with the predictable elements of leaders, participants, and curriculum and more as an interactive, dynamic *process* that seeks to change the institution one relationship at a time. And through this experience as participant, observer, researcher, fellow parent, and former teacher, I am part of this change as well.

JOINING HANDS: A LOOK INSIDE CLASSROOMS AND THE RELATIONSHIPS BETWEEN PARENT MENTORS AND TEACHERS

In this section, we look inside the classrooms of Funston Elementary School from the viewpoint of two rather new parents. One parent is completely new to the idea of parent mentors; the other parent is entering her second year of the program, but in a new school. Each woman experiences different things as she begins her work as a parent mentor.

Graciela: Finding the Way

At first glance, this classroom is like any other kindergarten classroom, complete with children's drawings, learning centers, a circle-time rug, and a reading corner. The front half of the classroom is arranged in small tables where students sit in groups of five, chatting quietly to each other as they color an activity sheet. The sun streams in through the windows on one side of the classroom, lighting up the colorful mobiles that hang from the ceiling, decorated by young hands and budding artists. A teacher lingers with a student to talk about his drawing while she simultaneously keeps an eye on a nearby table of students who are beginning to bicker about some missing crayons. The morning announcements come through the loudspeaker, and for a moment, the students are shushed to silence and frozen in movement as the room listens to the voice of the principal. After the announcement, the room instantly returns to the low hum of activity. The teacher moves on to the next student, and the bickering over missing crayons continues.

What sets this room apart from many others like it is that a mother circulates among the tables, also checking on student work and keeping an eye on the group in the corner. She notices the squabble as well as the stray crayons that have fallen to the floor. She walks over to quiet the group and to turn their attention to the lost, now found, crayons. The teacher sees this interaction yet continues to listen to the student she is with, knowing that the situation is resolved, never once having to take her attention away from the student she works with.

In this classroom, the mother is *Graciela Lopez*, a Latina mother and first-time parent mentor. Graciela's son *Alberto* is in another kindergarten classroom, so it is the first year at Funston for both of them. Graciela is working in the classroom with *Patricia Connor*, a white teacher who has been at Funston for seventeen years. For two hours every Monday through Thursday, Graciela works with Patricia and her students. As witness to her first month as a parent mentor, I have arrived at the classroom to observe directly the work of new parent mentors and to talk to parent and teacher about the work they do together.

When I walk into the room that morning, I don't initially notice Graciela. Students are settling into their seats and getting started on the morning activity while Patricia circles the room to check up on student homework. Students start their day by physically checking in with Patricia. As she moves around the room, students tap her from behind to show her a new lunchbox, bring a tattered but completed homework sheet to win her approval, or ask for her help to unzip a jacket. With each child, Patricia pauses to give her full attention and softly encourages the child to put his or her things away or take a seat and begin the morning activity. Her soft, reassuring voice is just right for these young children, and as a teacher who seems to be in her fifties, she exhibits her years of teaching experience in the effortless way she manages a roomful of activity and excitement.

I take my seat in the back of the room, waiting for Graciela to arrive, when I notice a huddle of students at the pencil sharpener. There is Graciela, bent over the sharpener, taking one pencil at a time from the student in line next to her, focusing intently on working the sharpener, with few words or interactions with the children. The children, on the other hand, are waiting their turn, calling out, "Next me, Mrs. Lopez!" The commotion around the pencil sharpener only attracts more attention among students in the classroom, as one by one, each student decides to come sharpen a pencil as well. Beyond the actual condition of their pencils, the children are excited to get out of their seats and have the attention of the new parent in the room. However, Graciela seems uncomfortable with the attention of the rapidly expanding group of students, and she keeps herself focused on sharpening. With each sharpened pencil, she promptly urges each student back to his or her seat. From the other side of the room, Patricia notices the gathering students but chooses not to intervene, seeing that Graciela settles the group on her own. After all the pencils are sharpened and every student is seated, Graciela turns around, notices I am there, and sends me a nervous smile. She promptly walks over to Patricia to ask her what to do next.

It is the first activity of the morning, and the children are making story cards for two books they have just read: *Clifford the Big Red Dog* and *Caps for Sale*. Covers display the title, and inside the story cards, I see colorful images of unusually large red dogs and men sleeping under trees with enormous stacks of hats upon their heads. Students capture their favorite moments of a story through their vivid pictures, and I marvel momentarily at the artistic ability of young children to bring simple images to life.

Patricia circulates around the room, helping students who need extra support on the activity or who need help refocusing. Some students are well into the pictures they are drawing on the inside of the card, using crayons and colored pencils intently to illustrate the details of the story they remember. Others are still decorating the front cover, while some students struggle to copy the title from the front chalkboard to their paper. I notice a range of abilities in this room, and among those students who struggle with the activity, some abandon it altogether, moving on to distractions that are more entertaining, such as swiping a pencil from a classmate, kicking a neighboring student's chair leg, or poking around aimlessly inside their pencil box. While she works with students individually, Patricia occasionally spots these distracted students and urges them to return to the activity. But in a roomful of kindergarteners, she has to prioritize her efforts and energies, trying to stay focused on the students who need her support.

When Graciela asks Patricia what to do next, she simply replies that Graciela can be another teacher in the room, supporting students on the activity as Patricia does. As Graciela circulates around the room, she is reserved as she approaches students. While Patricia actively initiates conversations and probes students about their work, Graciela walks around silently, looking over students' shoulders and waiting for a raised hand or a question from a student. By nature, Graciela is shy and reserved. She has been quiet during our meetings, and I have often had to draw out more from her in our interviews, but in the classroom, she seems to be nervous. Her face is dewy and moist as if she is anxious about being there. She walks up to a group of students and looks to see what they have done. Two of the students are obviously off task and have barely started the assignment, but Graciela doesn't obviously help anyone at the table. She seems unsure how to initiate the conversation, choosing, instead, to wait for students to ask her for help. Meanwhile, at a table near my seat in the back of the room, students show me their pictures and ask for my help in writing. I call out the letters as a young boy, Isaac, writes them down on his story card. After a short while, another argument ensues about crayons at the table that has already bickered about them. One girl accuses a boy of using a crayon that he sneaked out of another girl's crayon box. He vehemently denies the accusation, at which point she fires back that he is lying. She immediately snatches the crayon from him, and this results in a sudden chase around the table. Graciela stands by the table, seeing what is happening but unsure what to do. Ultimately, she decides to stay out of it and waits for Patricia to settle the dispute.

Graciela is new to all this. She is unsure of how to support students and reserved in her interactions with them. She seems to use her time during this first month as an active observer—observing Patricia, getting to know students, and learning how to support them in the classroom. She does not yet know the students well, and during this first month, they don't seem to fully understand her role. Graciela looks to Patricia for her direction and instructions on what to do, as she is not yet sure what she should do at any given time. In our conversations, she notes that even classroom routines take getting used to—the expectations of students as they enter the classroom, what should be done with homework, which movements are acceptable and which are not. Rather than have Graciela stand on the sidelines or help in more administrative ways, Patricia invites Graciela to participate as she does, working with students. Graciela is not yet confident in her efforts to support students, but she is freely encouraged by Patricia to observe and learn until she is.

Toward the end of the morning, after the room has emptied and students have moved on to gym class, Graciela helps Patricia organize the homework that has come in that day. As she looks through homework folders and Patricia gets materials ready for the next lesson, the conversation turns to Alberto, Graciela's son. Graciela tells us that today was Alberto's first day in the new classroom. His previous classroom was over-enrolled with thirty-one students, so the school has moved ten students into another classroom. Graciela is concerned, because this change is occurring now, in October, after the children have become accustomed to the routines of their classroom and teacher. She asks Patricia if there is anything she should do to ease the transition for Alberto. He is disappointed to be leaving friends and a teacher he has grown fond of. Patricia agrees with Graciela that this will be a difficult transitional period for Alberto and sees that this is also a difficult transition for Graciela. Upon reflecting for a moment, the teacher offers, "Why don't you just go visit him right now? You can check on him in his classroom and see how he's doing." Graciela seems surprised and unsure about the suggestion, so Patricia offers to visit the room with Graciela now. "Why don't I go with you?" she asks. "He's probably used to this place enough by now. It won't be a big distraction to just check in on him." As I leave the room to visit another classroom upstairs, Graciela and Patricia wrap things up in the room and get ready to visit Alberto's new room. Graciela is giddy at the thought of checking in on Alberto, something, she admits to me later, she would have never dared do on her own.

As I reflect on this parting conversation, I recall my initial interview with Graciela just a month prior to this visit. I recall how visibly anxious she was when she talked about Alberto's first days in school. As she told me about his own fears and excitement in the new school, her hands were restless, her voice a near whisper, and her posture rigid. I initially accounted some of this nervousness to her quiet manner and her unfamiliarity with me. But when I began to explain that I, too, as a mother of a young child, anxiously anticipated that day when my daughter would go to school, I realized that much of Graciela's tense manner had to do with anxiety over Alberto. This moment of connection brought laughter to both of us when I admitted that my daughter was only one and a half—years away from entering kindergarten! The conversation then wandered briefly to our children and the surprising rate at which they seem to grow up. This moment released some of the anxiety Graciela had with me, but also confirmed to me how important it would be for her to be inside the school. It was important to her that Alberto feel comfortable, be liked by his teacher, and come home happy. The school was new and unfamiliar, and her fears and anxieties, as well as Alberto's, were pronounced. Being a parent mentor would allow her to do what I could imagine wanting for myself as a parent—to know for myself that the school was a place that cherished my children, nurtured their talents, encouraged new skills, and appreciated them for the multifaceted individuals they were. I understood Graciela's anxieties, and in that moment, as I left her with Patricia to visit Alberto's classroom, I realized how unsettling it was today—to have her son moved to another classroom. But through this experience as a parent mentor and specifically through the relationship with Patricia Connor, she would find ways to diminish her unfamiliarity with the school.

But as the many parents and teachers I have met have confessed, parents and teachers are often distant strangers, and the relationship between them can be strained, antagonistic, or, most frequently, absent. Developing positive relationships is often a mystery to parents and teachers alike, especially when language and culture stand as real or perceived barriers. As Graciela begins her journey as a parent at the Funston School, she admits, "This is all new to me. I'm not sure what the school expects of me, and I'm not sure what I'm allowed to do." She has the opportunity to build a relationship with a teacher who gives her some insight into the workings of the school, in essence, introducing her to the culture of the school and classroom. Through her experience, Graciela begins to understand the inner workings of a classroom, learns about teachers' expectations for their students, and generally becomes familiar with the school as an institution. And through it all, she will become more skilled in managing support for Alberto as well.

Isabel: The Difficulties in Moving Beyond Tradition

According to LSNA organizers, one goal in developing the Parent Mentor program was to move beyond a traditional model of parent involvement, where parents help teachers in the periphery of the classroom—merely building bulletin boards, making copies, and organizing the room. As we see in the case of Graciela, parent mentors are called to work with students and support the instructional needs of the classroom. But classrooms ultimately belong to teachers, and teachers have a variety of styles and approaches that shape the activities and interactions within a classroom. A teacher's working style and personality will inevitably shape the relationship he or she has with a parent mentor. And while many teachers, like Patricia Connor, may be comfortable having parent mentors work freely with students to support their learning, this is not always the case and sometimes requires a shift in teacher expectations.

This is *Isabel Diaz*'s first year at Funston, but her second year as a parent mentor. Her children previously attended a neighboring school that offered the Parent Mentor program, so although she is new to the school, Isabel is a second-year parent mentor who looks forward to returning to the classroom. She wants to support her children as they move through school, and being a parent mentor gives her greater insight into how to support them academically. Isabel explains, "When I am involved and interested in their school, they will value school and they have a better chance at staying interested in learning and doing well." She has a son and daughter who are just under a year apart, and they are each enrolled in different second-grade classrooms at Funston. Isabel looks forward to working in a first-grade classroom, because "it gives me an idea of what my kids could be doing. I can see what the teacher does and what she expects, and I can use some of those ideas to help my kids at home."

Upon first meeting Isabel, I am struck by how easy it is to talk with her. Unlike my meetings with other parents who prefer to speak in Spanish, Isabel is bilingual. By nature a self-described people person, she is friendly, engaging, and interested in getting to know people. At the training sessions, she is always one of the first parents to arrive. She sits front and center in the room, and as people begin to enter and take a seat, she makes conversation with everyone. She is Puerto Rican and converses in both English and Spanish fluently. As a result, she has the opportunity to connect with everyone in the room, and with her gregarious personality, she seems to make it her mission to get to know everyone in the group and often brings the entire group together in laughter. An astute observer of people—their sensibilities, whether or not they are integrated into a group—she often starts conversations with a quiet parent mentor who has yet to join a conversation or who sits off to the side alone.

It was often Isabel who included me in the side conversations of the early Parent Mentor training sessions, because she sensed that my momentary hesitations to join a group could be related to my novice Spanish-speaking abilities. And as I struggled to converse in Spanish, she made it comfortable for me to laugh at myself or would subtly correct me. Generally, conversations with Isabel usually involve light joking and laughing, as she uses her sense of humor to draw people in and make them feel comfortable. Around children in the school, I notice the ease with which she strikes up and maintains conversation. She has an uncanny ability to connect with any child—by remembering a name, waving across the playground, or remembering a small detail about his or her life. From these early impressions of Isabel, I look forward to seeing her in the classroom, because I believe she comes to her role as parent mentor with natural skills and abilities—as well as a facility with language—that would serve her well in the classroom.

On the day that I visit Isabel, I meet the teacher she works with. *Susan Johnson* is a young white woman in her twenties who stands with her class right outside their classroom as they prepare themselves to come inside and begin the morning. I am immediately struck by the formality of this first-grade class, compared with Patricia Connor's kindergarten class. The group stands in a line while Susan waits for a few students to settle down and get back into a straight line. When students try to share an interesting development in their day such as new shoes or a big, intact leaf they picked up outside, they are acknowledged but promptly shushed back to silence to begin the orderly entrance into the room.

Once inside, Susan prepares the front board while students put away their things and begin the morning activity. On each desk, there is an activity sheet with pictures, and students must color all the pictures of words that start with the letter *T.* Students begin to settle into their seats after they have put their lunches, backpacks, and jackets away. One by one, they take out their crayons, linger over which color they will use, and begin to start the activity. As students get to work, however, they are confused about some of the pictures on the sheet such as teepee, totem pole, and top (spinning top). These objects are unfamiliar to them, so the children begin to get distracted by fellow students or stray objects on the table. Susan continues to write on the board, but frequently calls students to settle down, quiet down, or start working, as noise and distraction begins to escalate. She looks around the class and finds that many students are slow to start the morning assignment, so she attempts to jump-start their participation by reading some of the pictures aloud and helping them begin the assignment. But every instructional direction to her class is interrupted by an order for a child to return to his or her seat, to stop talking to a classmate, or to pay attention. The pace of the classroom feels rushed as Susan attempts to simultaneously manage instruction and behavior. As I wait for Isabel to arrive, I reflect on how beneficial it might be to have Isabel help manage this roomful of restless first-graders.

Isabel enters the room late that morning. Today is class picture day, she hurriedly explains, so she spent more time this morning getting her children ready, frustrated in particular by how long it took to do her daughter's hair. Right away, she moves to a table in the back corner of the room and opens the grade book. She proceeds to check homework by looking into student folders that are kept in a stack of organized trays. She goes through each page of the homework—some filled and complete and some blank or unfinished—and then checks off the names of those who have completed the assignment, and closes the grade book when she is finished. Later, she tells me that this is how she starts each day in the classroom, as this allows Susan to know immediately who is behind and who is caught up on their homework. After she has checked the homework, Isabel waits a few minutes for a break in Susan's directions to her class, then asks her what Susan would like for her to do next. I am surprised by how formal Isabel's interactions are with Susan. I haven't yet seen this more reserved and formal side of Isabel. After a short interchange with Susan, Isabel begins to cut out some number cards from cardstock at the same table in the back corner of the room. She continues to cut these materials out as Susan reviews the morning writing activity with her students.

Throughout my time in the room, I see little interaction between Isabel and the students. She spends most of her time in the back of the room working on small projects and tidying up materials while the rest of the class either works at their tables or sits on the rug with Susan. When children move through the back of the room to get something from their cubbies, they walk by Isabel without much notice. In contrast to Patricia Connor's room, where the expectation is that Graciela will immerse herself in the activity of the classroom and slowly build a rapport with students, in this room, Isabel seems physically isolated from the rest of the class. When I talk with Isabel later that afternoon, she tells me that this is the usual routine for the mornings that she spends in Susan's room. Quite frequently, she will work in the back of the room on small projects. There is also a student with severe behavior issues, and Isabel often spends time with this boy, trying to manage his behavior and contain his outbursts. In fact, this morning, he has been moved to another room, at least temporarily. Isabel explains that some days are different, but for the most part, she is working in one of those two capacities.

Given what I know about Isabel—her ease in relating to others, her easy conversational style, and her willingness to support the needs of the classroom—I am disappointed to see her relegated to a passive role in the classroom. When she is used in this capacity, students do not directly benefit from the added resource of an additional adult in the room, and Isabel seems disconnected to Susan and her students. Isabel's work in Susan's classroom is not too different from the work of a traditional parent volunteer, where the expectation is that parents support the administrative needs of teachers and leave teachers to complete instructional tasks and work with students.

Teachers and Parents: Change Happens Slowly

As I walk through these classrooms during the month of October as routines are established and new parent mentors become acclimated to these new environments, my observations confirm my presumptions: changing schools and classrooms is a difficult and slow process. I recall the impossible stubbornness of teachers I have known—teachers who become set in their ways and inflexible to new ideas and changing practice. I have seen how just a few unwilling teachers can single-handedly undermine institutional change and progress. But I have also been the new teacher who has been overwhelmed with the seemingly endless demands and expectations of principals, students, colleagues, policies, and school districts. With so many demands, what is the utility of parent engagement? And wouldn't I feel exposed and vulnerable as a new teacher if parents were privy to my every move and decision? These are the everyday dilemmas and challenges that school reform efforts must confront. Are these challenges that LSNA acknowledges?

Although the intentions of LSNA's Parent Mentor program are to engage parents in classrooms in ways that are distinct from the traditional models of parent involvement, teachers and parents come to their interactions with one another in different ways that are guided by their own persistent beliefs and individual expectations. To change the nature of parent engagement in schools requires a change in the nature of relationships between schools and families. And as these parent narratives show us, relationships between families and schools can only be built when the walls of mistrust and misunderstanding are broken down. This will require schools that open themselves to parent participation. And while traditional models of parent involvement revolve around parents working in their child's classroom and with their child's teacher, LSNA purposefully moves away from that model of engagement, precisely because it is that relationship between a parent and a child's teacher that is most vulnerable to mistrust, skepticism, and defensiveness.

Across these two classrooms, Patricia Connor and Susan Johnson have different personalities, instructional styles, and approaches to engaging parent mentors. By working with parent mentors and developing a working relationship with a parent daily over the course of a year, these teachers make a commitment to include parents in the life of their classrooms. And while their styles and practices differ, it is only the experience itself—of parents and teachers working together—that provides any possibility of change.

BUILDING COMMUNITY

Rather than simply ensuring that parents physically get into the classrooms, the idea behind fundamental change in schools lies in building a community of families and schools. Objectives like trust and mutual appreciation, though more abstract, ultimately drive all the parties involved into a collective community bound by the common goal of educational success.

Feeling Connected

While Isabel's and Graciela's classroom experiences form the basis for their understanding of school life in ways that influence how they support their own children, both mothers explain that their sustained participation in schools is a direct result of their connection to a parent community. Isabel describes a sense of belonging she feels as part of a parent mentor cohort that "makes each day interesting" and something that she looks forward to: "I don't know if I would do this as much as I do if I wasn't part of this group. They are really nice people, kind of like a family, and when I come to school, I really look forward to seeing them and being part of the group."

Building a sense of family and community is an intentional strategy developed by LSNA organizers. Understanding that traditional parent engagement practices can restrict parents in their child's classroom to the role of merely supporting the administrative needs of the teacher, LSNA wanted to connect parents with each other. Parent mentor cohorts do just that: they connect parent mentors within a school through a common weeklong training at the start of the school year and continued weekly training sessions throughout the year. Joanna Brown, LSNA's lead education organizer, explains that for many of these parents, the Parent Mentor program is their first experience in schools. As a result, the training sessions are designed to invite them as a group with common goals and experiences. "This sets people up to go in feeling very positive about the experience as opposed to really scared when they first walk in," Joanna says. She understands that the unfamiliarity of the school environment can deter and intimidate many immigrant parents and parents who stay at home with their children, in particular, so the cohort model is designed to not only draw parents into the schools for the first time, but also to sustain their engagement over time:

> The whole idea of forming a group and a cohort is really important— especially for nonworking women with kids. For many of these women,

it is their first experience inside the schools and especially inside class-rooms, so if we were to just ask them to come in and do this work without providing them with a group and cohort that they can feel connected to—a place where they can ask questions and feel connected to other parents—then we might lose a lot of people who just aren't used to this or who are intimidated by the whole thing. The cohort sets them up to be successful, connected, and open to the experience. For a lot of immigrant parents, this is new territory.

As Ada Ayala has shared, schools can be new and unfamiliar territories that elicit anxieties. For many immigrant parents, a cohort that they can feel connected to may be critical to their sustained participation. Traditional strategies for parent engagement focused on a parent's willingness to volunteer in schools and classrooms fail to attract many immigrant parents. These efforts also struggle to maintain the participation of parents who are interested. LSNA's Parent Mentor program is rooted in the experiences of many low-income communities of color—where parent involvement is low, where schools may lack creative strategies to draw parents into schools, and where multiple factors such as linguistic and cultural differences often become barriers between schools and families.

At Funston, I have had the opportunity to witness the development of the cohort and how it supports parents like Graciela and Isabel. Each day of the initial week-long training consists of a series of interactive, engaging, team-building activities that keep parent mentors moving about the room, talking with one another, and sharing their stories about family, children, and education. Every woman in the room—they are all women in this group: mothers, grandmothers, and aunts—is connected through her children, and every story they tell begins with their family, their children. LSNA organizers who facilitate the training use these connections as springboards for discussion, as conversation starters among partners, and as the basis for many activities throughout the training. Day by day throughout the October training, these activities and conversations change the tone of the training sessions from the formal to the familiar.

I recall the first day of training, as sixteen mothers shuffle into Room 307. It is a cool, brisk October day, and classrooms are not yet heated.

As I walk into the room, I keep my jacket on and help Reynalda Covarrubias prepare the room. Reynalda is a Latina LSNA staff member who coordinates the Parent Mentor program at Funston. The room is large, and the walls bare; this seems to be an extra classroom that is primarily empty during the day and used in the evenings for adult classes. I see algebraic formulas on the blackboard, along with some instructions for homework. The furniture in the room is sparse; as a result, the high ceilings and tile floors cause all conversation and room noise to echo, creating an air of formality in the room. Reynalda moves briskly this morning, her arms full of plastic ware, plates, refreshments, and a big coffeepot. I offer my help, taking the coffeepot from her arms, and we chat about our expectations and anticipations for the day.

I have met Reynalda on several occasions since the start of my research project. She is energetic and gracious and has been central in making me feel welcome among the parents at Funston, but she is most fluent in Spanish and I am still finding my way in the language. As we move tables and lay out refreshments, we speak in short and punctuated sentences. She is anxious to get everything set up, and I am anxious to communicate well—with her now and with the other parent mentors throughout the week. In discussing her expectations for today, she admits, "I love new beginnings, but there is something that makes me nervous about them, too. I have met these parents, they are wonderful, and I have been thinking about what the group will be like this year. We are a community. This is what I am preparing for today."

As we arrange the last remaining chairs around the table, the first parent mentors begin to enter the room and take their seats. As the empty chairs around the table fill, I look around the room—at the coffee, the refreshments, the U-shaped table, the evenly spaced chairs, the journals that will be passed around, and Reynalda taking her place by the door to welcome parents. I realize that everything about this training is intentional—intentional toward building a group and community.

As each parent enters the room, she settles into a chair, keeping her jacket on, and taking her place at the table in quiet anticipation for the meeting to begin. The room is quiet and still when the session begins. Leticia Barrera and Ofelia Sanchez, both Latina and former parent mentors who are currently education organizers at LSNA, will facilitate this week's training. Leticia will lead the sessions in Spanish for the convenience of most parent mentors, and Ofelia translates into English for the few parents who do not speak Spanish.

Leticia, a veteran of these training sessions, quickly warms up the room with an enthusiastic welcome and an animated introduction. Her stride is confident as she walks across the room, looking each person in the eye as she speaks with enthusiasm and excitement, trying to bring energy into a roomful of quiet and observant women. Everything she says has a certain order or purpose and reflects her own knowledge of how parents may feel on this first day and the many times she has conducted these sessions. She begins by explaining that the hard work and dedication of parents were fundamental to the successful start of the Parent Mentor program years ago. She then talks about the important role that parents can play in their child's life and in the lives of other children at the school when they are involved in classrooms. Her language about parents is strong, assertive, and direct—she wants to let parents know that they are embarking on a critical journey and an experience that will make a difference in the school. Leticia gives parents a sense of why they will share this experience as a group this week and throughout the year: "We are here, because we have something in common. We are parents, and we care about this school. In this room, we will get to know each other and begin to care about each other. We will soon see this school as a family that is connected by the work we all do together."

Besides the goal of bringing parent mentors together as part of a larger community, Leticia wants parents to be open to the possibilities that this experience will bring and to hear her as someone who understands both their current situation and the possibilities that lie ahead. She tells these parents that she wants to connect with them from the very beginning:

Years ago, I was right where you are now. I decided to become a parent mentor, and I was part of this training, too. It was during this experience that I realized I had to make a decision. At the time, I was working in a plastic factory, and I knew that I had to keep working or go back to school and get an education. And once I started working in the schools, I realized that my place was in the classroom and that I needed to finish school. I realized I wanted to be a bilingual teacher, and this experience helped make that happen.

Leticia realizes that parents may be unsure or timid when they begin their work as parent mentors. As an organizer, she must connect with those feelings that shape their entry into the Parent Mentor program. She wants parents to feel positive about the experience and confident as they begin their work in the classroom. Consequently, she starts every training with a point of connection to relate to them and to open their minds to new possibilities. She admits to me later, "I would not believe it that I am here doing this, but here I am. I am leading these parents. I want them to know that this was a new possibility for me, something I didn't expect." She says that subsequently, at the start of every training session she leads, she tells parents about her own transformation:

I always let parents know, now I'm here doing this training in front of you, but before, I was like you. I was sitting in those chairs, very quiet, but now, I'm not a quiet person. When my son was in pre-K, and I first started the Parent Mentor program, I was very shy, too. I was a mom. Most of the time, I was spending at home cleaning and doing differ- ent things that moms are supposed to do. But I had an opportunity to be part of a program and discover some new skills that everyone has. We just need an opportunity to know those skills and know that this is what I can do.

The quiet that Leticia describes as part of her early days as a parent mentor is evident in the room on this first day of training. The room remains as quiet as it was at the beginning of the session, as parents be- come acclimated to the new environment. I observe the four newly involved parent mentors I met days before, and I recollect how parts of our conversation reflected the fears and anticipation about entering schools. Today, they, too, seem more timid, more reticent. Isabel, usu- ally gregarious and talkative, is a quiet but active observer on the edge of her seat during this first session, catching my eye periodically as if to check in with me regarding an unusually long silence in the discussion or a moment of laughter. Graciela rushes in to the first meeting late, takes a deep breath, and sits in the back of the room before she is ushered up to the table by another parent, who makes room for her. During these two hours, she has not made a single movement and quietly watches the proceedings. These are the typical interactions and exchanges during the first hours of the first session, as parents, not unlike me, decide to soak in the environment and get a sense of who is in the room, why we are all here, and how this is all going to turn out.

As Leticia and Ofelia share their experiences and draw their connections to the parents, others in the room become more comfortable and willing to share their stories. Role-playing and ice-breaker activities get parents talking, moving, and interacting more comfortably. They are supported by a small group of returning parent mentors who want to encourage their new colleagues and welcome them to the group. These returning parents have gone through this training and the parent mentor experience before and serve as an added layer of support for the new parent mentors.

It is a comic moment, however, that truly breaks the stillness of the new group. Parents are split into two groups, and one group is sent outside the room to wait while the remaining people in the room are instructed to completely ignore their partner during a conversation that will ensue. The other group returns to the room to be paired with a parent they don't yet know. Following brief instructions to share their personal stories about parenting, the conversations across the room are stilted and made awkward by the disinterested partners, who are under instructions not to respond. With the room in laughter after they realize they have been misled, the group discusses the ways students may feel when they are not heard or don't receive the individual attention from teachers and peers that they need. Energetic and lively, parents describe the potential role they can play in classrooms. *Shauna*, a black woman who is new to the program, suggests, "I can see how important it is for me to understand what that child is going through and being there, listening to them, giving them my full attention, so that they will feel that what they have to say is interesting and important."

67

During this discussion, a host of veteran parent mentors chime in about the rewards of the work they have experienced in past years, validating Shauna's point. Lisa Contreras, a Latina mother and former parent mentor, explains that "these students need you—your attention, your care, your eyes, and your ears, because many of them don't get the attention they need at home, and it's too hard sometimes for a teacher with a big class to be so involved." *Stella*, a Latina whose grandchildren attend Funston where she is also a veteran parent mentor, concurs: "You will realize that for many students, you are their chance in having that one-on-one attention that they desperately need."

Both for the new parent mentors who have never stepped inside classrooms to work alongside teachers and for the teachers themselves, the experiences of veteran parent mentors is reassuring and encouraging—and invaluable. Graciela admits, "I'm not sure what to expect in the classroom next week, but when I hear about the others, I feel better about going in. And I understand what I can do for the children."

This communication and relationship building across new and veteran parent mentors provides a positive network of knowledge and support for newly involved parent mentors and integrates the new people into an already-existing community. Leticia describes some of LSNA's intentions in bringing the veteran and new groups together and encouraging interactions between them:

> Well, I think that it's a good mix, because there's the knowledge that the former parent mentors can share. That's why I put them together— I pair them some new, some old, some according to the language, too. But I feel that if we have parents with experience and also new parents, for those new parents, it's easier for them to explore something and they can just help each other . . . or to be an example for the new parent. Former parent mentors can do a lot for the new parent mentors by being there with them in the training and then through the school year.

Eventually, as parents share their stories about children and family, the group dynamic begins to change. Light laughter fills in the quiet spaces, and there is a buzz of conversation before each session and during the breaks as parent mentors chat over refreshments. Parents walk in each morning to take their claimed spaces around the table, but as they settle into their seats, they are animated in their greetings to those beside them, and the conversations begin with more ease and familiarity. Even on the second day, the discussions are much more informal. Parents talk about their first impressions of each other and how they are breaking them down. Shauna admits some of her misunderstandings about *Renee*, a shy and reserved Latina mother who was Shauna's discussion partner for two days: "When I met her yesterday, I thought she was being cold and mean, because she didn't say much when I was talking to her, but then I realized afterwards, it was because she didn't speak English that well, not that she was trying to be rude."

She and Renee laugh in agreement, as others in the room concur that the icebreakers are indeed working and helping parents understand each other and feel connected. Shauna adds, "Without this, I may have just met her or maybe I wouldn't even meet her, but I wouldn't have a chance to change my first impression of her. She would have been just another parent I passed in the hall." LSNA organizers have often told me about the quick change in atmosphere and energy among parents during the training week, but it is quite remarkable to experience it firsthand. The change each day is noticeable as organizers work to build a community of parents.

I, too, am beginning to find my place among these mothers. In many ways, I am as much a newcomer to this school and group as some of them are. Each month, I travel from Boston to this Northwest Side neighborhood in Chicago to understand the parent narratives that shape the life of the school and community. As I share with these parents my own journey as a new mother and listen to their stories of parenting, struggle, hard choices, and immigration, I feel a growing affinity to them. While our life situations are different in some respects, I recognize the familiar echoes of immigration, educational dreams, personal struggle, and the common experience of parenthood that connects us all. In sharing their personal stories, these mothers build webs of connection that can bring a greater sense of community and purpose to a group that might otherwise be distant and disconnected. Day to day and over the course of the year, these are changes that take place through the Parent Mentor program.

Confronting Challenges

Through these conversations, it is clear that many parents face steep challenges in their own lives—challenges that influence their participation in schools and how they support their children's education. *Imelda* is a Latina mother who grew up in Chicago and just recently moved back to Logan Square from Minnesota with her son. As a single parent who struggles to meet the unforgiving demands of work and family, she has moved several times to find a better environment for her work and her son's education. Now back in Chicago, she admits her fears to her fellow parent mentors during a training session:

> When I left Chicago, it was hard to raise one child and become a single mother, and I didn't have anything here. Now that I'm back, I want the best for my kids, but it is just hard as a single mother. I have to stay on top of everything, but I'm not sure how, and the older he gets, the harder it is for me to help him at home. I am just hoping that this program is going to help us out, because sometimes I feel like there is so much working against this all working out for the best.

For Imelda, supporting her son is a challenge because of the demands of single parenting. She has tried to become involved in her son's schools before, with varying degrees of success, but has always felt that she is on her own: "I do what I need to do and what I have time to do, but I have never been part of a group like this before. Honestly, I felt a little uncomfortable with a group like this at first, but I am starting to see how this can help me—being connected to other people."

When I talked with Imelda earlier in the week, she told me that this group allows her to see that others have similar experiences. For her, these shared experiences offer support and encouragement. Upon listening to Imelda's struggles as a single parent, several fellow parent mentors admitted to having similar experiences that make the sheer act of parent involvement a seeming impossibility. But knowing that participation in this group will not dramatically alter the conditions within which many of these parents and their children live, Leticia reminds parents that this group, over time, can become a source of support: "This is your family now. LSNA is your family, and we are here to support you now. So you don't have to feel as if you are on your own or that you have to do this yourself. And at the same time, you are going to be a source of support for someone who needs it."

While the group will not solve all the problems that affect the lives of parents and families, Leticia believes the relationships between parents will encourage them to make some of the changes that are necessary and that they have control over. She finds that often, as in her own initial experience, parents become the parents who raised them, even when past models are not always ideal models to follow.

This point is made clearer during the third day of the training as Leticia and Ofelia begin to build on the personal stories parents have shared over the first couple days and to discuss the participants' role as parents and their involvement in their children's education. In one particular activity, parents discuss the activities that they do with their children to promote self-esteem and to encourage their development as learners. *Sarah*, a black woman whose nieces attend the school, says that she makes a point of telling her two nieces that she loves them every day: "Just that little phrase, I think, can make a difference in how they start out their day, how they show up at school, ready to succeed." She explains that she never heard this as a child, although she "desperately wanted it," and it is precisely for this reason that she does this for her nieces.

In this moment, I think back on the interviews I've had with the new parent mentors during the previous week. Isabel creates for her children's education a support structure that was absent for her as a child. Imelda still feels anger toward her parents for their neglect, although her passion for doing the best she can for her son comes from the same wellspring of anger that defines her childhood and education. *Sarita Flores* recalls how unimportant education was for her as a daughter in a poor, working-class Mexican family and how little attention she received from her family. These women all share stories of the support, love, and encouragement that was both missing in their lives and sorely needed. As a result, for them, education was stopped short, incomplete. Isabel and Imelda never finished high school, and Sarita never felt that her abilities amounted to much, because of the constant neglect and criticism from her own parents. Even Leticia, during this discussion that Sarah has begun, says that through her own experience, she has often used the excuse "that our parents didn't do it," and that this is often "why it is so hard for us, but that is why we have to do this—because it will give our children the confidence to succeed."

Amid this discussion, I am surprised to see Sarita's hand go up for a comment. While I know some of her personal story through an interview we had earlier in the week, she has not yet spoken during the training sessions this week, and I have often wondered how she feels about the training. She looks down at her hands nervously as she begins to tell us how hard it is for her to be affectionate with her children, as a result of her childhood. She cries as she recounts those experiences that have, unfortunately, become the basis for her own relationship with her children: "My parents never showed me that they loved me, and now it's hard for me to see my own children and say that 'I love you' and give them a hug. It's hard and very difficult for me. Sometimes, I feel bad, because I can't do it, but I know that I love my children."

This is the first time the room has heard her voice, and now she shares with raw honesty some of her struggles as a parent. The room is still as she speaks. As tears roll down her face, she is comforted by the new acquaintances around her, and others begin to connect to her story. One woman speaks of parents who taught her with tough words and actions that often left her wanting affection from them and inevitably having to find it elsewhere. After a long pause, Imelda recalls with overwhelming emotion that her parents were not present in her life at all: "My parents ignored us. And I will never ignore my kids . . . Now, every day, when I pick them up from school, I ask them about their day and ask them if they have homework. I am there for them. I show them love, and I'm learning every day."

These women admit that their parents only raised them in ways that were familiar to this older generation and that open forms of affection were often unfamiliar ways of interacting with children. Yet, as parents, the women in the room see how much children need and want affection, attention, and encouragement. During this conversation, however, the participants see that their actions as parents are greatly influenced by their own history, their family ghosts. Those whose own parents have failed to support and love them in positive and encouraging ways realize they must break the cycle and discover ways of parenting that will develop confidence and happiness in their children. Shauna tries to reconcile past mistakes with a more hopeful view that keeps the well-being of children in mind: "A lot of times, we make mistakes as adults, and because [our kids] are young, we don't always think it's important to apologize or express our feelings. We think that since they are kids, their opinions don't matter. But I think if we want them to come to us about the problems and let us know what's going on with them, it's important for us to acknowledge their feelings."

A NEW LEGACY: HOPE AND CHANGE

Shauna's comment during that discussion exemplifies a common characteristic of these training discussions—hope and change. These parents do not remain in discussions of past mistakes and current struggles. In support of Shauna's comment, Leticia adds that the motivation for change is the child who benefits—"our own children and the children in the school." She explains:

> Because that's not what we grew up with, but that doesn't mean that we can't change things now and raise our kids in an even better environment. Isn't that what we want? To find the best ideas for our children? So in this environment here as parent mentors, we are sharing our best ideas and helping us be the best parents and to be the best parent mentors who make a difference in these kids' lives.

Leticia, Ofelia, and other LSNA organizers encourage parents to see the resources that are available around them to bring about change and to use each other as pivotal sources of support for those daunting challenges. In doing so, these leaders foster a network of parents who clearly articulate their shared goals and experiences and begin to work together to support and encourage each other. By working collectively and keeping their goals set on improving the environment for their children, parents can, Leticia believes, "get rid of the negative things and try to break that cycle and start a new life."

Leticia explains that many of these transformative discussions—discussions that bring parents closer together and help them identify common ground—are spontaneous: "We never know what is going to be that discussion that changes the group." In reflecting on Sarita's description of her own childhood lack of affection, Leticia noticed how Sarita's sharing became an opening for other parents, in particular, Imelda:

> So when Sarita started talking, I looked at Imelda, and she—I think that was the moment for Imelda where she was ready to just break down the wall. Because the first couple days, she seemed like a very strong person. And the first day she said, "I've done all this parent work before and so I want to see how you do it here." And she was being very strong and kind of building a wall—protecting herself, almost—because she didn't really know anyone and she didn't know what they were going to be like. And I think when Sarita said what she said, it really gave Imelda an opportunity to break some of the walls down. And from where I was sitting, I could see that she started to cry.

Breaking Down Walls

During the training and throughout the year, parents like Imelda and Sarita will continue to overcome obstacles and break down some of the walls that they bring with them to the schools. According to Leticia, "they will just look at the world in a different color" as they work inside classrooms—getting to know students, teachers, and the complex culture of schools and classrooms. But as Leticia explains, each parent's journey varies, and "the change will be totally different in each parent." During the first week of training, she reflects on the change she has noticed in Imelda:

> Today, she was really expressing herself. Before that, she was participating, but not in that way. In order to open up like that, it's because something happened in the training. Something touched her very deep. It is the same thing in the classroom when they are working with a group of students or with the teacher. They may not be sure of themselves there, but soon they will do it. And they will just discover themselves, their skills.

Each new parent mentor arrives with an individual set of expectations, priorities, personal narratives, and school experiences. While Imelda has opened herself up to the questions and perspectives presented by LSNA organizers and made some powerful connections between her personal history and her goals as a mother, other parent mentors like Graciela and Isabel absorb the conversation but refrain from participating openly. Over the course of a year, however, I notice Isabel's growing openness with the cohort and her broadening involvement in school and community issues. And while Graciela remains a quiet participant in the year's training sessions, she gains a clearer articulation of the goals she has for Alberto, from her work in classrooms. For many parents, their experiences as parent mentors can be as much about connection to others as it is about self-revelations. While some may enter the program with clear intentions about how the experience will help them support their children in school, others come because they enjoy working with children or because it is an opportunity to be outside the home for the first time. Regardless of the reasons, the changes are apparent.

Over the school year, I witness some of the changes that Leticia has predicted. I see these parent mentors evolve—becoming more confident and assertive in their interactions with teachers and students, becoming friends who celebrate new babies, praying for the health of ailing husbands, and grieving the tragic events that unfold in their community.

Each Friday, as parents come together for their weekly Parent Mentor workshops, I sense the deepening relationships among them, the earnest and honest questions they ask of each other, and the enthusiastic agendas of parents who are committed to improving the school.

A Renewed Sense of Engagement

Amid the developing sense of a collective, where parents identify shared interests, work collaboratively, and support one another, the individual life circumstances of parent mentors often pose seemingly insurmountable challenges to staying involved. After two months at Funston, Imelda returns to Milwaukee, where she has greater family support and more economic stability. During the year, two other parent mentors leave the program because of increasing demands from family or employment. Isabel ponders leaving the program when an opportunity to babysit promises some needed family income. And Graciela suffers marital problems toward the end of the year, a situation that threatens her regular commitments to Patricia Connor's classroom.

While Graciela and Isabel ultimately stay on to complete their commitments as parent mentors, these situations are not unusual. To keep parents connected to a confidante or adviser who can help them navigate those decisions successfully, LSNA provides each school with a parent mentor coordinator to oversee the program and connect individually with parent mentors. At Funston, Reynalda plays this intermediary role by balancing the program's work at the school with the organizing and training agenda of LSNA. Reynalda is connected to each parent mentor—her struggles in the classroom, her successes throughout the program, and the life experiences that shape her participation in the program. As part of LSNA's organizing strategy, one-on-one relationships become a foundation for the development of a sense of community and shared interest. At Funston, Reynalda is often referred to as the mother of the parent mentors; she understands how these parents balance the demands of family and school, and she often serves as a confidante for difficult and challenging matters. Leticia explains that change in individuals is intricately linked to the connections people may make, often as a result of these one-on-one meetings: "It's not enough to train them. It's just the beginning. We have to be available to talk with them, help them figure things out. That's the whole reason why we have the one-on-one meetings with them. People change because they make a connection with someone or because someone helps them see a pattern that they cannot see by themselves."

For Graciela, who is shy and introverted by nature and does not connect as quickly and strongly to others as someone like Isabel may, Reynalda has been a strong and steady friend who listens and offers her advice. Graciela views Reynalda as a role model, someone who has challenged her to take bold steps, but who has also encouraged her abilities. At the end of the year, when Graciela endures marital problems that threaten to radically alter her family's circumstances, she tells me that Reynalda is the only one she confides in and that Reynalda has encouraged her to continue working in the school, in hopes that it will be a much-needed distraction. Similarly, Isabel, who comes to the Funston Parent Mentor program from another school, argues that Reynalda's leadership is distinctive and shapes the experience of all those who participate in the program:

> She is like the mother hen. What she does is she holds us all together; she makes me feel that we are capable and can make a difference here. I see her as a leader in this school. And by being with her and getting to know her, it definitely encourages me to think about what I might be able to do, you know, what kind of leader I could become.

And indeed, through Reynalda's support and guidance, Isabel has been active in school life and broader community campaigns. She has opened her home to a group of Funston families and teachers in support of LSNA's Literacy Ambassadors program; she has participated in balanced-development campaigns and rallies and has helped organize a Family Reading Night at the school. And when I ask her about next year, she admits that she has her sights set on being a parent tutor—an LSNA program where parents work individually with students throughout the school to support their reading skills. Rather than building a close relationship with a teacher and a group of students, as participants do through the Parent Mentor program, tutors work directly with students who need the added instructional support.

Through her participation, Isabel has not only become familiar with school culture, but also begun to take on opportunities to lead. When I ask her where she sees herself a few years from now, she describes a willingness to coordinate a program, be a parent tutor, become more involved in community campaigns: "I think I'm realizing I'm good at this, and this makes a difference for everyone—for the kids I work with but also for my own kids who need to see a role model in me."

THE REALITY AND POSSIBILITY OF CHANGE

In April, I schedule my last observation in Susan Johnson's classroom to observe Isabel at work. Just a few days earlier, over lunch, Isabel tells me that she and Susan have become comfortable with each other and often spend time talking about Isabel's daughter *Samantha*, who lately has had difficulty with her reading. Isabel carefully observes what Susan does with her students to support reading development, and they often talk about some of the strategies, resources, and opportunities Samantha could benefit from. Beyond the classroom, I have also noticed Isabel's own assuredness as a newly emerging parent leader. She attends and plays an active role in training sessions, goes beyond her required hours in the classroom to offer more support to Susan, attends field trips as a chaperone, and develops relationships with students she has come to know well. She spends four mornings each week in Susan's classroom, and by the end of the year, she has become an integrated part of the school community. But I secretly wonder how much, if at all, has changed in Susan's classroom.

On this busy morning in May, however, as I work my way into the new primary wing of the school, I see Susan walking her class down the hallway. I am immediately struck by her lightness and comfort with students—joking with a young boy about his homework and gathering two girls around her as another comes up to welcome her with a hug. My presence in her classroom this time is effortless as well; when I remind her that I will be spending the morning with them, there is no hesitation as she welcomes me to walk up to the room with them. As we make our way up the stairs and closer to her classroom, she begins to shush her students, abruptly ordering them to stand in line, eliminate the chatter, and calm down—in essence preparing for entrance into Room 200. Upon entering the room, I see Isabel organizing materials on tables, straightening up the room. On this warm and sunny morning as Chicago finally warms up to spring, Isabel looks radiant. I see her hair down for the first time, and she is dressed in a sharp, contemporary outfit of bold reds and blacks.

Students—girls in particular—flock to Isabel as soon as we enter. She is approachable, warm, gregarious, and caring. One student shows her a toy she has brought into school, to which Isabel responds with a laugh, "Oh, we call that bootleg—you better put that away!" A young girl passes on a message from her mother while another admires her long hair. The air between Isabel and these students is lighthearted, trusting, and familiar. This is a dramatic contrast from the beginning of the year.

Isabel goes right into her routine of checking homework, sitting at a small student desk in the back corner of the room. She goes through each student's folder, checking for complete homework, keeping track of who has fallen behind. She calls them over, asking them about their missing homework, to which each student responds with a short explanation or mild ambivalence. They acknowledge and accept Isabel's questions about their work and promise to her that tonight will be different.

When finished, Isabel puts away papers in students' mailboxes, tidies up some more, and then asks Susan what she'd like next, to which the teacher responds with a request to clean the tables. Susan helps Isabel find the cleaning supplies, and while the class is on the rug sharing journals with Susan, Isabel washes tables with a big scrub brush and a bottle of cleaner. This seems odd, for her to be so blatantly cleaning and organizing the room, with little interaction with students. As Isabel cleans the tables, the students are gathered in a circle at the front of the room, sharing their journal writing. As they read excerpts from their journals, it is obvious that a few students have misunderstood the assignment and will need to rewrite their entries. I saw these students, moments earlier, working independently without much support from Susan, who was circulating around the room. In all the other parent mentor classrooms I have visited this year, I see parent mentors support students' academic work—by moving around the room and assisting students as needed or by working one-on-one or in small groups for students who need support. As Susan's students share their stories on the rug, I can't help but feel that an opportunity has been lost. While Isabel attends to the minute details of the physical environment, students may stumble and fall academically, and the learning environment seems to be unnecessarily compromised.

For some parents like Isabel, the distance that remains between them and a teacher will sometimes be discouraging and may have an impact on their future involvement in the school. After months of working in Susan's classroom, Isabel tells me, "I'm not sure why Susan still uses me this way, but it is what it is. I think that's just where she is now, and I don't really think about it or expect more." When I ask her how this will affect her involvement as a parent mentor next year, she answers, "I'm not sure if I want to be a parent mentor next year. I have a great time with the students, and I love being with them, but maybe next year, I'll try to do something that gets me involved with students more, like maybe be a parent tutor. I think I'm ready for a change."

While Isabel is sometimes disappointed by the limits placed on her work in Susan's classroom, she is enthusiastic about the new community of parents she has become part of: "Being a parent mentor is just part of being in the classroom. A big part of it is getting to know these other parents, who you really start to care about. You get to know them, their kids, and they are really like your family when you walk into this place."

Her sentiments are shared by many parent mentors who feel connected to a broader community of parents, teachers, administrators, and families who share the common goal of improving the school and setting students on the path to academic, social, and emotional success. As parent mentors, they are widely recognized by students with whom they have worked in classrooms over the years. As Funston parent mentor Gipsie Santiago explains, many of these students feel a connection to parent mentors and a reassurance with this parental presence:

And because I live here and I know what they know, sometimes I really feel like they feel a connection with me. Maybe they see their mother or their neighbor or their aunt in me, but they see something in me that they can relate to, and I think that kids need that in school. So they don't feel like they are being taught by a bunch of people who don't really know what they're about. And the fact that we are parents in the school makes it even more powerful for kids, like this school is a place where people in my community are leading.

Just as schools become more familiar places for parents as they work inside classrooms and build relationships with teachers, Gipsie's sentiments reveal the possibility that as parents become active participants and leaders, the school becomes a more familiar and comfortable place for students. What results is a sense of community that forms around relationships, points of connection, and an ethos of trust, familiarity, and respect.

For Graciela, who is not naturally gregarious and often spends her time in training sessions quietly off to the side, she feels that her experience in the Parent Mentor program has given her a sense of confidence in the school. Through her time in the classroom, she has clear ideas about how to support Alberto at home. She admits an increased facility in striking up conversations with teachers—when just a year ago, she rarely approached them, often unaware of what the boundaries for conversations might be. She has gone beyond the expectations of the Parent Mentor program, committing more time to Patricia's classroom to attend field trips and assist her on classroom projects. While Graciela will always be a soft-spoken woman who encourages cooperation from students rather than demanding it, she has taken on a more assured stance in her interactions at the school. She quickly chides students who misbehave in the hallway. With fellow parent mentors, she begins to be a part of discussions. Although she remains silent for most of the meeting, during the informal moments between sessions and before and after the training, she is joking, laughing, and talking with the others.

But most notable is the profound effect the Parent Mentor program has on Graciela's sense of agency within the school. She feels an ability to advocate for Alberto—an ability that is directly a result of her experience as a parent mentor: "I think that when he is in the school, I can make sure he is getting what he needs. I know this is something that is my responsibility, and I think I know enough about this school to talk to people or just watch over a situation. I know what I can do."

Through conversations with Patricia, she gets a sense of teacher expectations but also an understanding that teachers and parents can collaborate on decisions that are in the best interests of students. In light of this experience, Graciela has learned that "decisions are not always final," and that there can be room for parents to ask questions and challenge. But through the classroom experience, Graciela is also enjoying the relationships she builds with students, the myriad ways she can support student learning, and as a result, she is pondering a career in teaching. Currently enrolled in a nursing program, Graciela finds elements of a teaching career compelling. Throughout the year, she begins to evaluate her work in classrooms and considers changing her own educational course and direction. She believes that teaching can be a worthwhile profession, particularly in a school like Funston, where parents and teachers feel they are part of a collective community.

Graciela is not the first parent mentor to feel drawn to the field of teaching through an experience in the classroom. These parent mentors value the connections that exist between teachers and families, believe that these connections should be more pronounced, and sense the promise of their own skills and abilities as teachers. As part of a collective community, parents see the many possible ways they can become integrated into schools. In fact, many parents attest to a more intimate sense of community, not unlike that of a family. On numerous occasions, I hear parents speak of the school community as a family, and their work in the school to benefit "not just my child, but all the children." Clearly, their work as parent mentors in classrooms and spaces outside of their child's own space has opened them up to the possibility that they teach, act, and lead on behalf of the many children and families of Funston. Lisa Contreras, a former parent mentor, emphasizes that over the years, she has felt a growing sense of responsibility toward all the children in the school, not just her own. While she previously looked at schools solely through the perspective of her children's experience, that is now impossible:

> These are all our kids, and if you see anything going on, or you see anyone who needs help, or you see a child crying—you are going to stop and you are going to find out what's going on with that child. That's one important thing that I learned as a parent mentor—that all of these kids are my responsibility, not just my own. In this school, that means that there are other adults and parents who are looking out for my children, too. If we see something that concerns us or troubles us, we don't look the other way because it's not our business. In fact, it is my business, and I have to let other adults in the school know, because this is the community that surrounds my child every day. It's all connected.

Lisa feels a responsibility to all the children in the school; she is invested in the broader community of the school. And she contends that through this network of parent mentors, her children are now watched and supported by many individuals, not just herself. If this is the case, and a sense of collective community and responsibility abounds, then students stand to benefit from a rich network of concerned adults who look after their interests.

4

SEEING THINGS EYE TO EYE

A Mutually Engaging Model for Parent Participation

IN THE BACK OF THIS light and airy classroom, I take my seat by the computer stations, which by contrast are dusty, dim, and seemingly unused. I pull out a small, child-sized chair from a small, child-sized table and attempt to get comfortable. The teacher, *Muriel Wolcott*, is a woman with a low voice that carries into every corner of the room. She keeps herself rooted at the front and center of the classroom, where she explains the instructions for a writing assignment. At the sight of students who are momentarily distracted, she stops midsentence for an abrupt moment of silence, waiting for their attention. This second-grade classroom is neatly organized into table groups of four. Despite the fact that students face each other in these arrangements, there are few distractions and the room is orderly. In marked contrast, one young girl, *Layla*, sits alone a few feet away from me. She is set aside from her classmates, and while they have open composition books in front of them, she does not. Instead, she has a book about Rosa Parks on her desk, which she pushes across the surface of her desk, occasionally opening the book to a seemingly random page, only to close it and slide it across the table again. She keeps an eye on me and watches as I pull out a pen and notebook and settle into my seat. While the rest of the class is focused on Muriel and the writing activity, Layla seems to barely notice. While Muriel again stops midsentence to address even the slightest of offenses by the other students, Layla's disinterest and lack of participation go unchecked.

At that moment, while I puzzle about this contradiction, *Sarita Flores* walks in. She is starting her morning a few minutes late and puts her bag behind Muriel's desk. She listens for a moment to get caught up on the activity, then moves over to my corner of the room and promptly pulls a chair next to Layla. Sarita asks her to take out her composition book like the others and quietly redirects her to the writing activity for the class. Layla voluntarily puts her book away and pulls out a pencil. All the while, Sarita whispers quiet words of approval and encouragement. As Muriel completes her instructions to the class, Layla, along with the others, readies herself to begin the independent activity.

DEVELOPING MUTUALITY THROUGH NEW RELATIONSHIPS BETWEEN SCHOOLS AND FAMILIES

In developing mutuality, that is, in creating a mutually beneficial relationship between families and schools, the needs of both parties must be considered. Mutuality is not a zero-sum process; addressing one participant's needs does not necessarily diminish the needs of another. Rather, by considering the experiences and desires of all those involved, school communities benefit from the added trust, respect, and reciprocity. Everyone stands to gain in developing mutuality. Let's look at how LSNA and area schools worked toward a mutually beneficial relationship.

Addressing the Needs of Schools

When LSNA first started working with Funston School to create the Parent Mentor program, students like Layla came to the forefront of LSNA organizers' minds—students who were sometimes lost in the midst of larger classrooms and a wide array of student abilities. LSNA sought a model that brought parents into classrooms in ways that would alleviate some of the current demands placed on teachers while providing an experience that would give parents insight into schools. With the early struggles of overcrowding and Chicago's diminishing use of paraprofessional support in classrooms, schools were dealing with larger classrooms that were sometimes difficult for teachers to manage. As a consequence, some teachers, like Amanda Rivera at Funston, were concerned that class size was impairing student learning. She explained that a program to involve parents in schools would have to consider the challenges in many classrooms:

> The whole idea was to get them involved in a significant way that would help create smaller class size in the classroom, where we don't have parents doing bulletin boards or grading papers or the typical peripheral things that need to get done, but to really impact student learning and student relationships. The parents were trained to work directly with students, so we were trying to address the issue of size and isolation in the classroom, and the issue of time. Teachers often don't have enough time to really work one-on-one with the different students. So, parents are able to assist with that.

While traditional parent programs might typically bring parents to work in the periphery of a classroom, LSNA's program would bring parents directly into working relationships with students to provide added support during the instructional day. These were the needs that the school identified, and the organization designed training sessions that would prepare parent mentors to support student learning in the classroom.

While these were the initial motivations for bringing parents into classrooms, parent mentors, principals, and teachers continue to identify classrooms as places in need of ongoing support. Ana Martinez Estka, principal of Avondale Elementary School, a Logan Square neighborhood school and LSNA partner, explains that she was ready to launch a Parent Mentor program soon after she was hired. She wanted to build additional resources that would respond to swelling enrollments and class size. Teachers feel this burden as well. Angela Vacco, a teacher at Mozart Elementary School, explains that with a parent mentor, "together we get everything done"—be it preparing for lessons, grading homework, administering tests for students who were absent, or passing out student work. Without a parent mentor, the daily routines would be overwhelming. Likewise, Ana Cabrera, who has been teaching at Avondale for three years, believes parent mentors meet a pressing need in the classroom. With twenty-nine kindergarteners and no teaching assistant, as well as her newness to teaching, she feels that having a parent mentor in her class is a "great deal of help." She admits just how much she counts on her parent mentors:

> I don't even think about it . . . The parents are like our assistants, because if I didn't have that, I would be like, "Oh God, what am I going to do?" They get me through the week, Monday through Thursday. They come in for two hours, so it's a big bulk of time that they can help out with the classroom. It helped me in a lot of ways.

But even for veteran teachers like Patricia Connor, who has taught for twenty-eight years, parent mentors "fill a need in the school," through their weekly commitments in the classroom. With the support of parent mentors, she explains, "my students have a better chance at meeting the expectations, and I can relieve some of the stresses that come with teaching larger classes." Similarly, Melva Patock, also a teacher at Funston, admits, "Now I really feel the stress of being alone in the classroom. Having a parent mentor in my room gives me the extra support I need to meet my goals."

Addressing the Experiences of Families

If these are some of the needs of schools, can certain family challenges also be addressed through parent engagement? The following stories suggest that parents are focused primarily on the personal domain— on matters concerning their children and their personal understanding of schools. Parents frame their work as parent mentors largely within the perspective of how their involvement shapes and influences their own children.

In addition to exploring the transformation at Funston, this chapter and subsequent ones will look at various other schools and parent mentors throughout the Logan Square neighborhood. Some ideas that emerged earlier in the book will be considered in more detail in the following chapters. In essence, we are moving beyond a portrait of Funston to a broader conceptualization of parent engagement across LSNA's eight partner schools.

For many parents, the mentoring program is their first foray into school culture. Many of the parents I meet are immigrants from countries like Puerto Rico, Mexico, Guatemala, and Honduras, and they often describe schools in their native country with distinctly different practices and expectations. For these immigrant mothers, their unfamiliarity with U.S. schools comes with their own inexperience with the new country. As Sarita, an immigrant from Acapulco, describes, "This is a different world for me, and much of it scares me." She explains that her experience as a parent mentor serves to eliminate some of her fears about an unfamiliar school environment. On the contrary, Isabel Diaz, who attended U.S. schools herself, is more natural and comfortable in her first year at Funston, because she is familiar with the dynamics of the school as an institution, given her own experience as a student in Chicago Public Schools. However, given her own inability to finish high school, she admits being especially sensitive to how she supports her own children in school. Isabel says she "never gave school a chance." She was raised by her maternal grandmother, a strict and traditional woman who lost two daughters to drug addiction and subsequently raised all five grandchildren on her own. Isabel's time in school was tedious, and she lacked encouragement from her grandmother. As a result, she left high school after her junior year:

> I didn't finish. I really wanted to. Like I was saying, my grandmother really didn't care, so I dropped out in my third year of high school. She didn't say anything about it. So she said, "Okay, better you stay home." That's it. "Just watch me and help me take care of the kids, and that will be fine." She didn't push me, so I really didn't care. I finished until my third year, and I dropped out.

This experience shapes the priorities she sets for her own children. A kindergarten graduation for her children was an elaborate family occasion, because she wanted them to know how much she celebrates their achievements and values their education. She still remembers the kindergarten graduation vividly:

> Well, obviously, I didn't graduate, so I'm excited to see my kids graduate. That's why I try to push them, but not too far, either. I don't want them to get frustrated and say, "I don't want to do this." I push them to a certain point that I try to make it fun for them, especially with the homework. I try to get that out of the way first, before they play or watch TV.

For Isabel, parenting is a balancing act—a process where she pushes and encourages but also holds back and supports her children's needs. And many of the activities she encourages at home to make learning fun for her children are activities she has learned working as a parent mentor. By watching teachers navigate this same balance—an attempt to make learning fun but to push some definitive standards for behavior and learning—she is better equipped to have the same expectations for her children at home. She contrasts what she knows now with what she failed to see earlier:

> Before I was a parent mentor, I really didn't know what my kids were doing in school, what their teachers wanted them to do, you know? I mean, they would tell me things about what they did in school, but I didn't know the details, and so I would make sure they had their homework done every day, but I couldn't really help prepare them for what they needed to learn and how the teacher would want them to learn it.

As a parent mentor, Isabel thinks about her time in the classroom as a kind of research—she observes the sorts of activities that teachers engage their students in, the types of behaviors that are approved and disapproved, the language of the classroom, and the strategies that teachers use to support student learning. From these daily observations, she will know what teachers expect from her children. Armed with these ideas, parents like Isabel can adapt them for use with their own children, bringing school practices into the home and helping their children develop some synchrony between the expectations of school and those of home. These are simple things such as "giving them a quiet space to work, reading with them, and giving them a snack when they come home and making sure homework is finished first before anything else."

Beyond the classroom insight that these parent mentors gain from the experience, their mere presence at school encourages their children. *Elena* explains that her children are excited to go to school, because they know she will be there: "Well, they're pleased, they feel happy, because they'll tell you, 'Well, my mom is here at the school,' and I see them from time to time, like just a moment ago, my son was around and he said hi. They look happy when they see me, and I'm also very pleased because I'm here at the school when they're studying."

Similarly, for Sarita, whose daughter *Emily* is in a pre-K class and used to cry every time Sarita dropped her off at school, being in school every morning is a relief. "I don't have to worry about Emily, because I can see that she is all right, and the people who are taking care of her in the school are not strangers." At the same time, it is easier for Emily, who is proud and happy to see her mother in the school. This theme of the children's reassurance recurs in many of the mothers I spoke with.

Besides reassuring their children, the mothers' presence in the schools begins to blur the stark divisions that previously existed between home and school. As parents become a regular presence in the school and bring some school practices into the home, children begin to see the separate worlds of home and school come together. Besides bringing a sense of familiarity and security to the school environment for children, it can also set a tone of accountability between parents and children. When schools and families are worlds apart, children are often the only ones who know and understand the culture and expectations of each environment. Communication between home and school can be distant at best, and this can hurt children, who need consistency between home and school to support their social-emotional and academic development. Isabel knows that her children are more likely to meet the expectations of teachers if the kids know that she is in regular communication with the teachers:

> I don't want them to be scared, like "Oh, my mom's here," you know, and to be on their tippy toes. But I like to make sure I'm here, that they can see me. And so then they are like, "My mom's there. I have to do my homework and not get in trouble." They like it. I do think they are on their tippy toes knowing for a fact that I'm there. Like, "Uh-oh, I can't do that. Mommy's around," or, "My mom will find out." So they are more cautious now of what they are doing.

This greater sense of awareness and accountability is apparent even in the informal conversations parents have with each other during parent mentor training sessions. Inevitably, parent mentors share stories about their classroom experiences, in an effort to hear about their child's teacher and the dynamics of that classroom. While they have these inside views into classrooms, these mothers also meet a standard of professionalism, where they keep the appropriate details of a classroom to themselves, sharing details that will encourage parents, not raise doubts. At the same time, the children know that their own parents are part of a larger network of parents who are active in the school—these adults are the eyes and ears of the classrooms, hallways, playgrounds, and cafeterias within which these children play and learn. I overheard one parent mentor explain this situation to a fellow parent mentor: "She [the daughter] knows I see you every day, so not only can her teacher talk to me, she knows that you see what she's up to, too. I know she thinks about that before she does anything in there." Time and again, the guiding motivation for parents' involvement in the Parent Mentor program is their children.

For many low-income families of color, schools are strange, unfamiliar, and assuming environments whose codes of behavior and guidelines for interactions are often unwritten and unspoken. Parents view schools with intimidation and fear, and their stances toward schools are often shaped by their own experiences—positive and negative. Their attempts to participate in schools may be defeating or frustrating as they struggle to understand a school's expectations for their child and for themselves as parents. As a result, many of these families spend little substantive time inside schools. In addition to the social and emotional barriers described by the newly involved parents at Funston, parents may also lack the time to become involved, may not understand how they can participate, or are not invited by schools to do so. Karla Mack, a former parent mentor at McAuliffe Elementary School, describes the often-hurried pace in getting her children to school, which precluded any interest in becoming involved: "And before, I was just in a rush all the time. Get the kids dressed, get to school, had to go to work. I've got to go make money—that's what we do. Your sole responsibility is to be responsible in all the technical ways."

But now, as a parent mentor, she understands what occurs within the school. Although she once believed her sole responsibility was to provide for her children in the material and technical ways, her experience as a parent mentor has broadened her view: "It's a whole new world you're going to explore when you are involved in your child's education and learning . . . I realize, wow, there's a lot more going on than what I thought, and it's not just about bringing your kid to school, dropping them off with teachers, and then rushing off somewhere."

MOVING FROM PARENT INVOLVEMENT TO PARENT ENGAGEMENT

These parent narratives suggest that effective, transformative parent engagement strategies must be rooted in the needs and experiences of both the families and the schools. But designing strategies that are merely built on the mutual interests of schools and families is not enough. While the preceding sections present compelling stories of family transformation, what kinds of changes must we see in schools? In the following section, we hear from parents like Karla, who argues that schools and families must begin to "see things eye to eye. It's not a 'what can parents do for our school?' attitude. It's a 'What can we do together?' way of thinking." Beyond developing a sense of mutuality, how can we move from parent involvement to parent *engagement*?

From the Margins to the Center

By devoting their skills and energies in support of classroom learning, parent mentors are more than volunteers. In the words of Joanna Brown, they "become essential to the teachers and to the kids and to the school." By moving from the periphery to the central focus on students, parent mentors begin to more intimately understand the struggles, accomplishments, and nuances of the classroom. Lisa Contreras, a Funston parent, describes this process as "starting to understand the life of the classroom—really seeing how things work." Despite having three school-age daughters and being involved in their classrooms from the beginning, she explains that in previous roles as a school volunteer, she did not interact with students often, and she departed from those experiences with a limited view of schools. Not until she became a parent mentor did she really understand the complex terrain of a classroom. In her early experiences as a parent mentor, she worked with a group of four students who needed the extra-individualized attention to make progress. Lisa recalls:

> I had four special students who, you know, they were kind of behind in their class work. So I would take them outside of the classroom, and I would sit with them and I would read with them or I would tutor them or would play word games. I had the ones who needed the most help. I would take them outside, and they were like my little classroom, and it made me feel good because I got to know them in a personal way.

She felt personally invested in their progress as students and, through her daily interactions with them, became intimately aware of their families, their hobbies, their working styles, their struggles, and their achievements.

Similarly, Maricela Contreras, a former parent mentor who was an administrative assistant for several years and is currently studying to become a bilingual education teacher, recalls her experience working with the same group of students who needed extra support. She recalls that she and the teacher worked with different groups:

> And I help them and sit with them, and work out problems and do one-on-ones with them. And the teacher would divide the groups, and we

would have a contest between her group and my group. And so every morning, I wanted to go to school and be there, because she created a really nice atmosphere for all of us, so it worked out perfectly. And then she was really good—good at making the most of my presence and good at sharing the classroom with me. I wasn't just her assistant, but we learned to work together.

Through her experience as a parent mentor, Maricela felt connected to the atmosphere of the classroom and now describes a collegial relationship with the teacher in contrast with a teacher-volunteer relationship in which the parents are relegated to a role of support and service to the classroom. These experiences go beyond what we typically envision as parent involvement. As these parents explain, they work directly with students, supporting their progress in the classroom and, in the process, often develop close relationships with students as well as clear insight into the children's experiences as learners. While these are obviously benefits for students, Maricela's story highlights the ways the experience can be advantageous for parents as well—through a collaborative approach with teachers and the development of an inviting classroom environment. Silvia Gonzalez, the parent mentor coordinator at McAuliffe Elementary School and a former parent mentor, adds, "These parents also do the patrolling outside and help children cross the street—they're becoming very active in their community. So, this is all new. This is the exposure that LSNA gives. You're exposed to all of these learning experiences. You're not going to get that at home. You're not going to get that just as a regular volunteer."

Through its Parent Mentor program, LSNA conceives of parent engagement as a process that serves the needs of both schools and families. Schools have shown a clear necessity for additional support in classrooms, and through their work, parent mentors address this critical need while also enjoying the benefits of more intimate views into classrooms.

Karla believes that when a school invites parents who want to become involved, it must find ways that appreciate "how new the situation of schools can be for them." In this way, the Parent Mentor program is designed for broad participation—parents with a variety of experiences within schools and parents with a variety of English-language abilities.

While many parents without English fluency might not be encouraged to volunteer in classrooms in typical school environments, LSNA pairs each parent mentor in a classroom where the person's abilities and experiences will be appropriate. A Spanish-dominant parent will often be placed in a bilingual classroom or in a pre-K classroom, where the language of instruction is Spanish or basic conversational English. For many of the parent mentors I have gotten to know at Funston, language is a critical concern. Many mothers do not have a firm command of English, or they understand more than they are able to communicate. A program that invites their participation, regardless of their ability to speak English, is a welcome opportunity. In fact, many of these mothers use their work in classrooms to practice and improve their English-language skills, and the experience often compels them to take ESL classes, a first step toward a personal goal of learning English. By meeting parents where they are, the Parent Mentor program is designed to invite those parents who have never been involved in schools and to create an environment where they can feel welcome, supported, and successful.

Reynalda Covarrubias, the coordinator of the Parent Mentor program at Funston whom we met in the last chapter, explains that many teachers work with parent mentors to design classroom participation that will match parents' abilities and comfort levels. Her own limited English skills and education posed barriers to how effective she believed she could be in the classroom, so she worked with the teacher to develop a plan for participation that would help her feel comfortable and successful over time:

> In the beginning, I was afraid, anxious, because I didn't have the preparation. I did not attend school for many years, and I only went up to sixth grade in Mexico. I didn't know if I was going to be able to work with the teacher. But since it was third grade and it was very easy to understand, she helped me. First, she asked me to feel comfortable, then she asked me if I could help her check the math, and I was able to do it. Then I helped her grade tests, and I was also able to do it, and then halfway through the year, she assigned me a child to help him with math, and I was able to do it and I felt good.

When parents and teachers work together to communicate mutual expectations and adapt their plan for working together, programs such as the Parent Mentor program can be more sustaining for both parents and teachers.

By working in classrooms, parent mentors gain a new view of schools and begin to understand some of the challenges teachers face. Kirsten Strand, who brought the Parent Mentor program to a school in Aurora, Illinois, explains that as a parent, "you think you know what goes on there, but you actually don't until you're a part of that, and you're actually working there." She explains that parent mentors often feel as if they have an inside view into schools that makes the school culture less intimidating and foreign. Eva Calderon, co-coordinator of the Parent Mentor program at Mozart Elementary School, has seen parent after parent begin to "understand the job of the teacher. They understand that it's not easy. They understand that the teacher is really doing a hard job." Often working in classrooms that have twenty-five to thirty students, these parent mentors feel the stresses of large classes that include a wide variety of students. According to Sonia Cortez at Avondale, her first experience as a parent mentor was humbling as she realized the task that teachers faced daily in educating children:

Oh, man, it's kind of stressful. I don't want to be a teacher. It's stressful, and kids can give you a lot of headaches. Some kids are good, and some kids are bad. And the teachers have a lot of stress with a lot of kids, because everybody's not the same. Some have tempers or act out. But it's because they have a lot of stress themselves, too—the kids. I never realized how hard it was to be a teacher until I started doing this.

With this new understanding, parents begin to change some of their expectations and are willing to share some of these insights with parents who do not have this inside perspective. When public sentiment toward teachers seems exceedingly harsh or critical, parent mentors are often the first to defend them, citing the difficulties in bringing such a wide variety of students together on task. Ines Diaz coordinates the Parent Mentor program at Darwin Elementary School in Logan

Square. She finds that parents who better understand the difficult work of the teacher often share this perspective with other parents, who may be more critical and less understanding of a teacher's situation. With this firsthand knowledge, the parent mentor becomes the "communicator to the parents to understand the education in the classroom."

In essence, parents begin to build relationships with teachers and students, and these relationships both provide the parents with a perspective of the broader school community and often influence their own goals in educating their own children. For Monica Garretón Chavez, a former LSNA education organizer who has trained parent mentors in the past and worked closely with them in schools, the Parent Mentor program provides parents with a "brand-new orientation to schools":

> When parents go into the classroom, they're learning a lot of things. They're walking into a school that they may have never walked inside before. They're seeing teachers as human beings instead of revering them as these gods that they would see before, learning how the system works, being more comfortable in English-speaking environments and more familiar with a system in this new country—when our school system is completely different than other countries' school systems.

For many of these parents, the unfamiliarity of schools is compounded by their experiences as immigrants, and U.S. schools may be vastly different in practice and in orientation from schools in their native countries. As these parents send their children to largely unfamiliar school environments, the opportunity to be a part of classrooms is an opportunity to become familiar with the institution that will surround their own children. Shirley Reyes, co-coordinator of Mozart's Parent Mentor program, describes this process as one in which parents learn more about schools as a way of developing trust and confidence in a new and unfamiliar institution:

> I felt this way, too, with my two youngest children, who are only one year apart. I remember a time when they went to a field trip, and I went to the field trip, not just to help the teacher but to make sure that my

two were safe. I wanted to watch them, to see if they were okay, that they were secure. So these mothers may feel the way I do, too. They are in a new country and they don't know anything about the school, but they have to trust that the school is taking care of their child. They can be involved so that they can see what is going on and feel more comfortable about it for their children.

While parent mentors gain invaluable insight into classroom life that, in turn, shapes their sense of comfort and familiarity within the school environment, the Parent Mentor program brings much-needed relief and support to schools that often struggle with the pressing demands of growing classrooms. By designing a program that both meets the needs of schools and addresses the experiences of families, LSNA creates a model of parent engagement that will be sustainable over time.

Parents As Vital Resources

As parent mentors play a more prominent and visible role in schools, they can be seen as important partners in educating students. Rather than viewing parent participation as voluntary or supplementary, schools may begin to view it as a necessity or a valuable resource. This stands in contradiction to a view that many parents may have, according to Patricia Lopez, a former parent mentor who is now studying to be a bilingual teacher: "You think the teacher is in charge of everything and she's the one who will be responsible for your child's education. And I think it's part of our job to let them know that it's not that way. They must be very important in their child's education." Parent mentors feel compelled to support their children's learning at home and in school, and according to Patricia, the message to families is that "they are needed. For children to succeed, families and schools must work together."

In classrooms, parents begin to develop relationships with students, often working regularly with an individual student or working consistently with a small group. During these daily interactions, parent mentors become role models and adult figures that students begin to rely upon and view as resources. Maricela recalls some of the relationships she built with students over the years as a parent mentor:

> If I am working with kids every day and I'm able to connect with a few because I work with them one-on-one or in a small group, then I feel myself making a difference for them. They have a person, a parent in their school who feels very much like someone in their own family, and they have this special relationship with that person. This is something that kids really look forward to, and for me, I have a better understanding of what's going on at the school—the families, the kids, where they are coming from, and what kind of issues my child is going to come in contact with every day. I feel comfortable knowing all this—and knowing that I can help.

As a parent in the school, Maricela believes that she has a special relationship with students, because she is a parent who lives in the community and is familiar with the kinds of experiences that many families within the school may have. And certainly, students have an affinity to the parent mentors they come to know, often sharing parts of their lives with these parents. She remembers that children would often find her in hallways or after school to update her on newly expecting mothers, passing grades, older siblings, and new teachers. She made every effort to remember each child, even after she had moved on to a different classroom, and over the years, she has come to believe that these parent mentor and student interactions "create a different atmosphere at school."

During my visits to the parent mentor schools on numerous occasions, I see the ease with which parent mentors interact with students. In hallways, I see mentors checking in with students about their parents, their siblings. In classrooms, I see parents help tie shoes, sharpen pencils, find homework, all while asking the children if their grandmother is doing better or if their mom has had the baby yet.

In one school-wide assembly organized by parent mentors at Funston, I see firsthand how popular and prominent the parent mentors can be in the minds of students, as I sit in the balcony, awaiting the start of the performance. Parent mentors have arranged a series of Latin American dance routines that they will be performing with some of their children. I have heard from organizers that the preparations were elaborate, that they will be incorporating traditional instruments and dress in the routines, and that the group has been practicing for months. I am surrounded by young children who are sitting on the edges of their seats in anticipation of the start of the assembly. As soon as the curtains come up and the first dance starts, I see the rows of students in front of me stand up or sit on their knees in their seats to get a good view of the parent mentors. As the children scan the stage and see the familiar faces of parents, they squeal with delight, waving their hands, and calling out their names. Their little bodies can barely contain their excitement as they continue to watch parent mentors dance and perform—dressed in beautiful colors and traditional clothing. These interactions between students and parent mentors reflect a sense that parents play a visible role within the life of the school. Through their regular presence in schools and classrooms, a parent mentor is a familiar face and another adult that students can feel connected to.

At times, parent mentors are confidantes to students as conflicts and other issues arise in school. In this role, parents potentially become an extra set of eyes and ears tuned in carefully to the culture of the school. Ofelia Sanchez, the LSNA organizer whom we met in chapter 3 and who began her leadership in schools as a parent mentor, recalls the many relationships she had with students in classrooms, her own children, or her niece. She remembers that her niece's friends would regularly greet her in school, "thinking that it was really great that I'm so involved in the school." But on one occasion, one of her niece's friends approached her, saying, "I don't know who to tell this to, but maybe you can help. I saw some activity going on right outside our classroom—there are these boys and they're bringing in drugs." On asking her for more details and finding out that they had approached this young girl along with others, Ofelia promptly went to the principal and her teacher with this information. As a result, the school checked students' book bags each day, and the problem was resolved. Ofelia believes that her presence as a trusted adult played an important part in the resolution: "I felt like if she had no one to actually go to, this could have still been going on and even gotten worse, to the point where my niece is actually doing stuff."

Because of the active role the mentors play in classrooms, many students view parents as teachers. In classrooms, many teachers introduce parent mentors as teachers or *maestra* (Spanish for "teacher"), prompting students to address the parents accordingly. Reynalda recalls her first experience as a parent mentor when she was introduced to the class as Mrs. Covarrubias, or Maestra. She remembers responding emphatically that she was not a teacher and shouldn't be called that way, to which her teacher responded, "For them, you are the teacher . . . I taught them that we're the same, you're a parent and you're giving your time, and we're both teachers, because somehow, I'm going to learn something from you and you're going to learn something from me and my children."

Similarly, Funston teacher Melva Patock explains that every year, when she introduces a parent mentor to her class, "the first thing I do is that I do not make a difference between her and me. I introduce them right away as a teacher so the children know we are equals." When parent mentors meet students in the community, on the playground, and in the school, they are viewed as teachers. At the grocery store, a child will see a parent mentor and explain to his grandmother that she is a teacher at his school. In school, children will introduce a parent mentor as a teacher to their own parents. Parent mentors are essentially teachers in these schools—seen as a source of authority and a resource within the school.

Rather than viewing parents for the skills and abilities they do not possess, such as English-language fluency, a background in education, or a knowledge of classrooms, the Parent Mentor program encourages school staff to view parents as assets. Parents become valuable resources under this model, as they show an ability to connect with students, support student learning in classrooms, and become partners in their child's education. By bringing parents into schools and classrooms to play an active role, schools give parents the opportunity to showcase their talents and abilities, transforming the way they are seen by students, teachers, school staff, and other parents. Schools can tap into a rich community resource with parents who reflect the experiences of students and who understand the issues that the children may face in their daily lives. In the words of Jossie Rivera, a teacher at Funston, through the Parent Mentor program, schools begin to view parents as "people who have talents, people who can be a positive influence."

But viewing parents as assets represents a basic shift in the institutional attitude of many low-income schools, where parents are seen as liabilities to their child's education. Individual parents or teachers alone cannot change institutional beliefs and attitudes. As a result, LSNA designs its parent mentor training to encourage parents to view themselves as leaders and resources to the school community. Silvia sees parents as a rich, untapped community resource. In the training, she wants parents to understand this as well. By preparing parent mentors for their work in classrooms and offering ways that they can support students and teachers, the training aims to develop parents as capable partners in educating children. She explains: "As parents alone, they have a rich set of talents in interacting with children and understanding what children need. In the training, we want every parent to think about every strength they bring into this work, and we try to build on that."

From the training, parents have a base of knowledge and encouragement that they will build on as they begin to work in classrooms. According to Leticia Barrera, who trains parent mentors for LSNA, this training builds great confidence in the parents:

> Well, I think that the training at the beginning of the year and as it continues will help them a lot. And then through their experience in the classroom, they will practice all the things that they were learning from the training. And when they see, "Oh, yeah, I'm capable to do this," they will start to discover themselves that "yes . . . it doesn't matter that somebody thinks that I'm not capable to do that. I'm doing it." When they discover themselves, they will just look at the world in a different color.

As Leticia explains, these experiences are new to many parents, who do not often believe in their own capabilities to work effectively in

classrooms. And in fact, many LSNA organizers believe that the training serves to boost the self-esteem and confidence of parents. Amanda
Rivera, a former teacher and principal who worked with LSNA to start
the first Parent Mentor program, believes that initially, low self-esteem
often inhibits this group of parents:

> Well, I think what we realized was, we needed to help develop the self-
> esteem of parents. I was so shocked to realize what low self-esteem a lot
> of parents had then. Most of them are women, and they're used to being
> codependent, and perfect nurturers, and they're doing for everybody.
> They're doing for the kids; they're doing for the husbands. They're not
> doing for themselves; they're not having time to be reflective.

To motivate and encourage parents, facilitators during the training ask parents to identify a personal goal that they would like to accomplish within a year. The goal must be focused solely on parents
themselves. Throughout the year, organizers and fellow parent mentors provide each parent with a network of support and resources for
achieving the personal goal. Silvia describes this process as transformative when she began as a parent mentor: "When I came in, I was at a
very low point in my life with wanting to do something more with my
time. The training to me was the foundation that you can make a difference. It boosts your self-esteem. It transforms, and they say everyone is a leader."

Similarly, Karla explains that the Parent Mentor program encourages parents to believe that "you as an individual and as a parent can
develop any of your skills." She adds that this encouragement, in turn,
gives parents the confidence they need to be successful in classrooms:

> That helps us in all areas, from parenting to any volunteer work to your
> day-to-day relations with people. To me, when I think of LSNA, I
> think of . . . us parents as maybe a little seed, and they're putting in some
> encouragement and support, and you don't get that [in] a lot of places.
> And it makes a parent realize, "Well, there are things I still can do, or
> hey, this matters." So, it makes you feel good about yourself. It makes

you feel good about your life, and then if you look at that as a parent, it's going good, I feel like, "Watch out, world!" because there's nothing they can't tackle!

The low inner confidence of these parents may be partly due to their isolation within their homes and the lack of opportunities to showcase their abilities. Leticia explains: "If you are in an environment that no one tells you that you are capable to do different things beside the things that you are doing at home or at your job, maybe, at the factory . . . then no one tells them that they have another opportunity to show their skills."

Across parent leaders and organizers, there is a common conception that many parents, immigrant parents in particular, come to the program with low self-esteem. Because of factors such as social isolation, an inability to speak English, or unfamiliarity with schools, these parents often approach schools with fear and intimidation and underestimate their own abilities to be resources to the school. But there seems to be a fine line between what LSNA organizers and leaders describe as parents' lack of confidence and my perception of parents' lack of institutional knowledge and connectedness. Because schools can be such intimidating and confusing environments, even the most naturally confident parent can feel challenged by the complex practices and expectations of schools. By characterizing parents as having low self-esteem, we view them unnecessarily against the standards of mainstream U.S. culture. From this point of view, they lack confidence, assuredness, and an ability to decisively navigate the institution. Rather, what parents lack is institutional knowledge and connectedness within schools. As long as schools remain rigid institutions that fail to develop meaningful connections with the families they serve, parents will continue to lack the institutional knowledge they need to engage with the schools more confidently. Schools must become welcoming and transparent in their practices, and parents must have access to other parents and school staff in ways that more clearly reveal school culture and open up relationships. In doing so, we come closer to viewing parents as assets— individuals with skills and abilities that are essential to schools—and demanding more transparency from schools.

Building Parent Presence: Every Day, Everywhere

Karla argues that in previous schools that her children attended, "parents were invisible, and it's just a fact of life." Today, at McAuliffe, you will see parents in classrooms, in lunchrooms, in hallways, on playgrounds, at crosswalks—parents are everywhere. Teachers admit that they are "less mystified, less suspicious" when parent mentors have such a regular presence in schools. To teachers, school staff, and students, parents are no longer an ambiguous, unknown entity. Rather, through the development of relationships, parents become individuals with goals and interests, mothers and fathers who are dedicated to their children, and colleagues who have the best interests of school in mind. These parents become a regular presence in schools, serving in any needed capacity and openly engaging in various aspects of the school. They serve as local school council members, watch over the lunchroom, work as crossing guards each morning, walk children who are sick home from school, and sound out words for young children learning to read.

As I recall the many schools that I attended as a child or where I worked as a classroom teacher, I remember glancing twice at the sight of newcomers in the school. In these school environments, the usual figures were staff and students; anyone who didn't immediately register as one or the other must be a visitor, a newcomer. To see parents in school would signify a special occasion such as an open house or a meeting regarding an issue with a child. In sharp contrast, as I get to know these schools in Logan Square, I come to expect the presence of parents in classrooms and hallways; they have become part of the school community. I talk with *Gilberto*, a Funston School parent we met in chapter 1, one morning as he tells me about his roots and upbringing in the neighborhood. As he looks at the school building, he notices the physical changes that have come about with the help of parents:

> You see, parents were involved in organizing to get this new playground on the west side of the building. And again, they were the ones who organized to get the community center up and running here—where we have programs and classes for parents and children. This annex was built because parents organized with LSNA for more space. If you were to

come here in the morning before the kids get here, you would see parents patrolling the sidewalks to get kids safely onto the property, you'd see them standing guard at the playground to make sure the young ones are safe, and you'd see them standing around talking to each other as the kids get ready to go inside. There's a lot they do, and I can just look at the building and see what they've accomplished.

After a year at Funston, I, too, can stand on the west side of the school during a quiet moment and conjure up the image that Gilberto has painted for me—an image where parents are everywhere, active, engaged, present, and vital to the life of schools. But as a former Funston student decades ago and a longtime neighborhood resident, Gilberto says it has not always been that way. He recalls that when he attended the school, parents "were not involved in school at all." Parents only came to drop off and pick up children, and there was almost "never any interaction between parents and teachers unless you did something really wrong." He noticed the first changes soon after LSNA arrived to increase parent participation: "I saw us swing around." The atmosphere, as he describes it, has changed as the school begins to feel "more like a community and less like a school."

Others have also noticed a shift in the atmosphere among parents as parent mentors become more actively involved. Ana Martinez Estka explains: "Parents are more aware that they're not alone and that the problems they have are shared by many other parents. We have friendship between parents—parents who are friends and connected to other parents."

This adds a sense of community and collegiality that makes schools more welcoming to those parents who might typically choose not to be involved. With this encouragement of parents, then, teachers and other school staff begin to notice the prevalence of parents and come to know it as a familiar and positive force. Melva sees this at Funston:

Now that we have a program that introduces them to the classrooms and schools, we have more parents who are in the school, who work with us on different events. You know, you really can't walk down a hall without seeing a parent, and the children see that, too. For everyone in the school—teachers, students, the principal, everyone—it is good to see that parents are a part of this place and that they are working together with all of us to make schools a better place. Our school is a better place because we have so many more parents involved in our day-to-day.

The "threat" of parent presence that many teachers described before parents became active partners in the school is transformed into a welcome attitude of partnership and collaboration for many teachers. They come to expect parental presence in schools rather than fear it. And for many parents who have yet to become actively involved in schools, the prevalence of parents is encouraging as well. Silvia notes that many of the new parent mentors she works with have often said that their curiosity was piqued by the regular presence of parents in the school:

When you look around the school and you see that other parents are in the school and they are very active, you also want to get involved, I think. When you see other parents involved and the school is a place where parents are not just welcome but very active, you start to think that this is something you can do and something you should do. I think that this kind of thing can be contagious, in a very positive way.

REAPING THE REWARDS FOR STUDENTS

These narratives reveal that when parents interact in meaningful ways in schools and classrooms, students can benefit from their presence. As vital resources, parents establish important points of connection with students as well as a sense of familiarity and trust that may be more difficult for school staff to attain. When schools develop mutually engaging forms of parent engagement that center parents, view families as assets, and integrate parent presence throughout the school, students benefit profoundly and in multiple ways. By their presence alone, parent mentors add familiarity and security to school environments where the worlds of school and community are distinct and separate. In this way, parent mentors become connecting forces—bridges—between students' communities and schools. By seeing parents as mentors and teachers within their school, children can not only relate to individuals within their school but also feel a sense of possibility and empowerment. Lesszest George, a former LSNA organizer, agrees: "For these kids to see firemen, policemen, teachers—anyone that has a very public job and something that they see every day—then to see a parent come in to do one of those jobs, actually makes them feel powerful."

For the children in the Lathrop public housing community that Lesszest describes, seeing a parent from the community as a teacher or public figure within their school can have a powerful and lasting effect. This is particularly true when we consider how influential teachers can be on the lives of students. According to Leticia, teachers, more than other adults, can offer students possibilities for change. From her work as a former teacher in Mexico and parent leader and organizer for LSNA, Leticia believes that when teachers take their responsibilities seriously and become effective in the classroom, the effects on students can be significant:

> I think that the teachers have a lot of potential for change. We are people who can make a difference in our children's education. Their parents . . . can do that, but . . . how many hours are children spending in our classroom? How much power does the teacher have over those children? We have to take this responsibility seriously, and we need the kind of teachers who can understand the lives of children at school, but also understand the lives of children at home, because these two places are usually so separated.

Even in her early days as a teacher in Mexico, she felt the immense potential of teachers "to make a difference in the lives of children." From this experience, she found that understanding the multiple dimensions of children's lives was critical in educating them successfully. When children's lives at home and school are distant and separate, Leticia believes that parent mentors can be powerful connecting forces between those worlds. For many of these students, she contends, the issues within their families and communities can often overwhelm them, leaving little room in their lives to meet the demands of teachers. According to Leticia, this requires a shift in how we understand students:

> I think that we tend to focus only on the academic things in a student's life, but we have to realize that students have many things going on at home that are keeping them from feeling happy, from feeling relaxed. And for every human being, we are not all capable of doing everything that is asked of us all the time, especially when our lives outside of our work are so hard. So you see, we have students who are thinking, "Well, my teacher is telling me to do this," or "She is assessing me and saying that I need to do this or I'm not going to pass."

As role models, mentors, or community figures, parent mentors concur that in their work, they feel that they are making a difference in the lives of students. Lisa Contreras recalls, "All of a sudden, you feel this huge responsibility, or maybe I mean possibility, because you are working with a child who really needs your help." In the larger classroom, these children may "be lost in the shuffle, not getting the one-on-one attention that they need," when teachers must navigate the many, sometimes competing demands in a classroom. Lisa describes her work with individual students as transformative as time goes by:

> When you first start, it doesn't feel like it, but you start off the school year and you have one little boy that can't read words, can't sound them out, and then you're a quarter of the way through the school year, and then all of a sudden, that little boy can read . . . That little boy can read words. And you know you had a part in it. And to me that is—that's the most important one for me is being able to help somebody—help a child read . . . I think that we make a difference; I really do.

By working in classrooms with students, parent mentors provide students with the additional instructional support they need to make progress. For parent mentors, this is a profound opportunity to make a difference in a child's life. Former parent mentor Maria Marquez describes her own experience working with students as a powerful opportunity: "I love the fact that I could teach a child something that day that would make a difference in his life." Her experience as a parent mentor was shaped by the time she spent teaching children to read, understand a math concept, or write. These experiences became the basis for her decision to return to school to become a bilingual education teacher. Even today, when she is out in the community, she is recognized by the many children she has taught; they call out to her and let her know how they are doing in school.

Through their work in classrooms, parent mentors admittedly become attached and otherwise connected to the students they work with. They become intimately aware of the children's struggles and achievements and learn to tailor their instruction to the individual needs of these students. At the conclusion of her first year as a parent mentor, Silvia realized the effect she had had on the children:

> I found out that I really could make a difference in a child's life, because [the] whole year that I was there volunteering, when I left the classroom, it was so hard for me to leave these first-graders. So, I do become very attached to the children, and you know what children are not being helped at home. You know which children have mommy and daddy working and where grandma is taking care of them.

Silvia realizes that for some children who do not receive the parental or familial support at home, she, as a parent mentor, is making a difference. Amid the busy routines of classrooms and the hectic lives of children's families, some students are sorely in need of attention. With parent mentors like Silvia, these students stand a chance at receiving the individual attention they need to continue on in their educational journeys. It is this calling to support students that defines Silvia's experience and her decision to become a teacher. As she explains, becoming a parent mentor was "how I became very involved, but really, I just love this calling for me, just to be helping other children."

The teachers who work with parent mentors also have this compelling sense that the mentors' presence is beneficial for their students.

Marlin Ortiz is a McAuliffe teacher who has worked with parent mentors. While she appreciates the support they offer to her in the classroom, "what I gain from this pales in comparison to what it seems to offer my students." She describes parent mentors who have a rare ability to connect with students—to interact with students as a "community mentor or teacher." Beyond the assistance that parent mentors may offer to students with their classroom work, Marlin explains, parents provide other sources of support:

> They are in the classroom providing my students with a much-needed sense that they matter, that their families matter. They often have children around the same age as the children they work with, so they are often naturally good with the young people in the room. They are a role model to the children, and they give them the kind of academic and personal support that they need. Sometimes, to teach the academic material, you need to make a personal connection first, and they can do that.

Parent mentors come into classrooms with the intention of finding out more about classrooms, to overcome some of their fears regarding schools, and to gain some insight into how they can support their child's learning at home. What they do not always anticipate is the effect that their presence and participation have on the many students who see them in hallways, hear them on the playground, read with them in small groups, and talk with them one-on-one. And in these large and small ways, parents are having a positive influence on classrooms, on the daily responsibilities that teachers juggle, and the learning and development that occurs in schools. When a host of parents is actively engaged in schools, few corners are untouched by their hard work and dedication.

On one quiet afternoon, after the crowds of students have left the school building and while the after-school groups are settling into their new groupings and classrooms at the community learning center, I wait in the hallway outside the main office for a parent who is coming to the school to meet with me. After-school announcements resound from the loudspeaker, the last students walk out with their parents, and teachers begin to walk into and out of the office to sign out for the day. As I stand and wait in the hallway, next to me is a young girl waiting for her mother, who is signing up for a class at the school's community center. The girl is sitting on the floor with her homework agenda open in front of her. I recall seeing her in class earlier that week when I had visited a parent mentor's classroom. She remembers me, too, and we start to talk about her class. We talk about the amount of homework and whether she likes fourth grade, and I'm struck by her seriousness when she tells me that the current year is a marked improvement from the last. When I ask her about this, she explains that she has always had difficulty "catching up to the class" and always felt "too shy" to ask questions. I explain that from my years as a teacher, I have certainly learned that everyone has her own pace in acquiring skills. Upon her asking, I mention that I used to teach fourth grade, also, and she suddenly asks, "Well, did you ever know anyone who couldn't read, even in third grade?" I stumble for a second on this unexpected question, trying to honestly recall whether I did or not, when she says, "Well, I guess I did learn in third grade, because one of my teachers taught me." Once again confused, this time by her reference to multiple teachers, I ask, "Your third-grade teacher?" to which she replies, "No, my parent mentor. She read with me every day until I could do it myself."

Her story speaks volumes to me as I recall my own struggles as a classroom teacher. Facing the challenges in teaching students with a wide variety of skills and abilities, I often found myself having to choose who would get my time and who would have to wait. Many students needed my daily individual attention, but in the real life of classrooms, this was rarely possible. Choices were made, and I often wondered how much a student would have progressed if I had had the opportunity to focus on him or her alone. In my own attempts to add individualized attention to my repertoire of teaching responsibilities, I often pieced together tutoring sessions after school with spontaneous one-on-one sessions during a quiet independent work period and "working" lunch sessions with a student who couldn't complete her homework. This was a compromise I could live with, albeit a hectic option for a new classroom teacher, and it allowed me to move some of my students along more effectively. But now, as I talk with this young girl, I am suddenly faced with the enormous potential that becomes available when parents are committed to classrooms to support student learning. When parent mentors spend two hours each morning in a classroom, the possibilities suddenly seem endless to me.

For many reasons, students like this young girl do not get everything they need from schools. There are too many students, not enough time, a wide variety of student abilities, persistent disruptions, well-meaning but ineffective teachers, parents who can't read to their children—the possibilities are endless in considering why this young girl was behind on her personal mission to read. But with the help of a parent mentor, she was able to persist in her goal of literacy, and, she declares, "I am finally able to say I can read. I was scared it was never going to happen."

CONCLUSION

By spending time with individual students and small groups of students who need the extra instructional support, parent mentors are making a difference in the lives of students—by teaching them to read, offering themselves as mentors and role models, and otherwise supporting the individual needs of students in classrooms. Clearly, by working in classrooms with teachers who are often overwhelmed by the demands of growing classes and high expectations, parent mentors provide invaluable assistance and support to struggling students. While students have much to gain from the relationships they build with parent mentors—socially, emotionally, and academically—parents also gain a wealth of experience, knowledge, and insight into schools and classrooms through their work in classrooms.

Through the creation of the Parent Mentor program, LSNA has designed a model for parent participation that is *mutually engaging*. Traditional models of parent involvement typically revolve around focused activities—such as volunteering in classrooms, organizing fund-raisers, or attending parent-teacher meetings—that are school-centered. Schools set the agenda for parent participation.[1] As a result, these models often fail to build broad and diverse forms of parent involvement. Parents may be perceived as hard to reach or lacking interest in school-based involvement when, in reality, schools may be the ones that are hard to reach.[2]

But how is the LSNA Parent Mentor program distinct from the traditional model of parent volunteering? What sets the work of parent mentors apart from the many schools that attempt to involve parents in a more traditional way? LSNA seeks out those parents who may not respond to school invitations—immigrants who are unfamiliar with expectations of schools, mothers who are not fluent in English, parents haunted by negative exchanges with schools—to find a means of participation that will be inviting, respectful, and eye-opening. While it may be more comfortable or familiar for schools to lay out the possibilities for participation and leave it to parents to respond, LSNA digs deep into the experiences of families to understand their experiences and create innovative strategies to draw them into schools. This is a direct challenge to the one-sided, school-centered forms of parent involvement that dominate urban schools today. This strategy defies the tempting expectation that we can develop a universal template for family engagement across school communities. Through a sense of mutual engagement, we must acknowledge that the varied and unique experiences of families and communities matter and are fundamental to the development of effective parent engagement strategies.

5

THE TIES THAT BIND

A Relational Approach to Parent Engagement

O N A COLD WINTER EVENING that was routine in every other way, Karla Mack sat with her children in the living room of their apartment in Logan Square, debating what to have for dinner. At the moment, the group seemed to favor something quick from McDonald's, when they heard a knock on their front door. Upon opening the door, Karla met a frantic neighbor who alerted her that a fire had taken over the back porch of the apartment building. Karla immediately rushed out of the apartment with her children, and "before our eyes, these four families that were there, everything burned . . . One minute, we're sitting there about to figure out what we want to eat, and the next, we lost everything." She recalls the moment that she realized she was losing everything. Those around her on the street encouraged her to get in touch with her family members, her mother, to which she remembers flatly responding, "But I don't have a mom. I don't have anyone to come and get me."

Upon losing everything to the fire and without renter's insurance to replace any of her family's belongings, Karla suddenly faced a future with little to offer her children. But a neighbor on the next block saw the raging fire and recognized Karla from her work as a parent mentor and as a crossing guard each morning. This neighbor notified Silvia Gonzalez, coordinator of the McAuliffe Elementary School's Parent

Mentor program. Karla remembers being received by members of the McAuliffe and LSNA community as they immediately organized an effort to temporarily house and provide for her family:

> And within two weeks—it was a rough two weeks. But I guarantee you, every day, we ate. Every day, we slept somewhere clean and safe. I had friends that helped, but that was, like, a place here or there. McAuliffe and LSNA—Silvia Gonzalez, Juliet, all of them—every day, they would have something for us to eat, a gift card. They told people at the school. They told people at LSNA . . . I don't even know these people, but they knew and they didn't care, and everyone came and gave us so much love and support.

Amid this challenging transitional time, she was faced with the possibility of leaving a neighborhood that she had come to know and appreciate and a school community that had become like a family. Karla recalls: "LSNA and McAuliffe were my family, because I really don't have any family. It's just me and my children, and I was like, 'What am I going to do?' I don't want to leave McAuliffe. I don't want to leave this community. My daughter goes to high school in this neighborhood. I'm starting to like what I do here and kind of see what my options are."

But with the support of individuals at LSNA and McAuliffe, Karla and her family were able to move into a new apartment after two weeks of temporary housing and abundant contributions from the community. Reflecting on this experience, Karla explains:

> This community saved me and put me on my feet again. My children cried not once. We lost everything. We got everything replaced back and so much more—toys, clothes, shoes, everything . . . What sustained me was this community, the love and support—everybody gave what they could . . . I didn't know half the people, but they heard. That's all they needed to hear. It was a family in need, and it came from their heart, so anything I can do to pass on that type of love, that type of support, that's what I'm here to do, because someone did that for me, and then you say, this is someplace I know I want to stay.

Karla's story confirms what we have learned earlier from the experiences of Funston parent mentors who attest to a sense of community and family that supports and sustains them. For Karla, the school became more than a place where she sent her children; it became a community full of friends, support, and meaningful relationships.

This relational strategy—a strategy bound together by the creation and sustenance of relationships—is a cornerstone to LSNA's education work and originates from its roots in organizing. Jeff Bartow, the executive director of the Southwest Organizing Project (SWOP), an organizational ally that has brought the Parent Mentor program to schools in Chicago's southwest side, has observed LSNA's approach in schools over the years and emphasizes that relationships are at the core of everything LSNA does: "Everything comes through the relationship first. They take time to listen and share and understand the reality of the lives of members of their organization, and there's a real deliberateness around that." Jeff explains that for many community organizing groups, "when we look at institutions, one of the things we try to do is figure out how you minimize bureaucracy, which has its place, and maximize and increase the relational component of the institution, because that's what brings it alive." When he reflects on LSNA's Parent Mentor program, he is struck by the centrality of its relational work: "My imagination goes towards things that are easily 'bureaucratizable,' and what specifically is important about parents as mentors is that it argues the importance of intentionality about relational work. That's the heart of it, and it can move where bureaucracy can't—it's probably the core reason for its success."

By prioritizing relationships—both creating them and maintaining them—LSNA's Parent Mentor program seeks to change the institutional nature of schools, moving from anonymous, rigid, tradition-bearing institutions to a community of individuals who are connected by relationships of trust and caring. As we have seen in the previous chapter, LSNA develops strategies to create and strengthen ties among parents. Through training workshops, on the schoolyard, and within the community, parents build new connections and develop a sense of collective community. In this chapter, we will see how this relational approach seeks to transform the interactions between parents and teachers.

NEW RELATIONSHIPS BETWEEN PARENTS AND TEACHERS

*I know because I've been there. I know the struggles. I'm a single mother
and I've had my tough moments with my own children in school, but if we
want to help our children, we have to have good communication between
teachers and parents, and so this is an important step that you're taking.*
                                                            —Jossie Rivera

During a training session at the start of the school year, Jossie Rivera, a
teacher at Funston, came to share her experience working with parent
mentors in the classroom. Although she gave parent mentors suggestions
to ensure a smooth start in the classroom, she also made a point of reaffirming the possible points of connection between parents and teachers:
"You will see—and I really believe this—we're the same: the parents and
teachers in this school. I really believe that you are your child's teacher at
home, and we happen to be their teacher in school, but we have similar
goals in teaching your children to be good adults and capable people."
    From the teachers they work with daily to the teachers they come
to know through their children, in the lunchroom, on the playground,
or at school events, parent mentors begin building relationships with
teachers. Even as parent mentors return to the program for a second or
third year, they are assigned to new teachers each year in hopes that individual parents and teachers continue to build a web of new relationships that will transform their interactions in schools.

Strengthening Ties and Building Trust

But how does an experience in a teacher's classroom shape the kinds of
relationships teachers and parents have? By working alongside teachers, parent mentors develop a greater understanding of the demands
on teachers—the academic expectations, behavior management issues,
the stresses of over-enrolled classrooms. According to Nancy Aardema,
LSNA's executive director whom we met in chapter 2, LSNA partner
schools have a unique characteristic: "hundreds of parents in our community who've spent two hours a day in the school [and] graduated as
parent mentors." The sheer volume and intensity of parental presence

brings a greater understanding of the myriad dimensions of a typical school day, she says:

> Parents here really understand in a deeper way what it's like to be in the school all day—what it's like for the kids, what it's like for the teachers. That opens doors for both the kids and the teachers, because if parents see things that they think aren't fair for the kids, they're the first to speak up. If they see things that they think are unfair to the teachers, they're also speaking up.

As parents become a regular presence in the classroom, not only do they help teachers manage the needs of a classroom and support students, but the relationships between parents and teachers begin to change. According to Amanda Rivera, over the course of working together and conversing, "parents began to understand the complexity of the work of teaching" as well as "the challenges that a teacher has with thirty to thirty-five students, the challenges they have with students bringing their personal issues to school, and issues that have nothing to do with the classroom, and how that impacted the classroom." At the same time, she says, "teachers began to develop a greater respect for parents and viewed them as an asset or a resource." Leticia Barrera adds that for some teachers, this represents a change in viewpoint about parents: "Probably, [the teachers] think that they [the parents] are just at home because they want to be at home or that they didn't pay attention." But because of the sustained time that parents spend in the classroom, the teachers "have all kinds of opportunities to chat, to talk about different things . . . for two hours"—to essentially challenge some of their own assumptions and beliefs about parents. As mentioned in chapter 3, Funston teacher Patricia Connor, who works with parent mentor Graciela Lopez, values the time she and Graciela have to "catch up and chat" when the students are in another classroom and the two women are preparing materials for the next activity together:

> When the kids aren't here, Graciela and I converse. We talk about Mexico. I've been to Mexico a few times. I've driven through the city that she came from when she was thirteen. So, we just kind of share experiences—experiences as women, as mothers. She's talked about going to

school, and not being certain what she wants to do in the future, but it sounds like she wants to finish college, and pursue a career—maybe nursing or teaching. We talk about these things, and I feel we can relate to each other more.

In these moments, Graciela and Patricia begin to build a relationship and a dialogue that does not center on a child. In traditional parent-teacher relationships, interactions and conversations center primarily on a parent's child—How is he faring in this class? What are some of the things we can do to support his learning at home? But by placing parent mentors in classrooms where their children are not assigned, the focus can be on many students instead of one, and the parent-teacher relationship becomes more of a relationship between two individuals. Through this arrangement, each person's focus—that of the teacher and that of the parent—can be on the broader dynamics of a classroom and school. Patricia explains:

> I see it's beneficial, because if your child is in the room, then that's going to be the area of your concern, helping your child. And the child will be aware of that; the other kids will be aware of that. So, I think it's great to have parents in other rooms, helping other kids, and for the parents—and they don't have to be bogged down with their own child. I would just say as a parent myself—I have two sons that are grown—that it's difficult teaching your own child, because of the vested interest you have, and they pick up on that—how anxious you are for them to learn and to succeed. So I think sometimes it's beneficial to work with other kids.

Taking the focus off a parent's child paves the way for simpler, more open relationships between parents and teachers. And while there are benefits for the students with whom these parent mentors work, one principal adds, "It also strengthens the bond between home and school, because parents are here, and they're working with us; they're not in opposition to us."

Changing Teacher Attitudes

But there are times when families and schools stand in opposition or when the relationship between parent and teacher is weakened with distrust, a lack of familiarity, and uneven power dynamics. While the Parent Mentor program seeks to build more meaningful relationships and develop greater trust between parents and teachers, individuals will vary in their willingness to change long-held assumptions and beliefs that will, essentially, affect the success of any relationship. Parents will often come to a new understanding of classrooms, teachers, and schools through their work in classrooms and their participation in the training, but the Parent Mentor program does not seek to explicitly change teacher beliefs. LSNA's Joanna Brown explains:

> The parents in the classrooms work for the teachers. Teachers choose to work with a mentor, and that power relationship is pretty clear. I don't think we change power dynamics. We break down the barriers between [teachers and parent mentors] in terms of prejudice and assumptions they have about each other, but I don't think we change the fundamental fact of power dynamics—we soften it, but it's still pretty clear who runs the classroom.

The emphasis of the Parent Mentor program, therefore, is on parents—introducing them to schools and building them as partners of the school and advocates for their children.

But parents alone cannot shoulder the burden of transforming parent-teacher relationships, and organizers and parents realized this a couple years after the start of the Parent Mentor program. The original intent of the program was to encourage mutual learning between parents and teachers as they worked together in classrooms. As Nancy recalls, "From the beginning, we always had this concept of parent-teacher mentoring—the teacher was mentoring the parent, but the parent was also helping the teacher understand more about the culture of the community. That's the unusual part, because teachers teach, but teachers aren't looking to learn the culture of the community necessarily."

Although the Parent Mentor program was successful in helping parents understand the classroom environment, the opposite goal—in which teachers learn from parents—was a more challenging endeavor. Through focus-group conversations with parent mentors, LSNA found that if teachers were to truly understand the experiences of families, they had to experience the children in the kids' homes. Acting on a desire to also reach out to families that had little connection to schools and little exposure to classroom expectations, LSNA designed the Literacy Ambassadors program. Created through the vision of parent mentors who, according to Joanna, wanted to "build a bridge between the school and home," the program brings teachers into a student's home to talk with families about reading to their children at home. The hosting family invites other students and their families from the school to join in conversation over a meal. The classroom parent mentor who serves as a bridge between the teacher and the families accompanies teachers on the home visit; together, they plan activities for parents and children. These activities support the goal of literacy and give parents ideas on how to support their child's reading at home.

The families that participate get an opportunity to meet teachers in a more familiar environment—within the community. They learn how they can support their child's literacy, and they establish connections with fellow parents at the school. According to former Literacy Ambassadors program coordinator Lisa Contreras, whose experiences as a parent mentor were detailed in chapter 4, "students are so excited to see teachers at their home, and families often feel less intimidated by teachers and the school environment because of this experience." By interacting with teachers in a more informal environment and getting to know them, "these parents don't have to feel intimidated, because now they know the teacher . . . they have been actually having a conversation."

But Lisa also believes that the benefits for teachers are just as compelling. She has seen that teachers who participate in the Literacy Ambassadors program for the first time are "nervous to be out of their comfort zone and into a family's home." But as teachers become immersed in the activities and interactions with the families, "that nervousness just goes away, and they leave excited to do this again." For many teachers, the sheer act of entering into a family's home, often for the first time, can "get teachers to understand in a small but meaningful way how [the student's] family lives, what they might struggle with, why it might be difficult to help their children at home." Melva Patock, a Funston teacher who has often participated in the Literacy Ambassadors program, agrees:

> It's hard to build that connection with parents when you don't know them. And when you only meet them in school, you don't really have to think about it. But when you come to a student's house and you sit down together for dinner with his parents and you can see where they live, then you can really focus on the family and the community that they are a part of. You start to see everything in a different light, but especially from that student's perspective.

As Melva implies, most parent-teacher interactions take place in schools, where the traditions and culture of the school may be overwhelmingly oriented toward white, middle-class norms. Within that environment, power relations are often undisturbed and unexamined. By bringing parents and teachers together into a student's home and into the community, LSNA facilitates the relational work in a setting where parents may be more comfortable and where teachers can examine some of their own assumptions and relinquish some of their authority.

I get to see these newly located interactions firsthand during a Literacy Ambassadors home visit that has been arranged by parents at Mozart Elementary School. One day after school in late April, we gather inside a warm, welcoming apartment—six young children, four mothers, one teacher, a parent mentor, a Literacy Ambassadors coordinator, and me—to spend an afternoon reading with each other and getting to know one another. The event starts with a gracious meal that is served by the hosting family. All of us help ourselves to a home-cooked meal of rice, beans, fried plantains, and stewed chicken and sit in the living room—on the couch, in chairs, and on the floor. Children are on their best behavior as their mothers watch them carefully, make sure they eat well, and thank the host, *Jessica*, enthusiastically. During this first hour of the home visit, the atmosphere is subdued as parents and teacher look for ways to begin conversations and get to know each other. *Eva*, a parent mentor and the only one who knows everyone in the room, slowly engages all members of the group. In this setting, the teacher, Susana Rojas, begins to talk with the parents seated beside her. First, the conversations are focused on the classroom—what students are learning and doing—but as Susana starts talking about her own children, the conversation quickly turns to raising children, cooking, family narratives, and the delicious meal put together by Jessica.

After the meal, Susana gathers the children together for a reading of *Love You Forever*, a book about the evolving relationship between a mother and child, in preparation for Mother's Day. At first, the reading is like any other classroom reading—children are gathered on the floor, sitting on their knees to get a good look at the pictures. Susana reads the book aloud with enthusiasm and animation, asks the students to repeat the refrain with her, and peppers the reading with questions to elicit discussion. But all the while, she also engages the parents, who sit behind the students. As their children raise their hands and enthusiastically share their responses, mothers look on with pride. During this reading, Susana is modeling literacy support at home—reading and discussing books in ways that parents and children can do in their own homes. As she reads the book a second time, this time in Spanish, children are up on their knees, chanting the refrain with their parents:

Para siempre te amare,
Para siempre te querre,
Mientras en mi haya vida,
Siempre seras mi bebe.

By the end of the late afternoon visit, the atmosphere in the house is transformed. While children work on a Mother's Day craft activity—making decorative flower baskets—Susana and the other mothers in the room oversee the projects and chat informally with each other, sharing past Mother's Day experiences and fondly sharing memories of handmade presents from their children. For the remainder of the afternoon, "the ice is broken," Susana later remembers; parents approach her, and she comfortably engages with them, sharing stories about their children as they scurry about the house with their friends. As everyone gathers to leave, children continue to run around the apartment while their mothers attempt to slow them down to say good-bye to Susana, who hugs each parent, reaffirming, "So I will see you in school now—come say hello."

As I walk back to the school with Susana, she explains that with each home visit, she feels she understands the families more. She is always moved by how carefully they prepare their homes for this short week-day visit—making space for a large gathering and cooking a full meal to satisfy adults and children. She admits, "Initially, I didn't think I had the time for something like this, but if I think about what I gain—getting to know my students' families and breaking the ice with them—well, that's why I keep doing this." By experiencing children in their homes, she attests that "everyone lets down their guard," which allows for "the kinds of relationships we want between parents and teachers—the kind that benefit our children."

BRIDGING COMMUNITIES

Maria Marquez is the parent coordinator for the Ames Middle School Elev8 program for adolescent youth. She is a former parent mentor who is currently studying to be a bilingual education teacher. Like many parent leaders at LSNA, she has participated in most of the education programs—starting as a parent mentor, then moving on to become a literacy ambassador, then a parent tutor. She recalls her own experience in the Literacy Ambassadors program as a parent mentor who would accompany teachers to the home visits. Because of her bilingualism, she was often paired up with teachers who only spoke English. During her four years with the program, she was always placed with the school's new teacher, someone in his or her first year of teaching at the school, who often didn't speak Spanish. Early in the year, during the first home visits, the teachers were often anxious. She recalls, "They actually told me, 'Ms. M., I have no idea what to expect,'" to which she would explain that it was like teaching a class at the student's home, but that they would have to anticipate that the home environment would be one that could be new and unfamiliar. A neighbor might drop in, the group might be surprisingly large, there might be children from outside the school community. As a parent in the community, Maria knew what to expect, felt comfortable going into the homes of students, and often worked with teachers to plan activities that would be appropriate for the children and families that would attend the home visits. She recalls these conversations where she would try to "ease teachers into the situation, because they were scared to go to the home and scared to do the activity. They didn't know what they were scared of, really, just the unexpected. They knew they were going to be out of their comfort zone."

But after each session of reading, meeting parents, sharing a meal, and leading an activity for the group, teachers were always "so happy and relieved as we walked [back to school]." She remembers their reactions, their excitement to participate again: "They would say, 'Ah, I was so worried! And this is so great. I've got so many ideas on what I can do in my classroom. I feel so much better about communicating with parents,' and all of a sudden, they're hooked." While teachers would often ask Maria to help them plan and facilitate the first home visit activity, after the success of the first visit, "they came back with different books and different activities, and they had already run off the copies . . . and would now tell me, 'Don't worry about the activities. I'll take care of the activities.'"

For the teachers Maria describes along with the many other teachers who are unfamiliar with students' home lives and communities, parent mentors like her play a bridging role between teachers and families. LSNA understands the distance that exists between schools and families, so across its programs—the Parent Mentor program, the Literacy Ambassadors program, the community learning centers, and the Grow Your Own Teachers program—it emphasizes the need to bridge that gap. Through the development of parent leaders who are comfortable and active within the community as well as the school, LSNA builds a generation of leaders and members who connect the sometimes disparate worlds of home and school. The Literacy Ambassadors program, according to Joanna, "was an attempt to build a bridge between the school and the home by using the experienced parent mentors as the bridge, so that there were teachers who said, 'Oh well, I'll go, but only if my parent mentor goes with me. I don't want a parent I don't know. I want my parent mentor.'" By building relationships with teachers throughout their time in classrooms, parent mentors become uniquely positioned to facilitate a dialogue between teachers and the many parents who have yet to participate fully in schools.

Many parent mentors admit that becoming involved in schools was not easy. The newly involved parent mentors at Funston discuss their negative experiences with schools or their intimidation and fear of schools as prominent sources for their own lack of participation. They understand that for many parents, these issues persist as obstacles for their own involvement in schools and their willingness to build relationships with school staff. Maria believes that parent mentors anchor the school community through their connections to both parents and teachers. She explains that being a parent mentor "gets you closer to the community and the teachers and the parents. You're like a bridge between them." On numerous occasions, she has encountered parents who were afraid to ask teachers questions or whose questions remained unanswered until they noticed her in the classroom. At that point, parents approached her with their questions, which she then took to teachers on behalf of parents. But she insists on encouraging parents to come to the teachers themselves: "I tell the parent, 'Listen, don't be afraid to ask the teacher. Go ahead.'" The distance between teachers and parents is a reality—one that can be affected by a dissonance in cultural values and expectations. Maria explains:

> You know, it's not uncommon for our parents to feel intimidated by the teacher or feel that there is a distance between them, especially our parents who don't speak English—that have recently migrated to the country, maybe one or two years in the country. They would be mostly the ones that I would think would be fearful of asking. And in a lot of Latin cultures, it's not acceptable to ask a teacher, because we assume the teacher knows. A parent has no right to be asking questions of the teacher.

Because parent mentors like Maria understand both the experiences of parents and the expectations and practices of schools, they can play powerful bridging roles between the families and school staff, groups that are traditionally distant and separate. In many schools where the school staff not only reflects middle-class, white culture but also educates low-income students of color, there will be few individuals who are well connected to the worlds of both home and school. While schools may understand the importance of building relationships with parents, many parents may be hard to reach or schools may lack the skills and resources to connect with them in meaningful ways. LSNA's Parent Mentor program shows us how parents themselves can mediate relationships between families and schools and potentially become catalysts for broader parent participation.

Lesszest George, the former LSNA organizer mentioned in chapter 4, believes that trust forms the foundation of the relational strategies fostered by LSNA. In the midst of a school environment that often struggles to engage parents and teachers, Lesszest believes that parent mentors open up the possibilities of building trusting relationships between them. Because mentors send their own children to the schools that they, the parents, work in, it is easier for outside parents to trust parent mentors when they see them in classrooms. This, in turn, says Lesszest, "allowed the parents on the outside to trust what was going on in the classroom, because parents didn't trust the teachers. They didn't trust what they said; they didn't believe what they said about their children in the classroom." For many of the parents Lesszest meets, parent mentors are a less threatening voice and are better able to build a connection between families and teachers. The mentors can propose to parents suggestions that teachers would or could not make, can encourage conversations between parents and teachers, and can offer some insight on perspectives that might be overly critical. By establishing trust with parents, the mentors can ease some of the tensions that might interfere with the relationships between teachers and parents. As Lesszest explains, "it brings a connection between parents and teachers that probably wouldn't be possible without [parent mentors]." In essence, parent mentors become the bridge that is desperately needed to close the distance between families and schools.

While cultural differences may often put teachers and parents in sep-arate worlds, the diversity among families within a school will often also pose challenges. Many families are Latino or Spanish-speaking, but there are often further divisions among these families, depending on the countries of origin (Puerto Rico, Mexico, Guatemala, etc.), in-come, or English fluency. As one organizer attested, "it's not unusual in some places for different Latino groups or people from varied expe-riences to have some initial difficulties in getting connected." While the parent mentor training programs are designed to generally encour-age points of connection among parents, "sometimes you really have to work through some different ideas that people might have about each other." In schools across the country—and certain Logan Square schools are no exception—we find parent associations that are fractured by racial or ethnic groups. The intense relational approach that runs throughout LSNA's education programs and campaigns allows for par-ents to build connections across race and ethnicity—no small feat. As Karla recalls, during her family's challenging situation with the fire, she was moved by the outpouring from the community. As a black mother who was supported by a generous outpouring from a primarily Latino community, Karla admits, "It was nice to see all these people—who knew me, who didn't, who were Hispanic or not—coming together to support my family. I didn't expect that." But Karla is not alone. The Parent Mentor program provides opportunities for conversations that may lead to early relationships across groups that may normally be di-vided. Reynalda Covarrubias from Funston explains:

> Part of the wonderful thing about the Parent Mentor program is that it can bring everyone together, no matter who you are. I will be honest, sometimes it's not easy to get the different groups together, but even so, we try to make it happen. And even when there is difficulty, we are trying to build this connection across us—our children learn a lot from watching in this way.

In the parent mentor trainings I have seen across the schools, while most parents are Latino and many of them Spanish speaking, in some schools, the proportions of black parents are comparable. Even despite the language differences, I see parent mentors who build relationships across racial groups. At the larger neighborhood-wide workshops, where parents come together across school sites, this is oftentimes more visible. As a hundred and twenty parents rally together in support of a local ordinance, it seems to matter very little who is speaking out in Spanish or English, who hails from Mexico or Puerto Rico; the collective goal bands the group together. This provides opportunities for parent engagement that are diverse and integrated; parent mentors are themselves bridges across difference.

AN UNLIKELY BUT ESSENTIAL PARTNER: THE ROLE OF COMMUNITY INSTITUTIONS

When schools and families are worlds apart and relationships between parents and teachers are fraught with tension and misunderstanding, the task of building relationships of trust and reciprocity often seems an insurmountable challenge. Through their work in schools, parent mentors closely interact with families, school staff, and the community. While parent mentors can be seen as bridges between school staff and the many families that have yet to feel a part of schools, on a broader level, LSNA also acts as a mediating force between schools and communities. Nancy Aardema underscores how challenging that can be when schools are steeped in traditions that rely on the separation between schools and families. Within these situations, she says, the relational approach is nothing less than necessary:

> For these principals, you have people who come in, who use your building, whose work might mean that the chalk is missing the next morning—it means you're sharing space. And that's not something you set out to do when you started your work in schools. We're used to having students in here and parents over there, for the most part. So what we're asking them to do is very difficult. And so you have to be relational.

When schools are accustomed to working in isolation, they often have few resources that will support them in developing relationships with families. Lissette Moreno-Kuri, LSNA's director of community learning centers, has worked both in community service agencies and in schools in support of developing resources for youth and their families. She understands that when schools and communities have distant relations, it is not necessarily "because schools don't have good intentions." Engaging parents is often one goal among many goals that schools do not always get to: "It's a full-time job for someone else to be thinking about making connections to the community and actually doing it," says Lissette. "A lot of the teachers have so much to do outside of the teaching . . . so it's hard to get them to think about how to get parents in the school." Schools that are overburdened with intense responsibilities may have insufficient resources and skills to engage parents. These schools may also lack staff who speak the languages necessary to connect with families, and they may lack individuals with experience in the local community—people who could help the school design culturally appropriate strategies for engagement.

But organizing groups like LSNA that center their work around building relationships and developing community capacity for change bring a set of assets that possibly fill the voids of schools. According to Stephanie Garza, a former SWOP organizer who worked closely with LSNA organizers to bring the Parent Mentor program to schools in the southwest side of Chicago, the relational component is a critical strength that organizing groups bring to their work in schools:

> I wouldn't make the gross generalization that schools aren't good at building relationships. But as organizers, that's what we do. Our primary goal is to get people together, to move forward on X, Y, or Z . . . And we're good at it because we're really intentional about it. And I think schools can do that, and there's teachers and staff and some issues that can do that, but I think sometimes, they need a little help.

While groups such as LSNA come to their work in schools with a relational approach that is central to the practice of community organizing, Stephanie also underscores the value of groups that come to their work from outside schools. For these groups, she says, the "set of interests are different." She explains the difference for her, as someone who works in schools from the outside: "I don't have to worry about losing my job as a teacher depending on how I relate to the principal or the other parents or other teachers."

But even to those who work inside schools, there is value in an outside organization like LSNA. For example, Edwin Rivera, principal of Monroe Elementary School, says that not only does LSNA offer resources and programs "that I simply couldn't offer on my own," but the organization comes with an understanding of how things work within the local community and the school:

> They have got this valuable expertise in the community. They are well connected to the families and the needs that they have. At the same time, they are able to come to this school with some clear ideas about the kinds of programs they are capable of offering. For someone like me, I'm looking for these kinds of partners to help move us in a direction that is positive and to help us with some areas that we are committed to but maybe don't have all the resources for.

At Monroe, LSNA runs a fully active community learning center for adults and children after school. During the school day, there are parent mentors, parent tutors, literacy ambassadors, and the many other parents who volunteer or who are involved as school leaders through the local school council (LSC). The school has an active parent presence that is "supported and cultivated by LSNA," Edwin says. "And these are all opportunities to build a better relationship or understanding between families and the school."

With a deep commitment to the Logan Square community and expertise in, and knowledge of, the issues that families face, LSNA approaches schools with an understanding of community history and context. But schools are complex institutions, and organizers looking for solutions to problems such as low parent engagement must also understand the context of schools. While it may be tempting for community institutions to enter schools with deliberate intentions and clear plans to improve the schools, LSNA understands that schools have a set of practices, values, and traditions—a school culture—that it must intimately understand to create positive change.

Educators may view an outside organization like LSNA with skepticism. Is the organization's knowledge about schools too shallow? Aren't schools complex institutions that require a trained eye and expert attention? But many of the organizers come to the work in schools with deep commitments to education and a willingness to mediate complex and conflicting interests.

Joanna Brown is a case in point. With a rich experience in journalism, politics (working in Mayor Harold Washington's administration in Chicago), community activism, and international education, she made her foray into Chicago public education as a local school council member and an active parent of two children in the public schools. Her ease and familiarity with community politics has allowed her to understand the complex interactions between public institutions and local residents, in particular the many newcomer residents that Logan Square schools serve. As a mother of two Latino children, she understands the complex terrain where race, inequality, opportunity, and ethnicity collide. In the many meetings and conversations we have had together, stories of her children—her son's experience at the university, the family's search for the right school for her daughter, the care for and frustration toward their teachers, her unabashed faith in education as a human right—run alongside the stories of LSNA campaigns and program developments. With decades of experience navigating educational institutions as a parent and community organizer, she has, over time, learned the careful art of mediating the interests between the often-conflicting cultural institutions of home and school. The relational approach that she encourages among her staff is the very same one she practices.

THE NATURE OF RELATIONSHIPS: MOVING TOWARD RECIPROCITY

While it is important to build the necessary relationships among parents and between teachers and parents, what is the nature of those relationships? The conversations are critical, but how do parents and teachers engage with each other? Power and authority are reflected not only in actions but also in relationships between individuals. Do the relationships reflect the traditional power dynamics between teachers and parents—where teachers wield the most power and authority over parents? What is LSNA's approach in supporting the development of relationships between schools and families?

Early in the school year, during an October parent mentor training session, new parent mentors ask questions about the kinds of activities they will perform in classrooms. Stella, a veteran parent mentor mentioned in chapter 3, explains that she spent time each week working with the teacher in the classroom to prepare materials for upcoming lessons while students were in art or physical education class. These opportunities were "nice moments where I could get to know the teacher. We would basically just talk while we were working the whole time— about the students, about our families, all kinds of things." She explains that these opportunities would allow her to get to know the teacher; with the two women establishing this rapport, they became more comfortable around one another.

During this training session, I am sitting in the back of the room with Graciela. While Stella tells us about the personal connections she has built with teachers, Graciela turns to me and says, "You know, I don't think I've ever really talked with a teacher like that before. That makes me nervous." Other parents talk about the relationships they have built with various teachers over their years as parent mentors, giving the new people the idea that parent mentors have an opportunity to engage with teachers in new and different ways. Later, during the break, I ask Graciela whether she looks forward to that opportunity, given her hesitations, and she admits that her reason for being involved is to be in the school, learn more about the classrooms, and consequently support her son. She consistently talks about wanting to "learn from the teacher" and feels uncomfortable with the idea that she could build a relationship where they would connect on a more personal level. "Teachers are busy people, and they want our help. I don't think they will want to know all these other things about my life."

Graciela's stance is a common perception of newly involved parents, who often talk of learning from teachers and helping teachers in their classroom. The relationship between parents and teachers, as it begins to develop, is one where parents see their work in support of teachers and often defer authority to them. But throughout training sessions, LSNA organizers emphasize to parents that they have an equal voice in school matters. LSNA organizer Ofelia Sanchez explains to parents during a training session that "your voice is important and this school is here for your kids. If you see or hear something that makes you wonder, it is your right to say something about it." As parent mentors become privy to the interactions and practices within classrooms and across the school, they are encouraged to take a critical perspective, all with the goal of improving the school. Nancy sees this as a form of advocacy on behalf of the school: "If there is one class where no one does their homework or a classroom where there aren't enough textbooks, parents know that, because they are in the classroom and they see it, not because they hear it from their children. So they feel they have to change that culture and feel that they can intervene and make that happen."

As parents move from the periphery to the center of school life, they begin to take notice, speak up, and intervene in ways that change the nature of relationships. Rather than viewing teachers and school staff as final authorities on school practice, they begin to see them as partners. Through the relational work that LSNA fosters during the year, trust is built and a sense of reciprocity emerges as parents and teachers redefine the terms of their relationship.

Lisa Contreras reflects on her changed views of teachers as "a move from thinking that they are on a different level to thinking that we are working together." Through her experience in classrooms as a parent mentor, she has a wealth of knowledge about students, their struggles, the interactions among peers in hallways, their home lives—"all things that contribute to me having a say. My child is here, I am a parent, and I am here to look out for our kids." While she may not have been so assertive before, now she is quick to intervene when she sees something troubling in the classroom, on the playground, at the school crossing, or in the community. She explains, "If it has to do with this school, it is my business." As she shares situations in which she has confronted a teacher, intervened for a student who was being bullied, or went to the principal to raise a concern about something she saw or heard, I hear the voice of a parent who feels entitled to speak out and have a say. At times, she is outraged by the actions of those around her, and even though most of those situations do not directly involve her daughter, she still cares.

By building a base of experience in schools and developing relationships of trust and collegiality with teachers, parent mentors become vocal advocates who stand up to school staff or parents in defense of students, families, and the school. Maricela Contreras feels that by "having a say and having a voice" at her daughter's school, she has taught her daughter to "have a voice, too." She notes that her daughter's confidence level is much higher when Maricela is present in the school, and Maricela has taught her daughter to view schools from a critical perspective as well—seeing teachers as human, as individuals who manage multiple responsibilities and could overlook a situation, and encouraging her daughter to feel comfortable approaching them with concerns as they come up. Her daughter learns this form of self-advocacy best, Maricela explains, when she models it herself. This was a skill she learned through her experience in schools and with LSNA's "belief that parents are powerful and should be at the table with teachers to decide what's best for their children." She adds:

> You would never have believed how shy I was before. I simply didn't have a voice in schools before, and I didn't think I had to. But as a parent mentor and then becoming a part of the LSC, I slowly began to see myself as a leader and as someone who had to speak up for my child and for those children I worked with every day. It was my responsibility to speak on behalf of my kids and teach them to have a voice, too.

For Maricela and other parent mentors, building relationships with teachers and fellow parents is a process that extends not only across various individuals (e.g., fellow parent mentors, teachers, principals, parents outside the Parent Mentor program), but also over time as the parent mentors become more experienced, confident, and assertive in their stance. While schools may implicitly or explicitly encourage parent participation that is more passive than active, and more supportive than challenging, LSNA encourages parents to believe that the relationship alone is not what is important, but the nature of the relationship. Through their work in classrooms, parent mentors learn that they can be equal partners with school staff, advocating on behalf of their children as well as those they come to know.

CONCLUSION

Every year when her son was in school, Nancy invited his teachers to her home for dinner. To her and other middle-class moms, this was a cultural practice that was natural. Although some teachers declined the invitation, thinking it was a boundary they did not feel comfortable crossing, for most teachers, it was a socially and culturally appropriate practice and a welcome invitation. Nancy explains that these teachers felt a sense of familiarity and connection with middle-class mothers like her, and the boundaries between the worlds of home and school could be blurred. In contrast, Nancy says, for many Latino families in Logan Square who may not be fluent in English, come from a different set of cultural practices, or lack a familiarity or connection with teachers, her yearly invitation to teachers would feel unnatural. And as LSNA organizers learned early in their work in schools and through their creation of the Literacy Ambassadors program, many teachers also feel a disconnect with families within the community, and the prospect of visiting a student's home elicits fear about the unknown and the unexpected.

Clearly, these examples illustrate a distinct gap or separation between the culture of schools and that of families. These differences may be attributed to variations in cultural group, race, immigration, or social class, among other possibilities. Whether schools are located within white, middle-class communities or low-income, Latino communities, as institutions, the schools often reflect white or middle-class norms and values, because of a predominance of white or middle-class school staff.[1] For schools in fairly homogenous, white, middle-class neighborhoods, the consonance between home values and school values contributes to a more "natural" connection between schools and families and a more easily established sense of trust and common interest. But in communities of color such as Logan Square, relationships between schools and families can be distant or adversarial, and a relational approach to parent engagement as illustrated in LSNA's Parent Mentor program is essential in bringing schools and families together.[2] To ease the entry of parents into the unfamiliar environments of schools and to encourage teachers and school staff to open their classrooms to families, schools must find opportunities for schools and families to build relationships of trust. LSNA, through the one-on-one working relationships of the Parent Mentor program and the intimate home visits of the Literacy Ambassadors program, creates opportunities for parents and teachers to become meaningfully engaged—making connections, gaining new understanding of each other, and challenging previous assumptions.

But insisting on relationships is not enough. Schools have perpetually struggled to build relationships with families in low-income communities of color. To bring together disparate, often-antagonistic groups, schools and communities need innovative strategies. Given these challenges, community institutions such as LSNA can play a potentially important role in bringing families and schools together. Through their expertise in local communities and their ability to collaborate with schools, these community associations become intermediaries that facilitate the engagement between schools and communities. This bridging role underscores the difficulties that exist in requiring either schools or families to tackle this challenge alone and offers groups like LSNA as potential catalysts for change. According to researcher Concha Delgado-Gaitan, groups like LSNA become "cultural brokers" that bring together groups that struggle with connection because of cultural differences.[3] But by building parents' familiarity with schools and recognizing parents' skills and other assets through the Parent Mentor program, LSNA bridges gaps between schools and families by developing parent mentors, who serve as a bridge between other parents and the school. In effect, by cultivating a base of parent mentors—a community of advocates and potential leaders who are immersed in schools and whose presence changes the very nature of school culture—LSNA displays how institutions *and* individuals can serve as cultural brokers.

Through these institutional and individual cultural brokers, coupled with the acts of bridging that enable new relationships, schools focus on the relational aspects of family engagement. Parent mentors maintain a sense of community and collective identity as advocates for their children and as staunch supporters looking out for the interests of all students within the school. Through their visible presence and ongoing experience in classrooms, parent mentors also become sources of connection to parents who are not yet involved in schools, thereby becoming potential catalysts for broader parent participation. But as we have seen, changing the nature of parent participation is not enough. By bringing parent mentors into meaningful collaborations and relationships with teachers, LSNA opens the possibility that teachers, too, will begin to challenge their long-standing assumptions about families, bringing schools one step closer to transforming the culture of schools.

6

NOT JUST DREAMS

Transforming Lives and Communities

O N THE NIGHT THAT Karla Mack's home was destroyed by fire, she never imagined that the school community would be such a source of strength and support for her family. When she began her work as a parent mentor, she focused primarily on the opportunity to gain insight into the school and into classrooms in ways that would benefit the three children she had in school. Although she was interested in the opportunity to meet other parents through the weekly training sessions, she did not expect the sessions to be a vital part of her school involvement. But as a mother of five children, she has experience with various school environments and she noticed energy in McAuliffe that felt inviting to her and that drew her into the Parent Mentor program. It was that energy, she recalls, that prompted her to "see what it was all about." She explains, "It was different than what I was used to. It was a nice atmosphere with a lot of opportunities for parents and community members." Upon joining and throughout the first week of training, she became hooked and began to build relationships with mothers who were interesting, who experienced similar issues with their children, and who were a vital part of the school community she was getting to know. Before the devastating fire, Karla began to see the school as "another community that I was a part of." After the fire, she says, members of the community displayed a startling commitment to her as "an extended family," to which she feels immensely grateful.

Despite the outpouring of support, Karla found the transition into a new life and new home challenging because of the real difficulties in finding affordable housing in the neighborhood. Having spent the past three years in a relatively stable rental unit but unable to buy a home in the community amid steadily increasing housing rates, she faced the prospect of moving out of the school's neighborhood to find affordable housing. For three weeks, during which she was "pressed for time" and juggling temporary housing, she attempted to find an apartment comparable in size and rent for her and her three school-age children. With few options, she recalls thinking, "I am going to have to move out of my neighborhood, or am I going to have to take something that's high and that's going to overextend me?" For the first time, she felt committed to a school and neighborhood that she wanted her children to be a part of. Through her work as a parent mentor, she had become connected to a range of parents, teachers, and families, so to be faced with the prospect of leaving those connections behind was a huge disappointment and an added source of frustration during an already challenging period of transition.

Karla ultimately found a suitable apartment that was only slightly higher than her previous rent and that would allow her to stay in the community, but the struggle of finding affordable housing revealed the broader housing and gentrification issues in the rapidly changing community. With the soaring real estate prices and rapid development that began in the late 1990s, LSNA began battling against large-scale condo constructions and redevelopment projects that were changing the character of the community and displacing many of the community's lower-income families. Given her recent struggles to find housing, LSNA organizers approached Karla and asked her to speak at an upcoming rally to promote affordable housing as a priority to Chicago Mayor Richard Daley. LSNA, along with Logan Square pastors and civic leaders, called on the local alderman and Mayor Daley to reverse a decision made by the city's Department of Planning and Development to reject a proposal to turn a long-vacant office building into the community's first supportive housing development. The project, initiated by two nonprofit groups, sought to develop apartments in conjunction with on-site social services to help residents move into permanent housing. Karla recalls the rainy Saturday morning when she decided to brave the heavy downpour and speak to a gathered crowd about her own experience and the importance of community involvement:

> We live in this neighborhood, and if people like me don't speak out about how high the housing is, how expensive it is, this is going to continue to happen . . . We're far west, and prices are still expensive. And they're building condos. Who's going to go in there? It's certainly not me. The prices that they have for all this new construction . . . it's like if you don't have a lot of money, they're pushing you out, and my point is, where am I going to go?

Through her experience, Karla understands the challenges that many low-income and working-class families face to stay in the community. With a vulnerability to housing prices, these families also become vulnerable to changing schools and unexpected displacement. Karla feels a personal responsibility to "get involved and speak out" on behalf of the necessary changes that are needed in the broader community. "This is not LSNA saying we want affordable housing for us. These are the people that live here. It was not affordable to them, and they live here and they pay rent, and they've been here for years." She believes that these changes will only occur if people like her who experience the struggles of daily living become involved in the fight for change. While Karla never previously felt a connection to her neighborhood or community before, she now feels a personal commitment that transcends her concern for an apartment, a school classroom, or a neighborhood block— her commitment "cuts across all the layers into the bigger community." When asked about her decision to become involved in LSNA's housing campaigns, she explains, "This, I committed to. It's not about pay. It's not about anything that I'm getting back." Karla believes that the struggle to attain affordable housing, quality education, and residential stability is fundamentally connected to her own struggles as a single parent and her own newfound commitment to the local community. As a result, her participation is grounded in a desire to change her own circumstances as well as those of her community. She recalls the early realization that she wanted to get involved:

> So, I told Silvia [Gonzalez that] in the future, I could see that I might want to do something with [the housing] part of LSNA, because that's something that means a lot to me. I plan on staying in this neighborhood. I plan on trying to get a house. And I haven't been able to. I've been here about three years, but the prices are steadily going up, so that was my example of—that really meant a lot to me to go and speak that day at that rally.

Karla is now committed to staying in Logan Square. Her struggle for home ownership is connected to a "refusal to displace my kids" and a desire to provide them with a stable, quality education. With her increased participation in schools, she sees this broader community issue of affordable housing as intricately connected to the issue of education.

Connecting schools and education to the broader issues of the community is an explicit strategy shaped by LSNA's perspective on community organizing. Community forces such as poverty, immigration, and inequality will inevitably shape the conditions of schools (e.g., teacher retention) as well as the conditions of the community (e.g., availability of affordable housing). Throughout their work with parent mentors, LSNA organizers encourage parents to view schools within the broader framework of community life. While parents traditionally view issues such as affordable housing and immigration reform as distinct from their concerns about schools, they begin to see and understand the connections. Shirley Reyes, a parent mentor coordinator we met earlier in the book, says these conversations with parent mentors must be explicit. While parents may be tempted to stay out of community issues such as safety and gang violence, "they have to understand that the gangs hanging in the corners that we don't talk about and that we don't work together on will continue to keep going in there and killing our people." For Shirley, children travel seamlessly from home to school to streets and through neighborhoods that are connected by the people they encounter as well as the environmental issues that cut across those settings. In order to focus a community's efforts on improving schools, Shirley adds, "we must improve the community." She agrees that *all* issues that affect children should be considered when thinking about education reform, "from security to difficulty in the community, from the life inside the house, and what they are doing in school."

While LSNA tackles many community issues, such as education, immigration, housing, and development, it believes that these issues are intricately connected. LSNA community center director Lissette Moreno-Kuri explains that "we try to take every piece of what we do in LSNA into the schools." During the weekly workshops and training sessions, parent mentors are introduced to a host of community life issues. Through the intense relationships that are built within the Parent Mentor program, "people already work so hard to get the families comfortable and bring them to the school." As a result, she says, "it's so much easier for us to bring more resources there and see it as the center to everything they do." In her experience with families, "Once they get comfortable, they want to stay there."

This view of school considers the ways in which schools are embedded within the broader contours of community and society. For this reason, LSNA views schools as central sites for community organizing. While other organizing groups and networks such as the Industrial Areas Foundation (IAF) use churches and congregations as the base for their organizing work, LSNA's lead education organizer Joanna Brown believes that in Chicago, things are different. Schools, she says, are the "only public institution in every mini-geographical area—every area has a neighborhood school. It's a public institution, it's built with public funds, it's a place-based institution." As public institutions that serve the full range of families within a community, schools pull together a representative section of the community. LSNA's director of the New Communities program, Susan Adler Yanun, compares the participants and leaders involved with LSNA with those in other community groups that are organized with more specialized interests: "So the thing about schools is, it's really more of a cross section, there's more of a representative slice of the community, so it just gives you a truer picture of who's in the community and what their issues are."

Joanna believes that by including parents and other family members across a range of experiences within the community, LSNA's approach draws new leaders and other new participants into community life. Through a relational approach to parent engagement that is based on the experiences of parents who are not familiar with public institutions such as schools, the Parent Mentor program invites community participation through school participation. Joanna says, "I think we should do everything out of schools, and we are moving to that, because that's where we connect with people. By coming into the program, people actually get pulled into the community. They get pulled out of their private houses, into the first public space that they've entered."

Schools become an ideal setting for inviting individuals into the work of the community, according to Joanna. A school is a familiar physical space within the neighborhood, a site that is visited frequently, and one that serves children and families. For groups that may be particularly hard to reach and draw out into community life, such as immigrant mothers and isolated low-income families, schools hold particular promise. "It's where people have their children," says Joanna. "So, for most of the mothers, it's where they're most interested and concerned."

For parents like Karla who have never been involved in community issues before, their participation is motivated by a sense of hope—a belief that their participation will make a difference and that their voice will be counted and heard. They realize that their own struggles, when seen through a collective lens, represent the struggles of a community that can work together to enforce change. As they become involved in schools and the broader community, these parents become more conscious of how schools are embedded within local communities and fundamentally shaped by the issues and circumstances of those communities. Through their school involvement, they gain a more holistic view of the community, and some parents begin to take steps into community life. For Karla, this has changed the nature of her participation in her community as well as her perspective into a neighborhood she now calls home:

I've been to other schools, from the north side to the south side. We've lived in a lot of different places. So, I've lived in neighborhoods, but I didn't really care about that neighborhood. I just lived there. And this is different, because I really feel like I have a responsibility to get to know the people around me and to work to make this neighborhood a better place. And all of this becomes real to me, because I'm involved in my child's school. Who would have guessed that school involvement could translate into community involvement? But it really does. The connection is really there.

THE LEADER WITHIN

While schools may be ideal sites for drawing parents into community life, participation alone will not prepare parents for the challenges in developing change in the community. In Logan Square, community organizing efforts focus on issues such as creating affordable housing, fighting for immigration reform, and putting a stop to real estate development that threatens to displace low-income families. And while LSNA often joins local community groups and elected officials in these efforts, it also often rallies in opposition to various groups and elected officials to win campaigns. Essentially, in a mixed-income community like Logan Square, there are competing interests, existing inequalities, and constant struggles to attain power. For parent mentors who become interested in community issues, developing leadership skills is a necessary strategy for successful community involvement. According to Joanna, "everything we do is with an eye toward leadership development, the development of people . . . Everybody is a potential leader, and our job is to help them reach their potential, as much as they want or come to want to do that."

Although the Parent Mentor program has produced many of LSNA's community and school leaders, the program itself is not solely focused on the end goal of developing community leaders. The program's first consideration is toward the many parents it seeks to involve: those who are new to schools, immigrants who may lack a familiarity with public institutions, mothers who may be isolated within their homes. In this regard, a first step for many parents is to become acclimated to a new environment. Through the training, parents are taught about school practices and expectations and are given opportunities to develop confidence in a new environment and personal goals that will shape their own development as mentors and role models. By working in the public space of classrooms, parent mentors engage in a host of activities that call upon skills of public speaking and interaction with teachers, students, and their families. They bring students together to work in a classroom, converse with parents who inquire about their children, work collaboratively with teachers to support students in classrooms, and become public figures in a public institution. These acts alone, according to Joanna, are acts of leadership. Through the Parent Mentor program, parents who are sometimes isolated within the larger community are placed in a public space where they continue to seek opportunities to develop their skills and talents.

Rather than viewing leadership as an outcome to be achieved solely for those members who go on to become community leaders, LSNA organizers view leadership as a process through which many kinds of leadership skills—with different levels of intensity—are fostered. By bringing parents into schools and developing their capacities for working alongside teachers in classrooms, the Parent Mentor program serves the very basic function of educating parents and introducing them to schools. This initial phase of leadership development, according to Leticia Barrera, "is critical, because before you can become a leader, you have to understand a lot about the environment—who is there, what is going on, and how things work." A training program that is focused on the development of personal goals and confidence in the public sphere of schools encourages parent mentors to think about their experiences and contemplate their potential contributions, their potential acts of leadership within schools and classrooms. Through constant connections with past and present parent mentors who lead training sessions, become LSNA organizers, coordinate the Parent Mentor program, or answer questions about the experience, new parent mentors gain a clearer sense of what those possible contributions might be. Silvia Gonzales, coordinator of the McAuliffe Elementary School's Parent Mentor program, explains:

> It pushes you to be a leader and to reflect on your experience—at home, at school, in your community—and to think about what you can do to contribute, what you can do to build yourself up, and what are those personal things, like the goals in your life and the dreams that you have, that you can work on. These are big questions that a lot of parents don't ever have time to think about, and we want them to start that conversation with themselves, because we believe that it takes that to get to action. And action will change the community.

By introducing parents to leadership skills, encouraging them to envision themselves as leaders, and educating them about the environment of schools, the program gives parent mentors an opportunity to interact and gain confidence in the new environment. Leticia observes that from this initial introduction, some parents "start asking questions. They start thinking, 'I want to be here.'" Through their exposure to the issues that schools and communities face, "these parents really think about other parts of the community life that they never think about." In light of their past experiences with leadership and through their work in classrooms, parent mentors respond in a variety of ways to the calls for leadership. "It's just the first step in the door," says Leticia, "and you don't expect most parent mentors to end up as community leaders. Some people want to work with kids in classrooms. Some people want to play a bigger role in the school. And then there are people who want to get trained [as leaders]."

While some parents aspire to become community leaders—becoming actively engaged in community campaigns and taking on leadership roles within schools—other parent mentors take on roles that require less time, commitment, and involvement, such as working in classrooms, supporting a school project, or serving on a school committee. Ana Martinez Estka, principal of Avondale, notes that these options make the concept of leadership more accessible to the full range of parents who participate: "I like the fact that it pulls parents out and makes them leaders or encourages them to become leaders, and I like that LSNA offers options for the parents to participate in ways that match their experiences and their wishes. There can be different ways to lead, and that leaves room for more people to be involved."

Not only do parents come with a range of motivations toward leadership, but LSNA organizers, as they spend a year in a close relationship with each cohort, also identify potential leaders who show an interest in added responsibilities and who otherwise have an outlook and disposition toward leadership. Many of these parents do not yet see themselves as leaders, so organizers must, in many ways, see the untapped potential of individuals, says Susan Adler Yanun:

> There's so much untapped potential as we've seen, because the Parent Mentor program has been successful for twelve years. There's always the opportunity to build and develop new leaders. And for whatever reason—some might be the natural influx of the community and new people moving in, some might be people who've stayed home when their kids are young, and now, when their kids go to school, now they're still at home—but they have a little bit more time to start becoming involved.

As Susan explains, many of LSNA's potential leaders have not yet developed their skills and experiences as public leaders, but through the intense relational work within the Parent Mentor program, there are opportunities to identify these individuals. With the encouragement of organizers and parent leaders, these individuals go on to join school committees, lead a group of parent mentors for a school project, run for the local school council (LSC), or work on a campaign.

But over the years, LSNA organizers have found the need for a more explicit leadership development strategy that takes parents beyond an introduction to leadership opportunities and prepares them for the real opportunities to lead. For this reason, organizers created leadership training for newly identified leaders. The week-long training session gives forty potential leaders grounding in the tenets and practice of community organizing as well as an understanding of power and accountability within the community context. Throughout the training, participants analyze community power dynamics, examine forms of accountability, explore the nature of publicly accountable and private relationships, discuss and enact potential actions, analyze their own strengths and weaknesses in the public sphere, and are called to design an action plan that would push an elected official to vote a certain way on certain issues. Leticia organized and facilitated the first leadership training sessions along with another education organizer, and she explains some of the intentions behind the training:

> There is some information that we as organizers and leaders have to know—about how decisions are made, who our leaders are, how we can push for changes. We have to educate our leaders about accountability and how we can use the power we have to push our elected officials to act in ways that are good for our people. And this cannot happen by just waiting and hoping that people will act. We have to show [our leaders] how we can take action together. And it is important that these leaders learn by doing and then go and share their knowledge with the others.

LSNA organizers understand leadership as a developmental process in which individuals are first introduced to the school and community environment to develop a base of understanding. Next, by identifying potential leaders or generating interest among members, LSNA offers an explicit leadership training that equips parents with the necessary skills and organizing framework to become effective in subsequent opportunities to lead. While the parent mentor training introduces parents to the skills of leadership, the focus is primarily on developing personal goals as well as confidence and knowledge in schools. The next step, and the focus of the leadership training, is to explore the traditions that are rooted in organizing, the nature of bureaucracies, the rights of community members, and the responsibility and accountability that elected officials owe to the community.

With the knowledge of community institutions and the development of explicit leadership skills, LSNA organizers provide potential leaders with the opportunities to lead, in effect, testing out their leadership knowledge and abilities. Whether parents are speaking to funders, speaking at a rally, sharing testimony in front of Congress, working on a door-knocking campaign, or reading with a first-grader, Joanna says, a wealth of opportunities are available for developing leadership. Part of LSNA's vision, she says, is to "bring people into the leadership of actions and campaigns that fundamentally matter to our work in the community." These opportunities bring individuals into public life, and Joanna explains that for many parents who have never spoken in public forums or otherwise led in these ways, they learn by doing. She calls this an "apprenticeship model," wherein individuals are given opportunities to lead and are supported by other organizers and leaders in ways that will ensure their success. Maria Marquez, an LSNA organizer and a former parent leader, recalls some of her early experiences in which she testified in front of legislators or spoke at community meetings. Although she learned by doing, she also felt well prepared for the task because LSNA organizers had briefed her on the plan for the meeting, helped her think through responses to potential questions, and listened as she practiced her speeches. In effect, organizers prepared her for success, and "after an event or accomplishment like that—whether it's leading the Congress or testifying to state legislators, you leave that event feeling like you have changed, that your voice is important, and that you have an ability to make a difference and can lead others to action."

In providing opportunities to lead, LSNA effectively creates a structure for leadership within schools. With each experience and the support that comes from LSNA organizers, parent mentors gain experience and confidence to intensify their work as leaders. Amanda Rivera recalls the way LSNA's leadership development strategies with parent mentors created a "pool for school leadership" that led to greater voice and decision-making within the school:

> Once parents completed the [Parent Mentor] program, then they were recruited to be members of the local school council, for which they needed to be elected . . . which is really great, because they were learning and making the major decisions of hiring a principal, and/or evaluating how we would develop the school improvement plan, or the rollback of the school, learning about budgets and approving budgets that are con-

nected to the school improvement plan. So, they were getting more involved in the greater life of the school, and the community . . . So the Parent Mentor program became a venue to not only attract parents, but to train them and better prepare them to serve in a leadership capacity.

The opportunities to lead can have a profound effect on parents—their perceptions of the role they can play in schools and the influence they can have within the broader community. Ofelia Sanchez, a parent and LSNA organizer mentioned earlier in the book, details her own personal transformation as she became committed to her work in schools and her subsequent involvement in the community. She describes herself initially as shy and reserved—not the kind of person anyone would depict as a leader: "Leadership was something that I definitely learned from being a parent mentor. I was really shy. I wouldn't talk in public, and I was really intimidated by that." Ofelia recalls that she became involved as a parent mentor solely for the sake of her child's education, but as she met and encountered other parent leaders who played an active role in school committees and the LSC, she began to think about the possibilities of leadership herself. Faced with her own shyness and intimidation, she recalls being challenged and supported by Maria Alviso, her parent mentor coordinator who encouraged her to open up in public meetings and practice the skills of leadership:

But Maria Alviso would take me to these meetings; she wouldn't even ask. But once I was at the meeting, she would tell me that I would have to talk. I was put on the spot, and I would have to talk. I would come for the education committee meetings—I would listen to what everyone had to say, and Maria would encourage me to talk, telling me to say something. She would say, "You were telling me on the way over here, so now say it."

Since these early days as a parent mentor, when it took the encouragement of Maria to prod her public involvement, Ofelia has become an LSC member, an active parent at the Monroe School, an LSNA organizer who coordinates parent tutors across partner schools, and a community member who has testified in front of state legislators to argue for passage of a statewide initiative for a Grow Your Own Teachers program. Amid these multiple commitments, Ofelia is also studying to be a bilingual teacher through Maestros Sin Fronteras, an LSNA-sponsored Grow Your Own Teachers program that, in conjunction with Chicago State University, will award Ofelia a college degree in education as well as certification to teach in the very Logan Square schools where she began her community involvement. This program and others like it will be discussed in more detail later in the chapter.

THE DEVELOPMENT OF PEOPLE

As the narratives of Ofelia, Karla, Leticia, among many others, attest, LSNA's approach to parent engagement transcends classroom involvement. The benefits are far-reaching—in classrooms, inside homes, within families. And while a parent engagement strategy might most obviously benefit schools and children, LSNA's programs show us that parents themselves stand to benefit. These women are on a path toward personal transformation, and as Joanna explains, the focus is on the development of people.

These parents move beyond the traditional expectation that parents should be passive participants within schools. And as parents become visible leaders within schools and communities, they set a new model for others to follow. When parent mentors are trained by individuals like Leticia, who attests to her own transformation and learned leadership through participation as a parent mentor, the possibilities for newly involved parents to imagine themselves as leaders become a reality. According to Shirley, the Parent Mentor program becomes like "a door open for other things." Parents have newly found motivations—to obtain a GED, to study to become a teacher, to learn English. Shirley reflects on the small stories of transformation that she sees around her:

> [Parents] have these goals, maybe to learn English or to finish their education, and this program allows you to do something about that. And then, their goals become bigger. They want to be somebody. They want to be something. They want to be more than a housewife, but they want

156

to be a teacher or they want to be nurses. So they have these dreams, but they are not just dreams. They can turn it into something real. And it's like they got awake when they're coming here, hearing all the other parents talk about their goals, seeing them as the leaders in school, and understanding how the things are working in the school and in the community. They are changed people.

Shirley admits that she never wanted to be a leader, and like Ofelia, she decided to become involved in schools for her children's sake, to "make sure the schools are a good place for my children":

I never wanted to be in the LSC—I don't know why—but then I learned more about it, and I also felt more confident and comfortable as a leader. But I never had an idea about something like this before. Before I started the program, I started to feel . . . like I don't want to do nothing . . . But when I came here, all of those things go away from me. So I have changed. It gives me confidence; that is what I feel.

As a Parent Mentor program coordinator, a member of the LSC, and an active member of the community, Shirley "definitely" thinks of herself as a leader. For parents like her, who do not imagine a call toward leadership, the Parent Mentor program—with its relational approach, its focus on community, and its awareness of "where parents are coming from"—pushes parents to imagine new possibilities.

As Shirley explains, part of the change is attributed to the presence of parent leaders. The dreams and hopes of new parents become real possibilities as these mothers and fathers come in contact with parent leaders who, like Ofelia and Shirley, speak of personal journeys and self-transformation. Shirley recalls being surrounded by inspiring role models who spoke of experiences and backgrounds that were similar to hers. At that time, she began to think, "Why not me? Maybe this can be my story, too."

Joanna agrees that much of the transformative effect of the Parent Mentor program stems from the individuals who carry their passion for schools and communities in the public space, where they engage with other parents and families: "Every time we have an opportunity to bring a speaker in front of a group, an opportunity for public exposure, why wouldn't we want that person to be one of our leaders?" The journeys of parent leaders are "completely inspiring," and in making their stories a part of the public domain, they also become "a role model for everybody else, so it's the way public life or community life works."

Through interactions with parent leaders and the explicit training sessions that introduce parents to schools, integrate them into a larger community, and expose them to leadership skills and critical knowledge, parents embark on a path toward personal transformation. As Karla reflects on her experience with LSNA, she realizes that participation in the Parent Mentor program "can lead you to a whole new path." The skills she has developed and the experience she has gained have put her on stronger footing in schools as she supports her children. But the advantages play out beyond schools and take hold in the home and within the community. Her leadership skills enhance her participation "in all areas, from parenting to any volunteer work to your day-to-day relations with people." And for busy parents like her, who are also unaccustomed to schools and to building relationships with parents within schools, LSNA's relational approach helps to sustain a parent's involvement and encourage his or her own growth and development. Most parents, Karla explains, are skilled in ways that schools and parents themselves don't recognize. "Parents are used to multitasking and doing all this, and we take it for granted," but unless they are recognized by fellow parents or schools, "you don't realize it, sometimes you just say, 'Oh, it's okay, it doesn't matter,' but it does." By viewing parents with the skills and assets to become leaders, LSNA recognizes, acknowledges, and encourages parents, setting them on a path to achieve their goals and build the confidence and skills to become leaders. She describes LSNA's positive view of parents and its process of encouragement and recognition as fundamental to the personal change and transformation that parents experience.

For Karla, the possibilities are nothing short of a "lifeline," a new hope for the future. With a renewed sense of hope and a newly developed capacity for leadership, she believes that parents can have dreams for the future and the skills to make them possible. "[The Parent Mentor program] gives parents a perspective into their real life and how important you are in your community, in your school, and in your child's life."

THE UNDERSTANDING AND DEVELOPMENT OF POWER

Nancy Aardema, LSNA's executive director, says that when parents build themselves as leaders and proponents of schools, they must also clearly understand the role that power plays in promoting community change: "Understanding organizing means understanding power." While she describes an organizing strategy that is built on cooperation and mutual interests, she also admits that sometimes, parents need to battle elected officials and school leaders to fight for necessary change in education. For many organizing groups that do not work directly inside schools and classrooms, a more aggressive approach can and often is the norm, but for a group like LSNA, she explains, "these are the challenges when you are organizing in schools, organizing in schools where you share space at the end of the day." For this reason, she finds that "the hardest place to work on power is within the schools." Nancy says that in designing programs that operate within schools—such as the Parent Mentor program and the school-based community learning centers, LSNA has to strike a balance between confronting and agitating schools toward change and working with school leaders in ways that would allow the organization to keep its programs within schools.

While the work within schools may lead to more collaboration, every parent leader who emerges from this work gains a critical understanding about the role of power and accountability in confronting school issues. But as Joanna Brown explains, "these parent mentors come to us from different experiences and backgrounds, and many of them are immigrant moms who are just coming into public spaces, so it's essential that we make the message in our [parent mentor] training—at least in the beginning—more about self-esteem and personal goals than about power." Joanna adds that for some of these parent mentors, who may be undocumented immigrants or who may not be familiar or comfortable with organizing practices in the United States, power is an inappropriate starting point.

But as parent mentors become familiar with schools and as they progress through a year-long training program that exposes them to the inequalities and problems within the local community, they become more comfortable with grappling with power issues and find ways to become involved in school and community change. Because of LSNA's broad work as a multi-issue organization, there are a host of ways—small and large—for parents to become involved according to their own readiness to try out skills of leadership and activism.

At Funston, I came to know a small group of parent mentors who meet regularly with other parent mentors across seven Logan Square schools to discuss safety issues in local schools. The Safety Committee seeks to address ongoing violence and the disturbing increase in school-related violence that resulted in the deaths of thirty-six Chicago Public School students during the 2007–2008 school year. The Safety Committee organizes block clubs to increase community awareness about violence, crime, and gang activity; conducts caucuses at schools to inform school communities about the ways they can identify and respond to community violence; and organizes a yearly safety summit to provide resources and information to community members through interactive workshops. In addition, the committee meets regularly with police department officials, and during these meetings, parents speak on behalf of the families and school staff of their schools, arguing to local officials about the need for greater vigilance around schools and more equitable resources in their community. Through involvement in a group like this, parents have the opportunity to attain a broader, more critical view of community issues and can find ways to become more actively involved. Lisa Contreras, a Funston parent who is involved in the Safety Committee, explains the importance of this critical understanding of community issues:

> Before you know the facts, you think that all schools are like this and they struggle with the same issues, but when you look at the numbers and you find that police presence is so much more lacking here than in areas east of us—towards the lake—that just completely infuriates me. Our community—there is one shooting after another, and yet we have to fight for the few police resources we can get. How can I not speak

up and get involved? Our community gets less here and less there, and when you add it up, there is a lot we have to fight for.

Through her involvement with others on the Safety Committee, Lisa realizes that her voice matters and that it is her responsibility to push against traditional structures that put her community at a disadvantage.

For Lisa and others at Funston, the problem of neighborhood violence is as much a school issue as it is a community issue. Because the school straddles the border of two rival gangs, parents have often been concerned for the safety of their children, especially on the school playground, an open, unobstructed space that has often been the site for gang crossfire. According to Rosita Delarosa, who has been organizing for the Safety Committee since its inception, the group's concerns for that street intersection have been long-standing. A community petition with three hundred signatures was submitted to request a security camera that would possibly deter gang activity. But in spite of the group's work and persistent efforts, a camera was never installed. Three years after the petition, just days after the end of the school year, thirteen-year-old Schanna Gayden, a Funston graduate who attended the nearby middle school, was fatally shot on the school playground—an innocent bystander taken by stray bullets fired by warring gangs. The security cameras that LSNA organizers and parents fought tirelessly to install at the street intersection bordering the playground were installed days after Schanna's death, a sad reminder that in many low-income communities that struggle with inequalities, the struggle to win over power is an uphill battle and one where changes come too slowly or too late. Rosita explains that for many community members, "it hurts to see here three years later that a young girl had lost her life there." Throughout the struggle for greater security and police presence, "the community came out to voice their anger, do a lot of vigils, and prayers, and marches." After those persistent efforts, Rosita believes the community's anger and disappointment is particularly intense following Schanna's death: "I think the reason they cry out so much—it was because we had requested a camera there three years ago, and they feel like someone did not follow through in getting that done before this happened."

For parents like Rosita and Lisa, a critical awareness of community issues and participation in organizing campaigns help promote a sense of individual empowerment. Through the exposure to issues within the school and within the broader community, Lisa has become more willing to engage in issues that are important to her and her family. And with LSNA's support, she has acquired the leadership skills and the knowledge to confront issues of inequality and power. Through her participation as a leader and organizer, Lisa is developing her own sense and awareness of power—of *individual empowerment*. LSNA, in forming close relationships with parents and introducing them to the issues that affect schools and communities, fosters a sense of power among individuals.

At the same time, through the relationships that are nurtured across parents and across the schools that LSNA works with, the organization also develops power through the community—*collective power*. Individual parents do not act alone in promoting change in schools and communities; the relationships that are created from the first day of training for parent mentors are sustained throughout and become the basis for identifying and carrying out community actions and campaigns. Instead of having a small group of Funston parents act alone to push for greater security around the schools, LSNA provides an opportunity for parents and community members across the school to organize and engage on an issue of collective concern. Parent mentors like Isabel Diaz at Funston describe the transformation: "When you bring parents together to push for some kind of change, it gives me a feeling that what I do matters and I feel a sense of power when I get involved. And when all of us feel that way, the whole group can be more powerful, because we all as a group feel unstoppable." In a sense, through LSNA's organizing campaigns, individual empowerment is integrally connected to a sense of collective power. Each source of power—individual power and community power—fuels the success and intensity of the other.

Because parents are connected to each other through their work as parent mentors, there are numerous opportunities for collective action, which begets collective power. During weekly training sessions at each school, parents are connected to community issues. Housing organizers come to inform parents about a campaign to challenge the city's definition of affordable housing. Organizers talk to parent mentors about the concerns for new testing requirements for bilingual students. Throughout the year, parents are exposed to a variety of community issues that they are invited to participate in. Beyond the weekly meetings, parent mentors across all LSNA partner schools come together once each month for neighborhood-wide workshops that focus on broad issues that affect schools and communities, such as the No Child Left Behind Act, literacy, bilingual education, housing, and immigration. These meetings are opportunities to connect parent mentors across schools and develop a larger sense of community and common purpose.

During one neighborhood-wide workshop in May, before the viewing and subsequent discussion of a segment of the civil-rights-movement documentary *Eyes on the Prize,* three organizers—Leticia Barrera, Monica Garretón Chavez, and Bridget Murphy—update parent mentors on the balanced-development campaign. After many of the advances made through tireless efforts to preserve rapidly developing communities in Logan Square with fair and just allotments of affordable housing, LSNA and other community groups are concerned with the most recent news that City Councilman Ray Suarez, head of the Housing Committee, along with Mayor Daley, has decided to call an extra meeting immediately before the new City Council will be sworn in. The meeting is designed to push through the Affordable Requirements Ordinance, which would call for 10 percent of new developments in the city to be sold at affordable prices, which the ordinance has set at $220,000. With the "affordable" benchmark determined by an average of incomes across six counties—not just within Chicago—organizers argue that units with this "affordable" price tag will simply be unaffordable to 75 percent of Chicago families.

When Leticia and Monica explain the definition of affordability and ask parent mentors whether they or many families they know can afford a condo for $220,000, the organizers are met with a resounding "No!" Leticia explains that parents can take one or more of three actions. They can call the alderman's office to ask him to stop the meeting. Parents can also distribute flyers in the 31st Ward and talk to residents about the ordinance. If the community is not able to stop the meeting, the parents can also be part of an organized group to attend the City Hall meeting and show their presence.

Leticia, Monica, and Bridget then distribute flyers with information about the ordinance and instructions on calling the alderman's office. Across the room, as organizers circulate, answering parent mentors' questions, parents begin picking up their cell phones to call the alderman's office. The room begins to buzz with conversation as parents leave messages for the alderman and discuss the meeting and the ordinance. For many of the parents who have participated in the balanced-development campaigns over the year, the new ordinance threatens to "send everything down the drain," says one parent mentor. By setting an affordability standard that is truly unaffordable, the ordinance "lost all its value," she explains. Other parents are concerned that an impromptu meeting scheduled for 8:30 on a Monday morning will discourage public participation.

As parents call in to Alderman Suarez's office, his phone lines become tied up and those who can leave messages to call for a stop to the meeting. Frustration mounts in the room over an inability to communicate with someone at the office and the threat of the pending ordinance that can potentially null some of the advances made by LSNA and other community groups. Amid the phone-in, a group of parent mentors approaches Leticia, putting forward a suggestion for the rest of the group to consider. One parent mentor asks, "Why should we spend this time watching a movie when all of us are here, ready to do something?" Parent mentors in the small group agree that the issue is pressing and demands immediate attention. Shouldn't they capitalize on the fact that interested parents are gathered, informed, and ready to organize? As other parents listen in on this conversation, they all agree that they should act.

Within half an hour, parent mentors decide as a group to go to the alderman's office to address him directly about the ordinance and to use the remaining time to distribute flyers in the 31st Ward and talk with local residents about the ordinance. They are gathered in groups that will drive to the alderman's office. Meanwhile, organizers pull together flyers to be distributed and call media outlets to let them know of the action.

In the midst of this activity, I can see the different leadership roles that parents are playing. Established leaders like Funston parent mentor coordinator Reynalda Covarrubias, who has also been involved in organizing for the balanced-development campaign, explain to undecided parents the details of what the group will do. New parent mentors like Isabel, who has been taking on more responsibilities and branching out into new leadership roles, attempt to energize the group and build excitement for the action. She shares what she knows about the balanced-development campaign, expressing her disapproval of the affordability terms and trying to convince others to join the protest. At the same time, many parents are hesitant to participate, or they follow the suggestions of the larger group with little response.

Within the room, there are a range of leadership styles and stages, and the action reveals the opportunities parents have to try out leadership skills, from the one-on-one conversations I see parents like Isabel engage in, to the small-group and large-group interactions where parents lead conversations and initiate plans to support the action. Throughout the meeting, LSNA organizers facilitate discussions, but encourage parents to drive the decision making behind the morning's agenda. During these neighborhood-wide meetings and the Friday workshops for parent mentors at each school, organizers provide opportunities for parents to lead, make collective decisions, and encourage critical action. In this May workshop, it is obvious that parent mentors have developed a collective identity, using the workshop spaces to freely ask questions, collaborate, and move to action.

About thirty parent mentors decide to move the meeting over to the 31st Ward while the remaining group stays on-site to complete the agenda for the meeting. For the next two hours, parent mentors lead a protest at the alderman's office after a failed attempt to meet with him. They distribute flyers in the 31st Ward and inform neighborhood residents and business owners about the alderman's meeting and the scheduled vote on the ordinance. Throughout each stage of the action—from choosing representatives, to requesting a meeting with the alderman, to deciding the next course of action when his office refuses to grant group representatives entry, to deciding the details of the public protest—parent mentors make decisions and lead the action. To the chants of "*Si, se puede!*" (Yes, we can!), the group uses its presence to express dissent to the alderman and inform residents about the community issue.

Ultimately, the scheduled City Council meeting will go ahead as planned, and the ordinance will be passed by the departing City Council with the contested affordability terms, but as one parent mentor explains during the protest at the alderman's office, "What matters most is that we are here and we are showing that we know what's going on and we feel something about it. Even if [the ordinance] passes on Monday, we will feel good knowing that we tried." And for many parents, like this parent mentor, who are usually not involved in public life and community activism, the opportunity "to come out of your house and be involved in something bigger" can make them feel more invested in their neighborhood, leaving them with a renewed sense of power and possibility:

> I feel I have some power—power that I can make a difference. And even though myself, I am not a leader or not someone who can change a lot of things in the community myself, when I am part of a group like this, we all feel different. We feel that together, we can do this, and that is what we were saying in the circle—we can do this together.

With an active core group of 150 parent mentors across eight Logan Square schools as well as leaders, members, and former parent mentors who are active in many of the other education programs and campaigns at each school, LSNA has built a base of parents who form the core for many of the group's organizing efforts. And because the work in schools has fundamentally been connected to the broader social issues in the community, members and leaders see the community organizing efforts as integrally connected to school issues. John McDermott, a housing organizer for LSNA, describes the power in numbers—the sheer mass of support from parent mentors accelerates and accentuates LSNA's work in the area of housing:

> If it weren't for the parents, a lot of these campaigns—some of them—would not happen and most of them would not have the kind of power and impact that they have. On the balanced-development campaign, LSNA has been one of the key members of the coalition, and when there are citywide actions or some major hearings at the City Council Housing and Real Estate Committee, the education leaders, parent

mentors, and, to some extent, the community center students, are really the lion's share of the turnout of the force.

Because parents are the core members who will be part of school- and community-related issues, organizers like John McDermott and Elena Hernandez (Elena also works on housing) come to schools to build relationships with parents and to spark their interests in issues beyond schools. Elena explains, "It's really important for me to try and build relationships with the parents, because ultimately, when there are big public meetings, when we have to do an action, whatever it is we have to do, we're going to go to them first and ask them for their support." Elena attends neighborhood-wide workshops, facilitates discussions at schools during the Friday workshops, and attends education events to meet and maintain relationships with parents. Chicago Alderman Rey Colon, who has worked with LSNA in the past as a community activist and who continues to work with the group as an elected official, agrees that LSNA's ability to mobilize parents is fundamental to its success within the community and across the region. Through regular contact and established relationships with parents at eight Logan Square schools, LSNA can identify issues that are pressing to the community and can bring a broad array of parents into involvement in those issues. In effect, Rey explains, "LSNA can mobilize its parents—they've got people working in the schools who can get other people together and if they need to send people to the alderman's office, then it's a lot easier, because you have people in all these different schools."

This power of mobilization is illustrated in the parents' action to stop the City Council meeting, as described above. John explains that because parents come to the organizing work with already-established relationships, connected to each other and to the issues, the organizing has a "tremendous impact." The parents who are involved in his campaigns come in with a sense of power, compared with the other individuals and groups he may organize:

> We have people who walk in off the street. And we have relationships that we build through other member groups like churches and block clubs. But the schools are these intense hubs, these intense webs of relationships.

There is such a huge level of trust and relationship between the educational organizers and the parent mentors, among the parent mentors, that the parent mentors at a given school are like this already-formed team. They have a common base; they have a lot of common experience in terms of life issues. They are moms, they have a school in common, they tend to have a neighborhood in common because they live around the school. So they are like a team that's already somewhat powerful.

TURNING POINTS: THE TRANSFORMATION OF COMMUNITY

Through a process of leadership development, an explicit understanding of power, and a pathway toward community activism through school involvement, parent mentors begin to act and collaborate in ways that seek to build positive change for schools and families. Moving beyond the role of passive participant in schools, they become critically engaged individuals who feel empowered to act, resist and challenge inequality, and push for change in schools.

While LSNA supports and guides parents into opportunities where they can lead—such as housing campaigns, immigration rallies, and door-knocking events—as the neighborhood-wide workshop illustrates, parents often apply leadership skills to situations that require these skills, building a sense of power and collective agency among themselves. In 2005, the Chicago school district reassigned the Monroe School's seventh- and eighth-graders to a nearby middle school, because of overcrowding at Monroe. The plan was announced to students and faculty without prior notification to families, says Ofelia Sanchez: "We were so surprised, because there was no advance notice, no discussion of the issue, and then our kids had to just hear that without us being able to prepare them with news which was pretty upsetting."

Immediately upon hearing the news that their children would suddenly be displaced from a familiar learning environment for their final years, Monroe parents came together and promptly took to action. Parent members of Monroe's LSC mobilized parents, contacted local aldermen, and reached out to local and state elected officials who were allies of LSNA and supportive of their goals in the community. As employees of the district, school staff supported the parents' efforts from the sidelines. Through a massive and quick mobilization effort, parent leaders gathered about two hundred parents to discuss the reassignment plan. Silvia Gonzalez, a Monroe parent, recalls the effort as an "inspirational success story in getting passionate parents immediately out there, ready and willing to fight a huge institution like the Board of Ed. You could say the odds were against us, but we never felt that. Once we heard [about the proposal], we knew we had to get together and stop this from happening." And as a result of the collective action and community resistance to the proposal, the Board of Education promptly withdrew its proposal, leaving parents like Silvia "feeling very powerful and very essential to the school."

As Silvia implies, without parent support and leadership, the Monroe School may have been unable to challenge the board proposal. And Joanna notes that while the parent group had the full support of LSNA organizers and staff, the effort was entirely led by parents on the LSC: "We [LSNA] had essentially nothing to do with that effort—the local school council organized and stopped that."

Ofelia and Silvia are among many parent mentors who never anticipated the leadership roles they would play within the school and broader community. Both parents stumbled into the Parent Mentor program as mothers who had young children, were curious about schools, and wanted to support their learning. But through their experience as parent mentors, they gained insight into schools, honed their leadership skills, and took on opportunities to lead—first in classrooms as parent mentors and then as parent members of the LSC, as coordinators of education programs, and as activists in the broader community. Through LSNA's emphasis on community organizing and the recognition of power and leadership in decision making and institutional change, they have learned how to challenge bureaucratic institutions such as schools and to mobilize fellow parents in support of institutional and community change.

While Silvia describes parent leadership and organizing as essential to the school, she also acknowledges how much it transforms each individual parent: "The school is a different place, but that's because each one of us [parent mentors] is a changed person—we see ourselves differently, with many talents and many opportunities to send the school in a positive direction." Years ago, when she started her work in classrooms as a parent mentor, she began to consider her strengths and abilities in working with students and the possibility that she could become a teacher. She felt a connection to students who were Spanish speaking. As a bilingual student who struggled with her early attempts to adjust in U.S. schools, she recalls "not knowing the English language, and not having anybody lending support, period. There was nothing." She decided to become a bilingual teacher, because she understood the experience that students brought to classrooms, and she wanted to contribute in ways that would improve the situation for bilingual students.

Silvia is now studying to become a bilingual education teacher through a Grow Your Own Teachers program that was launched by LSNA. In the early years of the Parent Mentor program, as parents gained experience in classrooms, some felt a commitment to teaching—particularly in schools within their community. Faced with the reality that cultural gaps and misunderstandings between students and teachers and between families and schools created challenges in classrooms and barriers to student learning, these parent mentors began to see the potential role they could play in classrooms. According to Joanna, these parents—as teachers—could play potentially powerful roles in bringing schools and communities together, because "maybe they've acted as bridges between the school and community [as parent mentors] and so when they become teachers, they bring that experience, and they know how people think on both sides of the divide."

As parents came out of the Parent Mentor program with a desire to teach in their own classrooms, LSNA began a partnership with Chicago State University and then Northeastern Illinois University to create a Grow Your Own (GYO) Teachers program. The program brings individuals from the local community into a teacher education program that certifies them to become bilingual education teachers in the city of Chicago, the goal being ultimately to return these teachers to their communities to teach. While many school districts struggle with teacher retention and turnover, with many teachers leaving urban school districts for teaching jobs in more affluent and well-paying suburbs, GYO programs train individuals who already have a commitment to these local communities. Through LSNA's success with its first GYO program cohort, Nueva Generacion, its model became the basis for a successful initiative led by community organizations and funded by the state of Illinois to implement GYO programs across the state. In 2010, there were sixteen such programs. According to Anne Hallett, director of the statewide Grow Your Own Illinois, the GYO program initiated by LSNA "creates a pipeline of teachers who are really very connected to the kids, to communities, to their cultures, who want to be there, who passed the zip code test. They already live there."

Through their experience as parent mentors and subsequently through their training and experience as teachers, these GYO candidates look at schools from a holistic point of view, understanding the struggles of students, their families, and teachers, and teaching and communicating in ways that would serve students and families well. Maria Marquez, a former parent mentor and current teacher candidate, underscores this unique outlook:

As a parent mentor, I saw the necessity there was for more bilingual teachers. I saw the struggle the children have when they just come from their respective countries only speaking one language, and how hard it is for them to blend into the customs here, the way the school is taught, and the language barriers, mainly. Some of the teachers I saw were frustrated diagnosing kids, or misdiagnosing them, telling them that they were special ed kids when what the child really needed was an explanation in Spanish so that he could understand what it meant in English . . . We know what the community needs, and what our community lacks is a lot of communication between school and parents, and I think that as a Grow Your Own teacher, I'm going to be able to diminish that gap or that need at least a little.

Parents like Maria bring a unique combination of perspectives from classrooms and from families. This combination will serve the students well and attempt to close the gap between schools and communities.

Ofelia, also a GYO teacher candidate, explains how her work and observations in classrooms as well as her experience growing up in the community solidified her desire to teach: "I want to be a teacher in this community, because I know this community. I grew up here and I know what problems . . . are coming up every year . . . But a lot of these teachers, they just pack up and go home. They don't know what's going on . . . I want to use what I know about the community as a resource in my classroom." She promises to bring her classroom experience and community experience together to create a vision for teaching that is community based: "Once I am in that classroom, I will understand every single student because I would have that sense of all this knowledge about how schools work, what families need, prior knowledge of the community surrounding the school, as well as what's involved within the system. It's that knowledge that I'm going to take with me to better educate them and to be a better and more effective teacher."

Although her time in classrooms has shaped her ideas about teaching, Ofelia's leadership and activism in schools and within the community has influenced her community-based conceptualization of teaching. Among her many commitments, she was a parent mentor at Monroe who was elected to serve on the LSC. She also became a parent tutor who worked individually with Monroe students who were targeted by teachers throughout the school, and she moved on to coordinate parent tutors across LSNA's partner schools. She currently coordinates the Parent Tutor program, which is now in its third year as an AmeriCorps program, and has been involved in a Bilingual Education Committee, organized by LSNA. To achieve her goal of teaching in the community, Ofelia is also working toward an education degree in the second cohort of LSNA's GYO program, Maestros Sin Fronteras. Through these experiences, she expects to be "the kind of teacher where the lines between schools and communities are blurred."

As a committed teacher-education candidate, Ofelia feels that her training as a teacher strengthens her ability to organize on educational issues. Through her involvement with LSNA's Bilingual Education Committee, she has confronted elected officials and the Illinois Board of Education on bilingual education issues. Although she recalls being "nervous and intimidated" when she first started organizing in schools, she is no longer fearful of the interactions with elected officials. "Because of the fact that we are in Grow Your Own and have been taking those classes, we have knowledge," she explains. "We know what we are talking about. We are powerful." Policies, classroom practices, school approaches to bilingual education—these topics are familiar to Ofelia as she takes on groups and individuals to promote positive change in schools.

For parents like Ofelia, the parent mentor experience becomes a catalyst for personal transformation. Parents become experts on school matters, understanding the culture of schools, but with the development of leadership skills and community awareness, they also become transformative figures within their communities. As a collective organizing group, parents stand to change the dynamics of schools, banding together as a force for positive change. But as individuals, they create a vision for their leadership and participation, as in the case of Ofelia, who is working to become the teacher she wishes and wants of schools. And with LSNA's support, her dream to become a teacher becomes a reality. As she and other GYO teacher candidates graduate and enter Logan Square schools to teach, the schools move one step closer to a different form of transformation: a new teaching force, with community-based conceptions of teaching, enters classrooms to close the gap between communities and schools.

CONCLUSION

When an individual like Lisa Contreras both views the inequalities that threaten the safety and well-being of her community and challenges those inequalities, she is exercising her power as a member of the school community. While she may act in ways that are more collaborative by nature *within schools*—by helping to organize a Family Reading Night, serving on a school committee, or recruiting teachers to conduct home visits in support of the Literacy Ambassadors program—she has greater freedom *outside of schools* to rally for change and take on a more confrontational approach that seeks to uproot existing power structures. These contrasting approaches allow parents the freedom and flexibility to engage with schools in largely positive ways that help to build their relationship with schools while also developing a critical outlook through their understanding of the broader community. Nancy Aardema explains that this serves parents well—particularly those parents who may hesitate to organize through a more traditional, confrontational approach inside schools, where their children may be vulnerable to backlash. She describes the change in thinking of those who are accustomed to this more traditional approach to organizing: "[Skeptical parents] think, 'Well, how powerful are these parents when they're working in classrooms and playing to what the school really wants and needs in the first place?' [But] those very same parents become the people who lead rallies and who have the Friday workshops, and who lead in the classroom every day."

LSNA's organizing approach also seeks to meet the various needs of parents as they gain an understanding of school environments and prepare themselves to become leaders. There is an emphasis on relationship building—connecting parents to other parents and teachers, in an effort to develop a collective identity and voice with fellow parents and build a familiarity in interacting with school staff. At the same time, this relational approach also trains parents to become cognizant of power issues. As a result, parents build a collective identity, a sense of shared interests, and a growing sense of their power as a collective group.

The goals of LSNA's education work are multifaceted—building relationships, connecting parents to school culture, developing leadership, and realizing and exercising power. However, these strategies are part of a holistic and comprehensive plan that reflects the needs and experiences of the neighborhood families. For many of these immigrant families, building power is not the most effective or appropriate starting point. They are unaccustomed to schools and first need to build a base of knowledge of schools as institutions before they develop a sense of their own power and potential leadership. For this reason, LSNA designs a strategy that first introduces parents to schools and to the various dimensions of community life that shape their experiences in schools and within their homes. By gaining a facility in schools as institutions, parents are better able to move successfully into more explicit forms of leadership development and organizing. LSNA develops a culturally appropriate organizing strategy for parents' work in schools.

By cultivating parents as leaders and engaging them in school and community life, LSNA seeks to transform communities. As parent leaders, some parents take steps to organize on broad community issues, and for parents like Karla, school involvement translates into community involvement. As a result, neighborhoods and communities become places where parents understand the issues, work together toward shared goals, and transform the leadership and dynamics of a community. According to Karla, who talks about "the love and support from McAuliffe and LSNA," this can change the nature of community life: "I've been in different neighborhoods . . . Everybody is off to themselves. It's their unit, or their home, and they're off to themselves. [But in Logan Square] they still have block parties in these blocks in the summer. They still try to work together . . . So, I said, I think I'm going to stay here a little—help out, and grow with this community."

CONCLUSION

AN ECOLOGY
OF PARENT ENGAGEMENT

I know every face in this classroom.
These bright, shining faces are how I start each day.
There isn't a face in this school I can't put a name to. I know them all
by name.
When I think of this school, I think of all the familiar faces that greet me,
reminding me that this is a family to me.
   —various parent mentors at Funston Elementary School

WHEN I READ THROUGH the preceding comments, which are culled from various conversations I've had with several veteran parent mentors at Funston, I am reminded of my first day at Funston, in September 2006. As I parked my car on Central Park Avenue and walked toward the school building, I tried to guess which of the large, closed doors might be the main entrance. Without a sign to help me, I walked briskly to an entrance where a young woman was just leaving, and I motioned to her to hold the door open for me. As I approached the door, she looked at me for a moment, as if to hesitate granting me entrance through what I now realize was the back door. To reassure her, I asked her to direct me to the main office, which she promptly did. When I first stepped into the school, with the rush of students and the commotion of movement, I remember feeling vulnerable and exposed. I was and have always been, to my knowledge, the only Asian American in the schools I visited in Logan Square. I was at once unfamiliar and notice-able, and as I encountered children and adults in hallways, I knew nei-ther who they were nor what they thought of me as I passed them by. Not a face was familiar; amid of sea of strangers, the school became a field of anonymity.

My feelings of strangeness and vulnerability as a visitor—although intensified—could very well be the norm for many parents. For them, school encounters are intimidating and overwhelming. Not only are these parents inexperienced in navigating dominant institutions, but they are frequently rebuffed or elicit antagonism. Precisely for these reasons, sociologist Sara Lawrence-Lightfoot argues that it is critical for low-income parents of color "to find faces in the crowd."[1] She adds, "Not only does the school feel like an alien environment with incom-prehensible norms and structures, but the families often do not feel *en-titled* to make demands or force disagreements."[2]

When the culture of school is unforgiving and foreign, it comes as no surprise that parents are involved in limited ways and feel ill pre-pared to challenge the school. The subordination they experience may be exacerbated by acutely painful and negative experiences in schools as well as the long history of alienation, racism, and inequality that has plagued home-and-school relations in low-income communities of color. These persistent struggles that many families face often lead parents to throw in the towel, abandoning hopes of participating in schools. Consequently, schools despair of parents' lack of involvement or apparent lack of caring and abandon their hopes of connecting with parents. Thus, the vicious cycle continues, and educators remain mysti-fied about, or apathetic to, how things might be changed.

Now, after four years of observations, visits, conversations, and ex-periences in classrooms, assemblies, and hallways, I no longer see an anonymous sea of strangers. Rather, I can identify the familiar faces of parents, teachers, principals, secretaries, crossing guards, and students I have come to know. These faces represent relationships and connec-tion; they are the faces that come to mind when I think of Funston to-day. When the parents quoted at the beginning of this chapter describe the faces that meet and greet them, these parents are referring to the familiarity, the comfort, and the sense of community they have gained in schools. Schools become a place where individuals begin to strip away the masks of insecurity, distrust, and strangeness, instead building personal connections.

A NEW VISION FOR PARENT ENGAGEMENT

Acknowledging the steep climb and weighty task of fostering relationships between families and schools, I sought to examine a successful model that would shed insight into how schools and communities can begin to tackle this problem. Through LSNA's Parent Mentor program, we can understand both the limitations and the challenges of schools as well as how the struggles and experiences of parents lead to persistent problems in engaging parents. I decided to look to a community organization—well positioned to both understand families and navigate schools—for some of the answers that might close the ever-widening gap between families and schools. In the end, I tried to reenvision parent engagement and develop a model of action that reflects the realities of urban schools and communities. This allows us to understand how parents have found ways to make the strange familiar and to see faces from the crowd.

LSNA organizers have created a model of parent engagement that is rooted in the experiences of the immigrant mothers they know. For many of these immigrant families, schools are foreign and intimidating places. While the development of parent leadership and power is the goal of organizing, LSNA understands that parents come to their participation in schools from varied experiences and attitudes.

The following section answers some important questions that will guide a new approach to parent engagement. The approach is guided by three key questions. First, *what* should schools explicitly do to more effectively reach parents? From LSNA's family- and community-based model, I have designed a framework called the *ecology of parent engagement* that answers this question. Next, I address the question *How* can we put these recommendations into practice? That is, which key processes must be used to engage parents in these ways? The section will end with a brief return to the multiple layers of family, school, and community transformation, answering the question *Who* must be involved in the transformation?

What Do Schools Need to Do? The Ecology of Parent Engagement

Parents are not a tabula rasa to be written upon by schools that know what is best for their children. Any form of parent engagement must be based on a mutual conversation or dialogue between school staff and families. While it may be tempting to understand parent engagement in a simple, linear fashion, where we focus on outcomes and activities and set guidelines that parents will follow, this will only invite the participation of select parents who agree to the terms that schools create. In effect, schools will fail to reach out to the parents who, arguably, matter the most.

In response to this limited view, Angela Calabrese Barton and her colleagues support what they call the "ecologies of parental engagement."[3] Arguing that a view of parent engagement as a series of outcomes or activities is overly simplistic, they propose that parent engagement is "a set of relationships and actions that cut across individuals, circumstances, and events that are produced and bounded by the context in which that engagement takes place."[4] They argue that parent engagement is a process and propose that we must move beyond analyzing parents' individual actions and instead examine their interactions with a range of school- and community-based individuals. As parents become more involved in schools, they will develop a complex web of relationships with other parents, teachers, and school leaders, positioning themselves to become advocates for their children.

This book builds on the view of Barton and her colleagues and shows that parents can be active, not passive, participants in schools, working in ways that reflect their needs and expectations. Like Barton and her coworkers, I describe parent engagement as a dynamic process that cuts across relationships, events, and settings. Parent engagement is a process that *evolves* over the course of a parent's participation in schools—as parents become more acclimated to schools, find opportunities to become involved, develop a sense of place and belonging in schools, and discover the different roles they can play.

Based on these conceptualizations, I propose a three-phase framework, which I call the *ecology of parent engagement* (figure 7-1). The framework considers the multiple settings, contexts, relationships, and levels of engagement that shape a parent's participation in schools.

INDUCTION: INTRODUCING PARENTS TO THE COMPLEX WORLD OF SCHOOLS
For many parents, school-based participation begins in an unknown environment. For those who view schools with fear, suspicion, anxiety, or uncertainty, parent engagement can be a process of *induction*—to school culture, the expectations of teachers, the regular interactions between students and school staff, the curriculum, and the complex social world of schools. Particularly in immigrant families who have little understanding of U.S. schools, parents are often surprised to find that the expectations schools have of families is quite different from those in their native country. For example, LSNA organizer Leticia

FIGURE 7-1

The ecology of parent engagement

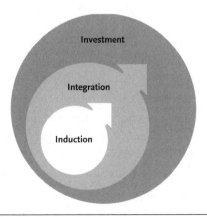

Barrera finds that the expectation that parents can be involved in schools is distinctly different from her experience in Mexico:

> In Mexico, it is totally different than here in the United States. That's why I give applause to schools here in the U.S. Through this program, you have an opportunity for parents to be in the schools, but in Mexico, schools are for students and teachers. That's why when I saw parents outside, I was worried for those who were inside, wondering, What are they doing? It was strange for me.

When parent participation, or the lack thereof, is influenced by cultural norms and values that run counter to the expectations in U.S. schools, parents can be judged by school staff for their decisions. These misunderstandings often result from a lack of communication, so when parents become involved in schools for the first time, their experience presents opportunities to answer questions and fill in the gaps in knowledge between schools and families, creating greater transparency.

Induction, by definition, describes an initial experience or entry into a new environment, and for many newly involved parent mentors, the initial experience in schools is greatly influenced by their desire to support their children. Newly involved parent mentors discuss the ways their participation benefits their children, their families, and themselves. For the sake of their children, these parents gain greater insight into the expectations and experiences the students will have with teachers and in classrooms. Many parent mentors find ways to better support their child's learning at home, as a result of their interactions with students and teachers in the school. The experience also allows parents to shed some of their fears and anxieties about schools and to feel more able and willing to engage with the school in ways they didn't anticipate. While language may be a barrier to many parents, LSNA has designed a program that invites any parent to participate, regardless of English-language fluency. For parents who are not fluent in English, this is an opportunity to feel that their skills and resources are valued as well.

Parent engagement as a process of induction can be a personal experience where parents view their participation in terms of the benefits and opportunities it provides to their child and family. Many parent involvement programs serve this purpose—encouraging parents to become involved in ways that give them insight into school expectations. With this information, parents can better support their children at home. The Parent Mentor program, however, has also shown us that shared experiences can be equally effective, if not more so. Parents begin their school experience through well-connected cohorts that are built on shared experiences and trust. Through this experience, they find that they have common concerns and struggles, and this, in turn, eases their entry or induction into the school.

LSNA's work has shown us that induction into schools should not be guided by traditional practices or by the desires and conveniences of schools; rather, schools must understand the varied experiences of parents within school settings. While many of the Latino immigrant parents who were part of this study expressed fear, intimidation, and a lack of knowledge about U.S. schools, the Latino parents who were raised in the United States faced different issues of access into schools. These parents were often negatively affected by distressing school experiences; their reluctance to participate in schools was shaped by distrust and resentment, rather than fear and intimidation. These experiences, in fact, are more similar to African American parent mentors, whose shared experiences in U.S. schools may lead them to reluctant and wary attitudes toward school involvement. Research shows that African American parents can often be more knowledgeable about school contexts, having firsthand experiences in U.S. schools, but may be more openly antagonistic in their dealings with school staff, because of a history of negative experiences, and may subsequently be more resistant to participating in school-based programs.[5] If parents send their children to school with a variety of beliefs, experiences, and expectations about schooling, then schools will have to find better ways to introduce the educational environment to these parents.

The various narratives of the parents throughout this book highlight the importance of a school's stance toward inviting families. In a study of parent engagement practices in one Boston school, Karen Mapp found that when she asked parents to identify the school practices that created trusting and respectful relationships, people consistently referred to a sense of welcoming, recognition for their participation, and a connection between families and the school that was centered on their child's learning.[6] Mapp calls this a "joining process" and emphasizes that without the right attitude or stance, schools will be unable to encourage parent participation. Inducting parents into schools will require a welcome and open environment that is centered on joining parents and school staff.

INTEGRATION: THE DEVELOPMENT OF PARENT PRESENCE IN SCHOOL COMMUNITIES

If newly involved parent mentors feel that the Parent Mentor program introduces them to a school environment that can often feel foreign, unforgiving, and unfamiliar, how do their perceptions evolve as their school participation develops? Although parents who are new to the program frame their motivations and experiences largely around their children and a needed entry point into schools, longtime parent mentors speak of their participation within a larger, cohesive community. Rather than thinking about their involvement in individual terms (my child, my family), they begin to understand their involvement in collective terms. The families in this study encourage a collective rather than an individual orientation.

As parents become integrated into schools—connected to a rich network of other parents, families, teachers, and students—some of the misunderstanding, distrust, and other barriers that plague school environments begin to erode. These parents move toward a sense of the familiar—a word derived from the Latin word *familiaris*, meaning "belonging to a household, intimate, friendly." For parents, teachers, and students alike, these relationships become a catalyst for change—the strange becomes familiar, and parents describe the broader school network as a family. Sara Lawrence-Lightfoot acknowledges these shifts in perception among teachers, but the same can be said about the parent mentors who were a part of this study: "For teachers, parents are threatening in large crowds; but when they can identify their faces and build workable relationships with most of the parents they see, then the parents begin to be perceived as individuals and some of the intrusive and negative images begin to fade."[7]

When parent engagement is seen as a process of integrating families into schools, the focus moves away from the activities parents can participate in to a broader presence within the school. As Barton and her colleagues found in their study, parent engagement can extend beyond what parents do toward a process of "becoming part of the fabric of the school."[8] Parent presence occurs when parents are integrated into schools and they find their own ways to mediate problems, advocate for their children, and build their own knowledge and expertise. As we've seen throughout this book, parent presence can also transform school culture. Beyond what parents learn to do in schools and at home to support their families—the individual benefits of parent engagement— a relational approach set on integrating parents can also change the nature and scope of relationships within the school, thereby building a collective sense of identity.

By moving away from the traditional activities and outcomes of parent engagement to becoming more integrated into the life and culture of schools, parents begin to gain a fuller perspective on schools. No longer confined to the narrow perspectives that result when they work to support school projects (e.g., helping the class within the context of a field trip, supporting teachers through administrative tasks outside the classroom, meeting with their parent groups outside the school day), parents begin to understand their child's experience within a broader framework of school interactions and practices. They gain connections to families, keen insight into classroom dynamics, and relationships with a variety of teachers and school staff—in essence, they begin to piece together a holistic view of the school. Through this more complete view, they have a better understanding of their children's schooling experience as the parents move across classrooms, into relationships with peers and teachers, and through an educational program. With this knowledge comes a sense of agency and authority; parents are no longer held in a subordinate role but instead can better communicate with school staff on equal terms about what they see and experience. By integrating parents into the life and experience of the school, schools can no longer close themselves off to outside perspectives that may challenge and disrupt the institution's norms and values.

INVESTMENT: EMERGING LEADERS ON THE CONTINUOUS JOURNEY OF PARENT ENGAGEMENT Parent mentors in this study have shown a lifelong commitment to their child's education. We met Ofelia Sanchez, a once quiet and introverted young mother who now trains new parent mentors, oversees a Parent Tutor program across multiple school sites, organizes campaigns on community issues, and is studying to become a bilingual education teacher. For her, parent engagement has also been a process of leadership development and personal and professional transformation. While we may be tempted to view Ofelia's example as the exception, why should our engagement strategies be limited to the shorter stack of possibilities? We should view parent engagement as a long-term investment in families.

The nature of schools, in some ways, encourages a temporal existence. With each academic calendar year, classrooms are shuttered and packed up, children say their good-byes to teachers and classmates, and a host of activities and events comes to a close. In this environment, parents can easily feel that with each new year, they are starting over and that their participation begins with a new set of invitations from new teachers and new classroom communities. But we have seen that it doesn't have to be this way. Instead, parent engagement can be an investment in the continuous and evolving journey that parents take as their children move across classrooms, schools, and educational experiences.

This investment approach, however, requires a radically different way of looking at parents. First, schools must recognize the valuable assets, skills, and resources that parents bring to a school community. Through meaningful relationships with parents, school staff can recognize their personal, cultural, and familial assets. For example, by recognizing Ofelia's skills and abilities as a parent, a community member, and an impassioned educator, schools and other parents must work together to find ways to support her long-term engagement. In Ofelia's case, LSNA provided her with opportunities to lead and to build meaningful interactions with school staff and students. Such an investment approach creates an atmosphere where schools emphasize the assets parents bring to schools and the central role they can play there.

Beyond the institutional recognition of parent skills and resources, parents must also see themselves as central figures and leaders in a school. When parents are outsiders to the culture and experiences of schools, they essentially become powerless—powerless within the context of school decision-making, powerless to advocate successfully for their children, and powerless to enact change.[9] To address this power differential, LSNA brings opportunities into schools and into the Parent Mentor program to build parents' knowledge of school environments, to develop skills of leadership, and to expand their opportunities to lead. By working in classrooms alongside teachers, interacting with children to support student learning and development, participating in school committees, and becoming active participants in the daily routines of schools, parents begin to view themselves and be seen as leaders within the school. Through a connection to broader issues in the community and opportunities to lead and organize, parents like Ofelia blur the lines between school and community and become leaders across those domains.

Rudy Crew calls these kinds of parents—those who have the power to become partners with schools on equal terms in support of educational goals and to advocate for the best educational outcomes for children—"demand" parents. According to Crew, schools are served well when they develop parents who are strong, are organized, and have a clear sense of their power:

> Good principals and teachers find it easier to work with strong, organized parents who know what they want and who operate with a sense of their power both as individuals and as a group . . . Most high-functioning schools have high-functioning parent leadership integrated into the workings of the school in ways that go well beyond bake sales and helping out on field trips. And underneath it all will be a structured yet open communication between parents and administration—in short, a partnership, challenging but not adversarial.[10]

Parent engagement as an investment in families and in parent leadership transcends our typical expectations of parent participation. It also moves beyond our usual focus on investing in schools. Rather than solely focusing on the ways parents can help invest in school projects—raising funds for a new playground or volunteering at a year-end carnival—we begin to see how parent engagement can be an investment in families. Parents build a set of knowledge, skills, and dispositions that stay with them wherever they go—across classrooms, school environments, and life experiences.

How Can We Move from Theory to Practice?

Understanding parent engagement as stages of induction, integration, and investment allows us to recognize the various experiences and stances parents will bring to schools. While some parents may be ready to pursue active roles of leadership, others may still be trying to understand how schools function and operate. The three I's of parent engagement—induction, integration, and investment—recognize that parent engagement is not a fixed set of activities but a dynamic, evolving, and context-specific process that requires us to break with tradition and consider multiple perspectives, varied experiences, and the myriad dimensions of culture and power. What are the core processes that must guide this multilayered transformation from a more traditional conceptualization of parent involvement to an ecological model that emphasizes the three stages? To explore this further, please refer back to figure 1-3, presented in chapter 1. The figure highlights the three key processes that will produce an ecological model of parent engagement.

These three key processes—developing forms of mutual engagement, building relationships, and sharing leadership and power—work across the three-part model of induction, integration, and investment. For example, while mutual engagement may be critical in an induction process, it should be thought of broadly across the entire three-part framework as well.

OPENING PARTICIPATION THROUGH MUTUAL ENGAGEMENT Schools and families must be willing to engage collaboratively and determine the terms of parent engagement together. LSNA's Parent Mentor program shows us that schools must open their doors to parents in ways that allow parents to gain insight into school practices and expectations. When parents work inside classrooms, they gain an invaluable perspective into school culture—a perspective that shapes their understanding of the institution of school. However, if engagement practices are to be sustained over time, parent participation should be designed in ways that meet the needs of schools. By bringing parents into classrooms as parent mentors, LSNA meets the needs of teachers, who can be overwhelmed with growing classroom demands, while providing parents with new opportunities to participate in classroom life. This *mutually engaging* model of parent involvement thus addresses the needs and experiences of schools *and* families. It is neither school centered nor family centered; rather, it relies on the intersection of both spheres. Schools develop a broad array of interactions and other experiences that encourage a greater understanding of families and the broader community. As parents become inducted into the culture of school, they decide how this new knowledge will influence the rituals and interactions at home.

With the support of LSNA, schools break past the more typical interactions that provide information to passive recipients (newsletters, open houses, parent-teacher conferences). Together with parents, these schools design experiences that are more engaging, accommodating, and inviting. We see parents working in classrooms, a principal hosting a weekly morning Café y Conversación session with parents after they drop off their children, and families borrowing books with their children and meeting other families during a weekly parent-sponsored lending library. These activities represent a more dynamic, experiential, and reciprocal form of engagement, and the experiences provide benefits to both families and schools. When a principal is open to regular and informal interactions with parents, he or she stands to benefit by learning of parent concerns early on. The principal is then more able to respond, by developing a communication style that is open and accepting and by gaining a better understanding of the families within the school community. Families stand to benefit from the access to school leaders who are willing to engage with them, from the relationship with critical school personnel who work beyond the more intimate sphere of their child's classroom, and from the greater understanding of a school's vision and practices that may be communicated in those conversations. Clearly, there is promise for sustained and meaningful parent engagement when families and schools can work together to determine what is in their mutual interests.

BUILDING SCHOOL COMMUNITY THROUGH RELATIONSHIPS AND ACTS OF BRIDGING In schools that have little to no understanding of the family and community experiences that pulse through their school community, how can we know what parents need and want? The intentionality of building new relationships and strengthening existing ones will be central to this task. This relational approach to school change takes time, patience, and understanding, but is required of any school that desires to work more effectively with families and communities.

Through a relational approach to parent engagement, parents have opportunities to enter meaningful relationships of trust and reciprocity with other parents and with school staff. In a study of social relationships within three Chicago schools, Anthony Bryk and Barbara Schneider suggest that successful urban schools build opportunities for teachers and parents to develop mutual understanding and trust to engage with each other effectively.[11] Because teachers spend the vast majority of their time with children and receive little professional development or preparation to engage families, Bryk and Schneider argue that teachers are often ill prepared to build relationships with parents.[12] As a result, these conditions breed distrust and misunderstanding.[13]

Trust between parents and teachers can act as a primary dimension of social capital. It becomes a catalyst for establishing relationships that carry resources and benefits. Parents become resources to students who view them as role models and as leaders who represent the students' community. Through close connections with other parents, a parent who may be isolated within his or her community finds a network of support, in turn developing a sense of community and shared responsibility for children. This highlights the potential of schools to become powerful sites for building social capital in communities. New relationships flourish in an environment where parents, teachers, school leaders, and students agree to work together.

Through their induction into schools, their increased knowledge and sense of familiarity with the schools, and their connection to a community of parents and teachers, parent mentors become bridges to parents who are not yet connected to the school. Their visible presence in schools and their interactions with a wide range of parents who view them as insiders also enables parent mentors to participate in *acts of bridging*—serving as intermediaries who build relationships that cut across the typical barriers of race, class, ethnicity, language, and culture. Through these acts of bridging, parent mentors expand parent participation and connectedness beyond the core group of parent mentors, drawing in parents who may not have the time, opportunity, or resources to join the program. Relationships become a key resource in opening parent participation.

Those who have studied the concept of social capital have argued that ties that cut across the boundaries of race, class, and ethnicity—what is called bridging social capital—are the hardest to establish.[14] LSNA's relational approach intentionally highlights those relationships that are difficult to build—creating strategies that allow for conversation, one-on-one connections, long-term working relationships, and acknowledgement of the cultural boundaries that may stand between individuals and groups. This fosters the development of trust and relationships that stand to be reciprocal—where both teachers and parents feel that they are passing on their skills and knowledge as well as receiving new insight into their own practices. Among parents, LSNA's weekly training sessions within schools and monthly training sessions across schools support the development of a rich social network where parents find support, develop a greater awareness about the school community, and maintain ties of friendship and collegiality that draw them into the school community in more lasting ways.

To address the challenges in bringing diverse groups of parents together, LSNA develops a strategy for parent engagement that is relational—that allows parents to build trust, points of connection, and opportunities to overcome misunderstandings. Organizers conduct training sessions, often in English and Spanish, and each program is overseen and organized by a program coordinator—often a former parent mentor—who works to create a sense of community within the cohort. Coordinators and parent leaders devote time at the start of each school year to identify new and interested parents and to recruit them into the program through one-on-one conversations. Within this context, the program consists primarily of mothers, many of them Latina. Although an outside observer may see this as a limitation, it is representative of the surrounding community. In this neighborhood, where many mothers in two-parent immigrant households stay at home to raise children, the Parent Mentor program is designed to be open and inviting to them.

There is value in the role LSNA plays in this relational work. To effectively integrate parents into schools and classrooms—connecting them to other parents and school staff—programs must not only consider the diverse groups of parents within a school community, but also strategically engage with families and community partners to build those connections. As an intermediary organization, LSNA serves as a cultural broker, helping to build relationships between the widely disparate worlds of home and school.[14] Schools must look outside the institution in search of mediating groups or cultural brokers who can contribute strategic intelligence in building parent engagement.

THE NECESSITY OF SHARING LEADERSHIP AND POWER True and meaningful change will not occur in schools if the fundamental imbalances in power and decision making remain untouched. Whether we are thinking of parent engagement in terms of induction, integration, or investment, these strategies must originate from a desire for shared leadership and power. When a school supports the development of parents as leaders, they become better able to engage with school staff, view schools critically, and advocate for their children throughout their time in schools. Through the twelve years of the program, LSNA parent mentors who began their involvement in schools while their children were in elementary school now continue to act as advocates for their children as they enter high school and college. These parents draw from their collective expertise and knowledge of the Chicago public school system to enroll their children in the appropriate high school, communicate with their child's schoolteachers, and connect with fellow school parents, in essence, becoming critical consumers of public education. This stands in stark contrast to a model of parent engagement whereby parents support individual classrooms or school projects and are left with fewer opportunities to exercise agency and leadership over their involvement within schools.

As discussed in chapter 2, a system of locally governed local school councils (LSCs) in Chicago provides added support for developing parent agency and voice. Through LSCs, parents have a formal avenue for leadership, becoming involved in a critical decision-making body of the school. Developing parents as an investment in the community will require that schools and school districts become open to more powerful forms of parent engagement and that district leadership open avenues for communication and involvement with community partners and organizing groups. Rather than waiting for existing parent leaders to take on active roles within schools, schools and districts must create opportunities to explicitly nurture parent leadership. Without developing this component of the model—parent leadership as a community investment—schools face the possibility that parent programs will continue to operate in ways that may change the activities of parents but fail to transform the power of parents.

By engaging parents in school and community issues through the Parent Mentor program and building community involvement through school involvement, LSNA attempts to break what educational philosopher John Dewey calls the "eclipse of the public."[16] In Dewey's estimation, aspects of modern society, the growing influence of special interests, and an ambiguous perception of the public threatened democratic participation into nonexistence. The public would only be called into being when individuals came together around a common interest of substantial or serious significance, and communication among individuals would be the catalyst for the renewal of the public and democratic participation. Present-day scholars argue that much remains the same since Dewey's early-twentieth-century claims. Institutions and agencies today must reorganize themselves to encourage, not inhibit, the creation of a public that will engage individuals to understand and participate in policy making and political action. To do so, we must take what Archon Fung calls a "public-creation approach" that is guided by the principles of participation, deliberation, empowerment, and equality:

> The basic elements of this public-creation approach are straightforward. Its first principles are participation, deliberation, empowerment, and equality: invite citizen participation in the direct determination of state action, organize that participation through deliberation between both citizens and directly involved officials, empower them by harnessing state action to the results of these deliberations, and assure that all citizens have equal opportunities to deliberate, participate, and exercise power in this way.[17]

By envisioning parent engagement as an investment within the broader community, LSNA develops parent leaders who, through their school participation, become connected to community issues and empowered to act as part of collective efforts to challenge, transform, and re-create community life.

Who Must Change?

This book presents a parent engagement model that is complex, context-specific, multidimensional, and dynamic. The three I's of parent engagement represent the kinds of approaches schools and communities can take in building parent engagement. Schools and communities can also strive toward the goals of relationship building, mutual engagement, and shared leadership and power. But as discussed, this change will be an uphill struggle for many schools and communities that have been defeated, diminished, and deflated from years of negative experiences, ineffective communication, or simple inaction. True transformation will require commitments and responsible actors across the domains of family, school, and community. Without the focus on all three, meaningful change cannot occur. If, for example, we focus on the changes that parents can make in their homes to support classroom environments, but we do not ask school leaders and staff to reshape their practices and interactions with parents, then we do not truly disrupt the system. The system still hands over all power to school staff and continues to ignore the valuable skills and other assets that parents could offer schools. To reach every corner of an educational system that is deeply in need of reforms that will alter the dynamics between schools and communities, we must commit to a multilayered, ecological approach to parent engagement. It must change *what* we seek to accomplish (induction, integration, investment), *how* we strive to attain it (building relationships, developing mutual engagement, sharing leadership and power), and *who* must be involved in the transformation.

A NEW ERA OF EDUCATION ORGANIZING: BRINGING POWER TO PARENTS

How is leadership relevant to parent involvement? What about the many parents who won't be positive role models to students? They've got substance-abuse issues, they don't speak English, they're not working. Do I hold them up as models and expose them to my students? The school is the one safe and responsible place these kids have in their life.

These are the words of *Karl*, an elementary school principal from a Midwestern city, whom I met at a conference. When he was first introduced to the three phases of parent involvement, he could understand how parent engagement could be a process of induction and integration, but he was more skeptical of the concept of investment. Some families were simply too troubled to invest in. This comment reflects a gross generalization that parents are incapable of supporting students. In essence, he has closed the door to working with parents. As communities struggle with poverty, racism, dire inequities, and the poor living and working conditions that threaten the stability and well-being of their families, the families are blamed for choices and actions that seem wrongheaded and dysfunctional. This principal's actions are guided by a deficit view of families. The view fails to understand the circumstances that shape a community's existence and the role that institutions such as schools play in perpetuating those circumstances. Any parent engagement strategies he may devise will only perpetuate divisions between the school and the vast majority of "those families" who are deemed unworthy of connection.

In environments like this, we reach a dead end if we wait for these schools to initiate changes in the persistently negative relationships between families and school staff. In an era where schools are deeply divided by race, ethnicity, and class and where educational opportunity is profoundly affected by poverty and prejudice, we need a school reform strategy that does not dance around issues of power, institutional racism, and equity, but confronts them head-on. Across the country, community organizing groups are making inroads in shaping school reform and educational policy. As we study these efforts and begin to draw important similarities and distinctions, what do we learn about the organizing strategies of these groups?

With almost two decades of experience, LSNA has discovered that working in schools requires strategies that move beyond the typical conceptions of community organizing and that consider the unique qualities and contexts of educational institutions. The same issues that shape strategies for parent engagement—power imbalances, tense relationships between schools and families, and the contextual forces of immigration, poverty, and racism—have also influenced LSNA's understanding of community organizing for school reform.

Organizing in Schools: A Hybrid Approach

Over the years, LSNA organizers have found that organizing and demanding change in schools requires a thoughtful blend of strategies. Schools are precarious places for parents to boldly confront and challenge authority. When the relationship between families and schools is strained, as it often is in school environments where parent participation is low, parents feel they do not have the power to challenge school practices. Parents feel vulnerable taking openly challenging stances, fearing the consequences for their children. For this reason, LSNA begins with a collaborative approach, seeing schools as potential partners. Education organizer Juliet de Jesus Alejandre describes just such an approach:

> I see organizing as partnerships—you're not going to get anywhere with any school being in-your-face with the principal. When you're organizing within the schools, you can't do that. They'll just close the door on you. So we've always learned how to give and take. It's about figuring out and anticipating the principal's questions, needs, concerns. And sometimes it means staying under the radar a little bit. And then a lot of it is just trying to figure out teachers that could become allies to get things done in the school.

As Juliet admits, organizing within schools can often require a balance between what organizing groups want to achieve and what schools need from outside groups. These conditions require a more collaborative and relational approach, where building relationships of trust and mutual respect is central.

Although LSNA's work within schools is largely collaborative, when the association works outside of schools on community issues, it takes a more direct and confrontational approach that is more typical of organizing groups. Through these community-oriented campaigns, it seeks to shift power and push leaders to promote equality in the community. As parents become involved in issues beyond schools, they become engaged in organizing tactics and strategies that are more openly confrontational. Even on educational issues such as school violence and testing policies for bilingual students, LSNA parents take on more aggressive approaches, openly challenging policies and public officials and demanding change. This hybrid approach allows for in-school relationships that are collaborative, and out-of-school actions that can be confrontational. In doing so, parents learn to navigate a complex range of interactions within and around schools—building trust and reciprocity while also agitating and advocating when necessary.

This hybrid organizing approach is increasingly recognized and used among organizing groups working on educational issues. Outside of schools, organizing groups may be intent on building power and winning campaigns. As a result, there may be little room for cooperation, particularly when campaigns center around what Nancy Aardema calls an "external enemy." This approach, however, is inappropriate for the Parent Mentor program inside schools. Consequently, LSNA developed a flexible approach, particularly for its education organizing, as Nancy explains:

> But the reason that this all happened is that LSNA didn't say, "Well, that's not an organizing campaign, so we won't do that." If I'm a straight community organizing group, which we were at that time, we wouldn't say, "Hey, we're going to take our organizing into a different direction." It's a really hard place to go, right? Because then the campaign isn't about an external enemy. It's about taking an issue and looking more internally at how are we going to address some of this . . . I think what's important is that you give yourself permission to do something that's not straight organizing.

For those in the community who work with LSNA, this approach is distinctive. Chicago City Clerk Miguel del Valle, who has worked with LSNA in the past as a local community organizer and longtime Illinois state senator, credits LSNA's success with an ability to evolve:

> At one time, LSNA was not primarily Latino. But they evolved as they saw the needs of the neighborhood change, and they kept their mission consistent. That mission was to address the needs of the residents of the neighborhood, and to do so in a more comprehensive manner using community organizing as a tool to address issues of concern to the residents. In doing so, they identified quality of public education as a key issue.

With keen insight into the daily struggles, wishes, hopes, and dreams of families, LSNA generates a series of programs, initiatives, and campaigns that are a product of the close ties it has to parents across the neighborhood. But to uproot traditional power dynamics and develop local leaders, LSNA also pays attention to the relationships it builds with school leaders and community officials. Jeff Bartow, executive director of the Southwest Organizing Project (SWOP) mentioned in chapter 5, explains: "The other factor that is important to their success is the care they've taken to cultivate relationships with decision makers in local schools. They're taken seriously as actors in the community. The relationships are not relationships that come out of really strong alliances or develop polarization. I sense that they really take time to develop an understanding of school staff and leaders and find out how they can work together."

To develop successful organizing strategies within schools, LSNA takes on an intensely relational approach in its interactions with schools and families. As a result, campaigns and programs grow organically and are, according to Joanna Brown, "based on what we hear and what people say and what people ask for." As schools devise strategies for engaging families, these conversations across parents and school staff will be critical.

What Can School Reform Efforts Learn from Community Organizing?

This organic model rooted in relationships and trust forms the basis for LSNA's transformative work inside schools and classrooms. In developing a hybrid approach that involves both cooperation and confrontation in its efforts to organize in schools, LSNA faces the twin realities that while school systems need accountability and direct demands from families, they also require the patient work of building relationships, trust, and collaboration. Although it may be tempting to dismiss the views of the earlier-quoted principal who has little faith in parents to provide leadership in a school, we have to devise strategies that seek to change the beliefs and attitudes of individuals like him. When I asked this principal whether he had experienced any positive interactions with parents, he replied, "It's very difficult meeting them. I honestly don't know how to get them into the school." As a result, his attitudes toward parents are formed in large part by a few choice encounters or general assumptions—not by meaningful and sustained interactions with parents.

Without these conversations, schools face the danger of creating approaches that are founded on baseless assumptions rather than concrete shared experiences. In the homes of families, we have seen teachers, parents, and children gather together in a living room for a Literacy Ambassadors home visit. The conversations move from informal introductions to stories about mothers, travels to Mexico, and the latest concerns in the neighborhood. By the end of the evening, these conversations have opened connections, eased anxieties, and sparked new relationships. These conversations—in parent mentor training sessions, between parent mentors and teachers, in one-on-one dialogue between organizer and parent leader—are at the center of LSNA's efforts to change school culture. Without them, baseless assumptions abound, and we face an uphill battle in developing the relationships and trust required to transform school-family interactions.

Conversations spark new understanding. For a parent like Graciela Lopez, conversation does not come easily, especially in environments that are foreign and intimidating. Throughout her first year as a parent mentor, she found that when she became connected to teacher Patricia Connor and her fellow parent mentors, Graciela gained new insight into the complexity of learning:

> I found that there were so many different ways to think about an issue. We talked about how just the behavior in a classroom is affected by so many things. There is how the teacher is handling the situation. Then you see the children with their parents, and you can see where they are learning some of their behaviors. And then you find out from another parent what the family is going through. And then, nothing seems so simple anymore.

Schools are complex cultural institutions that require multifaceted reform approaches. When I asked Graciela what could be done about the issue of classroom behavior, she paused and then responded, "Teachers have to know the families, the families have to know what's going on in the classroom, students have to feel that they are cared for, and we all have to talk about it." In her observation, Graciela believes that the issue is at once a cultural, social, and emotional one that requires collaboration, caring, and honest conversation. This multidimensional analysis of schools is an intentional part of LSNA's school reform strategy. While broader community issues may call for a more uniform approach that identifies a clear issue, an external enemy, and a strategy to demand change, schools are structured differently. LSNA's organizing strategies consider the complex and sometimes contradictory terrain of schools. As Joanna explains:

> We are working with so many tensions here. We have to think about our families as well as the school staff who are important to turning around schools. We have to think about what's happening inside the school building without losing sight of what's going on in the community surrounding it. We have to build trust among people who don't know or understand each other all the while keeping our eye on the goal of building parent power and leadership. There are so many things to consider when you want to build change in schools.

In any school environment, distinctions—between families and school staff, between schools and communities, between youth and adults—exist. How can we find ways to blur those distinctions?

When schools thrive, communities thrive. In this northwest-side community, LSNA has sparked a belief that school improvement should be connected to community improvement. Schools can be central sites for broader community organizing. From a practical perspective, schools can be places where parents can connect with others locally and gain a broader perspective into community life. In fact, for many parents, schools become a starting point for organizing within the broader community. Joanna agrees: "I think we should do everything out of our schools, because there's where we connect with people. By coming into the program, people actually get pulled into the community. They get pulled out of their private houses, into the first public space that many of them have entered."

LSNA's approach underscores that schools are intricately tied to community life. Schools can become places for civic participation and leadership development, but parents come to schools with a variety of leadership skills and experiences, different kinds of knowledge about schools, and varying levels of commitment to school and community issues. As a result, parent engagement can be structured as a "ladder of engagement," the term Mark R. Warren and colleagues use to describe a hierarchy of engagement wherein parents can decide what kinds of opportunities meet their needs.[18] Within this pyramid framework, large numbers of parents participate in smaller ways at the bottom, a moderate number of parents are involved in more substantial projects in the middle, and a relatively small group of the most active parents participate at the top.

Two parent mentors at Funston School are good examples of different rungs on this ladder of engagement. For Graciela, the Parent Mentor program offers a stable and consistent classroom experience with one teacher and is supplemented by opportunities to meet other parents. This level of consistent engagement may represent the middle of the pyramid. In contrast, Isabel Diaz takes on opportunities to become involved in neighborhood safety campaigns, invites teachers and parents to her house for a Literacy Ambassadors home visit, and helps plan family events at the school with other parent mentors. Isabel's participation represents a smaller group of parents who are more active and exercise greater forms of leadership. For parents like Isabel to move through the ladder of engagement, we must create explicit strategies that increase her familiarity with school, provide her with opportunities to lead, and enable her to build relationships with parents across the pyramid structure.

LOOKING AHEAD: IMPACTS OF PARENT ENGAGEMENT

Parents have attested to the transformative nature of the Parent Mentor program. The program has captured the relevant experiences of parents and created a model for parent engagement that sheds traditional practices and seeks authentic dialogue and relationships. Through this program, families' lives have changed: parents support their children academically and build a sense of community within schools, and children have role models who are from their communities and who are personally invested in the children's well-being and success. What's more, these improved relationships between school staff and families can dismantle misunderstandings and distrust, and schools come alive with the presence of parents. But the inescapable question for many—skeptics and supporters alike—will be, does this engagement strategy produce positive outcomes for students? This is certainly a valid question, considering that the urban, low-income communities of color that are central to this book often struggle to turn around the traditional measures of student achievement and success. In environments with alarmingly low graduation rates for high-schoolers and troubling standardized-test scores, will these parent engagement strategies set students on a path for success? This is the million-dollar question asked of every new intervention, program, policy proposal, and framework.

While the measurement of student outcomes was not the focus of this book, some narratives and other evidence suggest that schools and students improve when parent engagement is built and sustained in meaningful ways. Between 1999 and 2006, LSNA has reported an increase in test scores within partner schools. Scores have more than doubled, from an average of about 20 percent of students testing at national norms to nearly 50 percent.[19] David Pino, the principal of McAuliffe Elementary School, feels that he can confidently attribute the positive gains at McAuliffe to the intense and consistent involvement of parents: When he arrived in 2004, markedly smaller proportions of students were meeting or exceeding grade level expectations on standardized assessments. Those proportions have increased consistently since LSNA organized the Parent Mentor program and other programs in support of parent engagement.[20] David credits much of this improvement to parent engagement:

> You know, it's hard to say that the positive change we see here is related
> to just one thing. There is a lot that has changed in the past few years,
> but I see the difference it makes to our kids when the parents are in
> the classrooms, in the school, and truly invested in their success in the

school. But if I could, I would have to say that the parents—their involvement with their own children and the others they meet—has completely changed the way [we] are reaching students in this school.

Olga LaLuz, a former area instructional officer (AIO) for the Chicago Public Schools, notices a similar trend. In her role as AIO, she has overseen many of the schools in Logan Square. Through her informal observations and reviews of school data, she finds that schools with LSNA programs and other active parent-engagement programs not only are visibly distinct, with parents populating hallways and classrooms, but also seem to post measurable student gains over the years. She, too, is cautious in her generalizations, because it is a challenge to understand exactly what generates the positive trend—whether it is the start of new leadership, instructional leadership, changing school demographics, or parent engagement. But she insists, "Anytime you have parents in the school in a positive way, those kids, those parents, do better. I know that as a fact. They always do better." While she is cautious about making strong generalizations, she notes that for "all the schools where LSNA is involved, I can say for sure that they are definitely improving every year."

Students may individually benefit when parent engagement is widespread and significant, but how do the individual parents who participate benefit? How significant is LSNA's impact in these school communities? About thirteen hundred adults have participated in the Parent Mentor program since it began in 1995. The program has operated in nine schools in Logan Square, where many of the parent mentors are Latina immigrant mothers—new to schools and often new to community life. Many of these parents have pursued GEDs and English classes as a result of their experiences as parent mentors. Of this group, a significant number have moved on to become parent tutors, working in academically oriented individual tutoring sessions with students identified by teachers as in need of added instructional support. As we have seen, many parent mentors realize their interest in teaching during their classroom experiences. From this group of parent mentor graduates, fifty-six are pursuing teaching degrees and are well on their path to becoming bilingual education teachers through LSNA's Grow

Your Own Teachers program. Five candidates have graduated and become teachers. From a seemingly simple experience in schools that, for many parents, was meant to help them understand schools better or more effectively support their children, LSNA has charted a path that has also shown to be effective in developing the talents and professional possibilities of individuals.

Through the transformation of individuals and families, this model sets out to do more than create a culture change in schools. As parents enter and move through a program that fosters individual knowledge, interpersonal connections, and leadership development while also promoting participation in the broader school community and generating interest and enthusiasm among others, the resulting model for parent engagement serves a broader purpose of replenishing new participation and leadership. In essence, as parents move through the stages of induction, integration, and investment, they have the ability to participate in a model that continues to create and nurture new participation and leadership. This dynamic model of parent engagement is continuous and replenishes the very participation it seeks to encourage. The model is truly transformative—possessing the potential to generate a movement for change.

A SHARED CALL FOR CHANGE

Years of school tradition are hard to break. Although LSNA seeks to build schools as sites that are rich with relationships that move individuals to change beliefs and act in different ways, these shifts in school culture take time. Each year, if parent mentor cohorts reach approximately twenty parents and if Literacy Ambassador programs reach a dozen families and half a dozen teachers at each school, then the LSNA programs are considered to have made steady but slow improvements in school culture. Programs have the most success when school leaders buy into the program and its investment in parent leadership, but school leaders have differing attitudes toward, and experiences with, parents. Some educators may generate enthusiasm for building parent engagement, and some may turn away from the Parent Mentor program altogether. With programs that require the approval and longtime cooperation of school leaders, LSNA's education programs promise to be only as successful as those school leaders allow. Over time, the organization has found this to be true. For example, LSNA programs were withdrawn from one school site after growing tensions with a school administrator made the programs inoperable. Maricela Contreras, a former LSNA staff member and parent leader, recalls, "She [the principal] began to feel threatened by the parents. We tried to work with her, because our interest is in creating a better school for our children, but I think she became suspicious that parents were coming together against her. By having parents connected to each other, she felt threatened, and she began to do things in ways that would shut us out."

Maricela recalls that these incidents escalated to confrontations between parents and the principal, and some parents began to fear the consequences for their own children. She believes her daughter's removal from the school, justified in part by the school's discovery of her family's change in residence, was prompted by her own disagreements with the school leader: "So, that was the end result for my daughter. She was moved to another school. And in the end, things worked out for us, but this is what you're up against when you are an active parent and you are working to stand up for your children. It just doesn't always work out the way you expect." As this case shows, there are limits to programs that depend on the approval and cooperation of school leaders.

In addition to school leaders, these programs rely on the willingness of teachers to enter into working relationships with parents. Although the early years of the Parent Mentor program reflect reluctance on the part of teachers to invite parent mentors into their classrooms, coordinators across the schools testify to markedly improved, and often enthusiastic, responses from teachers. Nevertheless, as the narratives from Funston classrooms show, teachers have widely different styles of engagement with parents; as a result, the relationship between parent and teacher can be one of mutual learning and growing trust, but it can also persist in more traditional and hierarchical ways.

One could argue that many of the teachers who participate in programs like the Parent Mentor and Literacy Ambassadors programs are individuals with a more open and receptive attitude to parent engagement. What about teachers who might be resistant to these programs and the opening lines of communication with parents? These issues point to the need for parent engagement strategies that not only focus on the leadership and development of parents but on the attitudes and assumptions of school staff as well. Although teachers have broken down some of their previously held beliefs about parents through their relationship with parent mentors, these changes are not intentionally driven by a larger strategy from LSNA. To create a more transformative relationship between schools and families, training and education should also be part of the agenda for teachers. LSNA's strategies for engaging parents will be more powerful and effective if exercised in concert with strategies for engaging and challenging teachers.

These future directions, however, should not solely be the responsibility of groups like LSNA. While the Parent Mentor program may make deeper impressions into changing school culture if the beliefs of educators and school staff are explored, the importance of parent engagement should be emphasized in educator training as well. Teacher education and school leadership curricula often focus on reform strategies and practices within schools and classrooms, rarely offering coursework or other guidance on how educators can engage families or develop school-family partnerships. Teachers have little exposure to families and communities during their training or within their school environments. Beyond an arsenal of universal strategies for engaging families, teacher candidates often fail to understand the various stances that underlie those strategies. Without knowledge, experience, or practical insight into engaging families and communities, teachers and school leaders are left with the age-old, traditional views on parent involvement. As a result, they may be tempted to view communities from a deficit perspective without the communication and interactions with families that are necessary to challenge those troubling views. We need to build templates for teacher and administrator preparation, induction, and professional development that reflect knowledge, skills, and dispositions for parent and community engagement.

In my own work with aspiring teachers at a small liberal-arts college, I find that the young, energetic, and often idealistic individuals who are committed to urban teaching feel the most fear and anxiety about the unknown. As they read the latest studies in urban education that underscore the intense challenges and steep learning curves in the early years of teaching, they profess their deep anxieties about the very communities they want to serve. As one student in an urban education seminar shared, "I'm terrified, but I don't know what I'm terrified of." Each week, as she traveled to a predominantly black and low-income school in Boston to work in a kindergarten classroom with a mentor teacher, she began to unravel the source of her fear, understanding that what she feared most were the "unknown families and students" she would soon be teaching. By spending a semester with a mentor teacher whose communication and interaction with families was central to her goals of curriculum and teaching, she experienced a profound shift in her own mission and goals as an aspiring teacher. She would find ways to build relationships with families and within the community. She had seen how it could work, and this example offered her hope and promise as she looked ahead to her own assignment as a first-year teacher. While she still had the fear and uncertainty that any newly minted teacher will have about teaching, she had hope and confidence that authentic connections to families would allow her to understand her role as a teacher more clearly.

Although we may typically look inside the four walls of schools to generate ideas for school reform, LSNA shows us that community-based knowledge and experiences can be vital resources for school transformation. Joanna attests that local communities can hold valuable tools and resources for understanding school reform:

> When people talk about reforming education, they usually talk about it from the perspective of the teacher and the students and the school, but all of these things that we focus on lie outside of that framework. From our work, we know that an integral part of schools are parents and families. How can you talk about school reform without that important piece? These kids are raised and shaped by families and communities. We never forget that. So school reform can't be that simple.

As she suggests, parents and families are an integral part of students' lives and can be seen as potential partners in working toward school improvement. By bringing families into schools, LSNA also seeks to change the dynamics of how schools operate. When the environment of schools changes to one where parents are visible and actively engaged, there are greater opportunities for meaningful dialogue, mutual understanding and trust, parent appreciation and recognition, and a reconceptualization of school culture. These changes, however, need not be limited to the scope of schools. As in the case of LSNA, parents have used their newfound leadership in schools to promote changes in the broader community. It is a form of parent engagement that seeks to transform the dynamics of civic engagement and community life through its emphasis on community organizing—a tradition that knits together distant souls through relationships, has enduring hope in individuals, and is guided by a vision of a hopeful future. In the words of past Chicago community organizer and current president of the United States, Barack Obama, it is the healing and renewal of community:

> In return, organizing teaches as nothing else does the beauty and strength of everyday people. Through the songs of the church and the talk on the stoops, through the hundreds of individual stories of coming up from the South and finding any job that would pay, of raising families on threadbare budgets, of losing some children to drugs and watching others earn degrees and land jobs their parents could never aspire to—it is through these stories and songs of dashed hopes and powers of endurance, of ugliness and strife, subtlety and laughter, that organizers can shape a sense of community not only for others, but for themselves.[21]

As the narratives throughout this book have shown, it takes the joint efforts of *families*, *schools*, and *communities* to truly transform schools. In describing the strength and determination that results when families, schools, and communities band together for a common purpose, one parent leader quotes a biblical passage from Ecclesiastes: "Though one may be overpowered, two can defend themselves. A cord of three strands is not quickly broken."

APPENDIX

A LAYERED ETHNOGRAPHY

At the Crossroads of Relationship, Theory, and Methodology

SABEL DIAZ IS A MOTHER OF TWO. She is a parent mentor at Funston Elementary School and one of the mothers I have come to know well after four years of the study. As she navigates her way through a new school environment, I learn about her expectations, her accomplishments, her struggles, her family, and her goals for the time ahead. Though Isabel and I had different life experiences, as we came to know each other, we identified common interests and common experiences. These areas of overlap in our lives often fueled interesting conversations about parenting, children, cooking, and family. But in some ways, I was always a bit of a puzzlement to her. I recall a conversation we had a few months into the research project, when she told me about a potential opportunity to travel with some Logan Square Neighborhood Association (LSNA) organizers to New York. They would attend a meeting to talk about their experiences as parent mentors to a group of organizations that were interested in the program. When I encouraged her to join them, insisting that she would represent the group well and that her narrative would be an important one that would be well received, she simply answered, "Well, my husband will never let me go. Spending that much time away from the kids and traveling with a bunch of other people that he doesn't know—that just wouldn't be alright with him." In saying so, she was only speaking of her situation, but for some reason, in that moment, I was reminded that my life choices and experiences—as she perceived them—could be constant reminders to her that we are quite different. To Isabel, I am a researcher who, like her, is a mother. But I am a mother who travels monthly to Chicago for work that, while it introduces me to parents like her, also keeps me away from a young daughter at home. I am married to a husband who allows and might even encourage this freedom or this strange commitment to work. As we sat together during this discussion, we were reminded that we make different choices. We live in a world of contrast and connection.

Martin Buber discusses these moments of distinction and commonality as an "I-thou" relationship, where individuals establish a sense of self through connection but develop the I-thou relationship through contrast.[1] Alfred Schutz builds on Buber's concept of the I-thou relationship and claims that through these relationships, researchers begin to develop a sense of proximity and closeness, seeing others as fellow people, rather than a more ambiguous and impersonal type or category.[2] Each relationship is shaped by connection as much as it is by contrast. Over the course of my interactions with Isabel, our relationship is punctuated by moments of connection and distinction, and they have shaped the ongoing interaction we have as researcher and participant.

Amid these interactions and conversations, how does Isabel relate to me, if at all? How does she perceive me—the choices I make, the person I am, and the things I tell her? And how do those perceptions shape what she tells me in our conversations, what she chooses to withhold? These questions are fundamental to understanding the role of the relationships between researcher and participants as we attempt to excavate meaning from the many encounters we have with individuals in the field.

RELATIONSHIPS

The relationship I describe with Isabel signifies the greater relevance that relationships have in research and inquiry. According to ethnographer Michael Jackson, in his discussion of a methodological approach that he calls *radical empiricism*, relationships between a researcher and participants produce new understanding and knowledge. With this understanding comes an assurance that validity is met in research.

> Ethnography then becomes a form of *Verstehen*, a project of empathic and vicarious understanding in that the other is seen in the light of one's own experiences and the activity of trying to fathom the other in turn illuminates and alters one's sense of Self . . . To compare notes on experience with someone else presumes and creates a common ground, and the understanding arrived at takes its validity not from our detachment and objectivity but from the very possibility of our mutuality, the existence of the relationship itself.[3]

Relationships develop common ground between researcher and participants, and the mutual exchange drives new understanding and self-reflection for those involved. Through our interactions and our evolving relationship, Isabel and I re-create our own understanding of parenting and family choices.

Theorizing Research Relationships

For some researchers, relationships between researchers and participants are to be viewed with caution. Relationships have often been discussed within the context of gaining access to research sites, as if relationships must be managed in ways that encourage individuals to participate or that encourage institutions to open themselves to researchers. In an introduction to qualitative research that is geared toward the novice researcher, Corrine Glesne directs researchers to "manage" and "monitor" rapport in hopes of gaining access to information: "You manage your appearance and behavior in rapport-building efforts in order to acquire continual access to information . . . You consciously monitor your behavior so that people who are unaccustomed to the presence of researchers in their lives will be at ease in your presence. Your challenge is to fit in."[4]

According to this point of view, the relationship is something to be restrained and controlled in an effort to achieve appropriate distance and acceptable attitudes. The goal in these relationships is to ensure access and encourage accurate and independent reporting from participants in a way that is free of researcher bias and subjectivity.[5] Understanding relationships purely for their role in accessing data is a limited, reductionist view. In contrast, Joseph Maxwell argues that research relationships require a "continual negotiation and renegotiation," and "what you want is a relationship that enables you to ethically learn the things you need to learn in order to validly answer your research questions."[6]

Relationships are always shaped by a confluence of factors. The goals of research relationships are not to create a formal distance, to become detached observers, or to leave encounters unaffected by the researcher's presence. In my own experience, for example, how my participants view me (as an Asian American woman, a mother, a Harvard graduate student) will clearly shape their interactions with me. Throughout the research relationship, my goal has been to highlight the importance of our interactions and explicitly address the ways that interaction can be dynamic, complex, evolving, and authentic. My goal cannot be, as Glesne asserts, to "fit in."[7] As a graduate student and woman of color navigating the predominantly white institution of Harvard, I have neither made this my intention nor viewed it as a reality. Certainly, in this working-class, Latino immigrant neighborhood in Chicago's Northwest Side, my goals could be no different.

Such a reductionist view of relationships will tempt us to believe that we can manage parts of our personal and professional identities to reduce barriers and increase access. But relationships are more dynamic and constantly susceptible to the whims of our actions, conversations, interactions, and beliefs. Through every encounter I have with Isabel, for example, she learns more about me, and that knowledge shapes the interaction and experience we have together. The issue is not *whether* the relationship is influenced by our interactions, but *how* it is influenced by these interactions. What we may see as barriers to access can instead be seen as one of the myriad factors that shape the dynamic interchange between researchers and participants in the field. As a result, the goal is not to negotiate entry, for this assumes that one is either granted total access or denied entry into the field of study. Rather, the relationship itself shapes a researcher's understanding of the research question or the issues that emerge from the study. It may bring participant and researcher to a newly developed understanding of the topic under study.

Am I In or Out? Navigating the Insider-Outsider Quandary

If we attach monolithic identities to communities—seeing them as immigrants, black, Latino, or working-class, for example—then we may simply believe that researchers have *either* insider or outsider status. Many researchers believe that when this insider-outsider status is determined at the beginning of a research project, often before a researcher enters the field, access is granted and the research field is open for exploration.[8] These views, however, are too simplistic and do not capture the complex identities of communities and researchers. There are myriad dimensions of identity and representation, and the discussion of insider-outsider status must be a complex process that recognizes those dimensions.[9]

For example, from a superficial perspective, much about me and this Logan Square community is distinct and different. I am Asian American, and most of my participants are Latino or black. I am not a native Spanish speaker and prefer to speak English, while many of them prefer to speak Spanish. I live in Boston, and they live in Chicago. Many have not completed formal schooling, and I am a doctoral student at the time of this study. I have a comfortable, middle-class existence, and many of these families struggle to make ends meet. For all intents and purposes, I am the ultimate outsider to this community, and I face many barriers to obtaining access to the data I propose to collect.

While these are compelling distinctions, upon closer examination, there are points of connection as well. Like many of my participants, I am an immigrant, a mother, a woman, and a woman of color. I have experienced discrimination and other forms of prejudice. To the many teachers and administrators I have met and interviewed, I am a former teacher in urban schools. Many key leaders and organizers in LSNA are connected to and highly respect my dissertation adviser. One could argue that he was central to my own access to this organization as a research site.

So am I an outsider or an insider? What parts of my identity and experience carry more weight to tip the scale one way or the other? These are complex questions. There is no easy solution; relationships between researchers and participants must be regarded as complex, multifaceted, and dynamic. While it may be important to consider these traits of identification (race, ethnicity, class, gender), my role as insider or outsider can also be shaped by aspects that are more fluid and not as easily categorized. Throughout the two years of my data collection, might my role as an insider or outsider change as my familiarity with and connection to this community and the organization evolve? Will each individual, in light of how the person perceives and relates to me, have a different impression of my role within the community? As I get to know some individuals over time and build my relationships with them over multiple interactions, might their sense of me as an insider or outsider change? And how could my perception of my role stand in contrast to what participants believe?

Clearly, there is no easy answer as to whether I am an insider or outsider. I am both—my status may change over time, across contexts, and across individuals. But acknowledgment of how I stand in relation to my participants—the issue of reflexivity—is an important consideration, because it is inherently concerned with relationships, which also change across contexts, time, and encounters. William H. Schubert of the University of Illinois at Chicago says that reflexivity "helps us identify the socially and rhetorically constructed boundaries that delimit our view of the social field, to transgress those limits, and provide a basis for creative, ethical alternatives."[10]

Rather than reducing research relationships to strict, two-dimensional characteristics or matters of access, we should use our knowledge of relationships—and their multiple and dynamic boundaries—to move beyond traditional boundaries and, in essence, develop critical research strategies. In preparing for my entry into the field, I found that one of the major boundaries between my participants and me would be that of language. While many parent mentors are bilingual, many are more comfortable and fluent in Spanish. Prior to this research project, I did not speak Spanish. Although I pondered the use of a translator, I felt that speaking through a translator would leave me out of meaningful conversation with participants, lead to disconnected dialogue, and further distance me from the parents I wanted to know. As a participant observer, I also knew that I would miss many of the informal conversations in the field and would lose insight into the occasional meeting, rally, or training session that was conducted purely in Spanish. Ultimately, I felt that if I did not know how to speak Spanish or if I used a translator, there would be an added formality to any conversation I had or any interview I conducted.

As a result, I decided to learn Spanish. In the eighteen months between my decision to conduct this research project and my first formal entry into the field, I took on the Spanish language—primarily through independent study but with the occasional assistance of language classes. During this self-study, I acquired Spanish fluency that would allow me to understand and participate in informal conversations. Through the assistance of a translator who translated all my interview protocols into Spanish, I was able to conduct interviews, ask probing questions, and engage in conversation. Despite the concrete limits to my language abilities, I also accomplished significantly more—the sheer volume of data collection and a broader range of relationships in the field—by speaking Spanish. If I were limited only to conversations and interviews with English-speaking parents, my insight into the research questions would probably be skewed toward the experiences of parents who have a greater facility with and knowledge of mainstream U.S. institutions. Much would be missed, and my findings would be distinctly different.

My decision to learn Spanish was shaped primarily by a desire to broaden the range of parent relationships, develop a deeper and more authentic understanding of parent experiences, and collect more extensive data. Once I entered the field, I found that this decision would shape other aspects of the study profoundly. While I thought of language primarily as an issue of access—to individuals, to the "data" of conversations—it became an element that shaped my relationships with my participants. I approached interviews and meetings with feelings of inadequacy, anxiety, and insecurity. Although I had run through the interview protocols, possible probing questions, verb tenses, and vocabulary through careful preparation, with each interview, I doubted myself. I wondered if I would be able to express myself accurately, if I would sound "legitimate," if they would question my research skills because of my language inadequacies. In fact, I wrote about this very dilemma in my field notes on the second day of interviews at the school:

> I have run through all the questions, the possible probing questions in my mind, but I can't help but feel this overwhelming surge of anxiety. This is my first meeting with these parents, and while I want to give the impression that I am confident, self-assured, and articulate, I don't think I can do this in Spanish. I feel out of my element, uncomfortable. What if I don't understand what they tell me? What if I misspeak, and I confuse them? When I interview someone in English, I am always mentally multi-tasking. I listen to their response while I anticipate the next question, simultaneously trying to construct some of the themes of the conversation. When I do this interview in Spanish, I will have to multi-task but with the added dimension of English-to-Spanish and Spanish-to-English translation.

Ironically, however, I found that over time, my anxieties sometimes offered relief to the parents I interviewed. They would often confide later that they first approached our conversations with the same nervousness and anticipation I experienced—because they had never been interviewed before or because I was a researcher from an elite university, or because I wanted to tape-record the conversation. Myriad reasons exist for why parents approach the research relationship with caution, uncertainty, and skepticism. As I offer parents the choice to conduct our interview in Spanish, I also find this develops a sense of mutual trust and respect in the research relationship. By having the conversation in Spanish, rather than in English, participants acknowledge that I make a choice—to extend a sense of familiarity and ease to them, rather than establishing terms that put me at ease. In a conversation with Isabel, she offers her perspective on what this choice may mean to parents:

I think even a small thing like that can mean a lot to them. When someone says that you are going to meet with this researcher and she's going to ask you some questions, of course you are willing to do it, but you don't know what to expect. And a lot of parents are nervous about their English—they may speak it, but they are going to be self-conscious about it. So they are going to be really nervous when they speak to you, anyway. So when you come in and say, "Hey, we can have this conversation in Spanish," even if your Spanish isn't perfect, that is going to make them feel more comfortable. And they will see you in a different way. I think you get some respect for trying.

When participants are offered environments that put them at ease and allow them to express themselves fully, we honor them as vital contributors to the research project. However, this experience also shapes my perceptions and experience. By feeling uncertainty and anxiety in the field, I also become more attuned to what my participants may experience as part of my research project. This sense of empathetic regard is important as we consider not only *what* our participants tell us but also *how* they may feel in the telling.[11]

Language plays an important role in every encounter, but so does life experience. While my ability to speak Spanish often shapes the kinds of relationships and conversations I have with parents in the study, my experience and identity as a mother is the most profound point of connection. Upon first meeting me, many parents are kind and gracious, welcoming me to the meeting, the group, or the conversation. But at first glance, I am, in some ways, an obvious outsider. I am often introduced as a Harvard researcher or Harvard graduate student. I am an unfamiliar Asian American woman who is dressed more formally and who usually carries a laptop briefcase. But for many of these mothers, the most enthusiastic response and welcome comes at the acknowledgment that I, too, am a mother. Conversations immediately move toward the details—How many children do I have? How old is my daughter? Who is she with while I am working in Chicago? Do I have any pictures? What is her name? Over the course of my study, I uncover the profoundly important role that children and families play for these parents. Their participation in school is motivated by a desire to support their children. These parents value education, because they hope for better lives for their children. They become leaders in schools, because they want to create schools where their children will be nurtured, respected, and well educated. As they come to know me, I become a mother in their eyes, and the conversations we have often become punctuated with phrases like, "Well, you know, because you have kids," or "How would you feel if your child . . . ?"

Rather than viewing my questions and interests as pure research queries, they also begin to view my research in connection to my experience as a parent, as a mother. This is a question posed to me by *Shauna*, a Funston parent mentor: "Isn't that why you're here? I guess this means something to you, right? I mean, you understand as a parent that we have to be involved in schools for our children. We have a responsibility, and we need to make schools the kind of places where we can be a part of what's going on."

As a parent researching a community that values children and views families as central to community experience, I believe that my questions hold different meanings to the parents I come to know, and this can influence the relationships we maintain. Over time, interactions become the basis for an evolving relationship between researcher and participants, as can be seen in the final entry to my field notes, written on my last day at Funston Elementary School, where I spent extensive time over the two years of the project:

As I parked the car and prepared to walk across the street to the school, I felt a giddy excitement—to see parents I haven't seen in quite some time. While some are expecting to see me tomorrow, I wanted to drop in at this playground dedication, because I knew they would all be there. I remember just two years ago, I would be somewhat terrified to enter such a scene—nervous about speaking Spanish, walking into a room full of parents who weren't expecting me. I remember standing outside the Parent Mentor office door during one of those first visits, hearing all the noise, conversation, and laughter coming from the room. I paused outside the door. I wanted to go in, but what would I say? What language would I say it in? Would I ruin the moment and get everyone serious? They were strangers to me then. I remember standing outside that door—maybe for a couple minutes but it felt like an eternity—cautious to enter, practically forcing myself to go in. But here I am, two years later. I don't worry about the language. They are no longer strangers but people I feel deeply connected to and care about. And when they saw me today, walking across the street to the playground where they were all gathered, I saw that Stella was the first to spot me. And when she saw I was pregnant (this was the first time they knew), she waved her arms in the air, ran to the fence, motioning for a big embrace. She called to the others around her, and I was suddenly surrounded by a crowd of mothers—excited to see me, wild about the pregnant belly, glad to see that I had returned. What a journey it has been.

METHODOLOGY: AT THE CROSSROADS OF INTENTION AND REALITY

The interaction between the worlds of home and school is complex, dynamic, and even contradictory. Values, cultural beliefs, and attitudes shape these messy worlds, and the great challenge in understanding parent experiences in schools rests upon navigating the complex culture of schools and families. To tap into this complex world, I wanted to design a methodological study that would allow me to gain deep insight and understanding into these challenges. How do parents navigate their experiences and interactions in school, and how were these parents shaped by their personal and familial stories? And how does a community organization like LSNA mediate the complex relationship between families and schools? In particular, I wanted to understand how one program, the Parent Mentor program, supports the school-based involvement and leadership development of parents. Within that program, I wanted to understand the experiences of parents who were new to the program and school as well as those parents who had developed a sense of purpose and leadership over years of participation. But because this program is only one central piece of the larger vision and activities of LSNA, I also wanted to see how the other myriad projects and campaigns interacted with the Parent Mentor program. And to understand how the varied contexts of schools might shape how these interactions and activities evolved at each site, I chose to explore various school sites. I would balance this breadth with the depth I also hoped to achieve in getting to know new and returning parent mentors at one chosen school site.

Consequently, there are multiple units of analysis in this study—LSNA, its Parent Mentor program, a school-based cohort of parent mentors, and a group of newly involved parent mentors (figure A-1). These nested layers of analysis stem from the ecological nature of educational issues. Schools are embedded within local contexts—families; institutions; neighborhoods; and broader social, political, and economic forces—that inevitably shape the interactions that occur within schools and classrooms. Through this study, I wanted to explore the interactions between multiple spheres of influence—families, schools, and communities—and examine how those interactions can shape our understanding of parent engagement.

In the original design of the study, I used an embedded case-study approach, with the multiple units of analysis being LSNA's education organizing, the Parent Mentor program, the program as it was experi-

FIGURE A-1

The nested layers of analysis of this ethnography

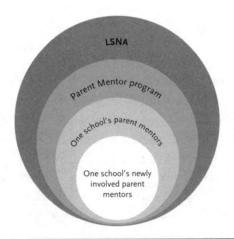

enced within one school, and the experiences of four newly involved parent mentors within the school. Case study allows for the observation and analysis of a single unit or bounded system such as LSNA.[12] In case study, understanding a group or individual's process within an examined context is critical to understanding the unit or system.[13] James Sanders agrees: "Case studies help us to understand processes of events, projects, and programs and to discover context characteristics that will shed light on an issue or object."[14]

My intentions to conduct research in this way—through an embedded case-study design over one year of study—began to change as I entered the field and began preliminary rounds of data collection. Qualitative research is not a linear approach to answering research questions; rather, it can be described as a circular approach or an emergent design.[15] The process begins with an established focus—a set of research questions and methods that are analyzed, interpreted, and revised as data is collected and a developing analysis emerges. This, in turn, directs further data collection, and the research design emerges through this process. As I entered the field to conduct this case study of LSNA and its Parent Mentor program, it became clear to me how central the process of change would be as parents participated in the program, but I also understood that my abilities to capture the process in all its complexity would not be met by a traditional case-study approach. Through conversations with LSNA organizers and parent leaders, I realized that my study could develop a richer representation of the program if I would analyze one school site with more depth and intensity, capturing more of the real-life complexity for the study. As a result, my research design shifted from an embedded case study to an ethnography.

Distinctions between a case study and an ethnography are often unclear and sometimes contradictory. R. K. Yin argues that while there are common methods and purposes between the two methodologies, ethnographies usually require longer periods in the field, emphasizing detailed field data that results from sustained observations of the participants.[16] Although case studies can certainly use ethnographic practices, the methodology does not require participant-observer data and can be accomplished without it.

With an opportunity to spend more time in the field, I planned to redesign my study as a multiyear ethnography, but I wanted to maintain the study's embedded units of analysis.[17] Because these multiple units could prove useful in an in-depth ethnographic study, I explored how I could conduct an ethnography with multiple units of analysis—units that were embedded or nested layers.

While the tradition of ethnography has much to offer toward a rich, complex, diverse representation of educational settings, I sought to achieve greater depth and intimacy within multiple settings that would capture the tensions, nuances, and rich character emerging from a close contextual study.[18] In choosing a unit of analysis, be it the school, community organization, classroom, or neighborhood, we can miss the details that are specific to an embedded sphere of experience. For example, in an effort to understand a school, our attention to a particular classroom may be focused on its traits or characteristics seen in light of the broader school context. As a result, the details of the classroom are examined and analyzed in support of a school study, and they may not stand alone to paint a deep, layered portrait of the classroom itself—its interactions, the relationships, the visual and aesthetic representation. Moreover, the representation of the classroom may be skewed toward the larger goals of understanding the school.

I wanted to create an ethnography that would richly and accurately portray the multiple foci of the study. By doing so, I could understand how each analytic unit (a school, newly involved parents, the Parent Mentor program) could be shaped by the multiple spheres of influence I was studying and by forces beyond the realm of my study. Consequently, the ethnography would serve multiple analytic purposes.

Every ethnography seeks to identify boundaries to the study, in essence, determining a study's focus—what the study has the authority to speak on and what it does not. In choosing the boundaries of study, ethnographers—through theoretical disposition and problem selection—will often decide between a micro- or macrolevel study.[19] A microlevel study is a close-up view of a small social unit or an identifiable activity within the social unit and will, for example, focus on a classroom or a series of interactions or relationships within the classroom. A macrolevel study, however, focuses on the large picture; its focus can range from a single school to worldwide systems. Either type of study involves detailed description and careful attention to the interactions, events, and relationships within a setting. Although a researcher who conducts either a micro-or macrolevel study can connect the findings of the study to related systems or the next larger system that affects it, often the focus of the study is singular.

Using this description of macro- and microlevel studies within ethnography, my study seeks to examine both the broad picture of a community organization and the smaller related units embedded within it. As I learned more about LSNA's work and the Parent Mentor program, I also understood the intense relational aspects of LSNA's organizing strategies and its work with parents in schools. To explore the smaller units of newly involved parent mentors and parent mentor cohorts and understand the change that LSNA seeks to nurture among parents and within the school, my relationship to the smaller sites would be critical. I wanted to design a methodology that would bring attention to the relationships within the field as well as my evolving relationship with participants in the study. For this reason, I incorporated the methodology of portraiture into the ethnography. I call this hybrid methodology a *layered ethnography.*

Portraiture, like ethnography, seeks to illuminate the rich, complex, yet also subtle dimensions of a subject that is embedded within a particular context. Established by Sara Lawrence-Lightfoot and Jessica Hoffman Davis as a methodology that employs the tools of qualitative research traditions, portraiture seeks to capture the complexity of human experience and organizational life through a careful blending of the art and science of investigation and through exploration of the depth, dynamics, interactions, and evolutions that shape that experience.[20]

While portraiture is influenced by the traditions of ethnography—the emphasis on "thick description," contextual forces, and phenomenological inquiry—what makes the methodology unique is the intentional presence and visibility of the person of the researcher.[21] Unlike ethnography, where researchers assume a more subtle and distant voice, the identity and voice of the portraitist is present in the inquiry, because of the acknowledgment that the research experience itself is a dynamic, interactive relationship between researcher and participant(s). Lawrence-Lightfoot and Davis elaborate: "The drawing of the portrait is placed in social and cultural context and shaped through a dialogue between the portraitist and subject, each one negotiating the discourse and shaping the evolving image. The relationship between the two is rich with meaning and resonance and becomes the arena for navigating the empirical, aesthetic, and ethical dimensions of authentic and compelling narrative."[22]

Given LSNA's relational approach to engaging parents, I felt I would have a more accurate and insightful perspective of the Parent Mentor program and parents' experiences as part of the program if I could immerse myself in one school environment. Portraiture would provide me with methodological strategies to examine the program in depth while allowing me to articulate and define my own relational approach to the research site.

As a result, I have developed a methodology that joins the two forms of ethnography and portraiture, acknowledging the distinctions across the nested layers of analysis and providing methodological strategies that allow for the appropriate levels of depth, intimacy, and examination at each layer of analysis (figure A-2). To analyze the macrosystem of LSNA's education work as well as the Parent Mentor program broadly across various schools, I use an ethnographic approach. To analyze the microsystem of the program as it is experienced within the Funston Elementary School, I use portraiture. Through this hybrid approach, or layered ethnography, the conceptual design—a belief in the ecology of education—mirrors the methodological design, bringing synchrony to the framing and process of research. These mirroring approaches are also reflected in the research design, which emphasizes the layered units of analysis within the organization under study.

Armed with the tools of these ethnographic methodologies, I embarked on four years of active interviews and conversations with myriad individuals in the field—from parents to teachers, school administrators, students, organizers, community activists, and elected officials. I attended training sessions and community rallies, visited classrooms, met children and family members, and sat in meetings between orga-

FIGURE A-2

The hybrid approach of layered ethnography

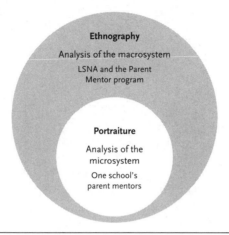

nizers, new parents, and parent leaders. As a relative newcomer to Chicago, I found a sense of place and familiarity in the Northwest Side and beyond as each new school, home, community center, and public space I visited became punctuated with vivid research experiences in the field. The Funston study became a microcosm of the broader community study, and I began to identify the distinct learning and discovery that occurred within the realm of one school and the broader community. Concepts such as parents as bridges or teacher-parent trust—concepts that resonated across schools and parent groups in the broader community—could be understood with greater clarity within the Funston experience. At the same time, messages and findings that emerged in Funston would often echo out in the broader community. The intimacy of portraiture would complement the careful community study of ethnography. With these dual interests in ethnography and portraiture as well as a clear examination of the multiple layers of field analysis, this study became an honest reflection into both the potential limits and possibilities of research. As field experiences evolve, research questions change, and the tools and methodologies we use must become subject to the very same process of inquiry that guides everything else.

NOTES

Introduction

1. Through the course of ethnographic data collection, conversations and interactions range from the informal (casual conversations, chance encounters, unplanned observations, and informal meetings) to the formal (scheduled interviews with participants granting consent for participation). The names of participants who have agreed to be part of the study and who have chosen to use their real names will appear in regular font. Names of participants who have requested the use of pseudonyms or who were part of more informal conversations will first appear in italics. Subsequent referrals to the participants in the book will appear in regular font.

2. While practices vary, I have chosen to represent racial identifications such as black, brown, and white in lowercase, reserving capitalization for ethnic or national identities such as Asian American, African American, and Latino.

3. Mark R. Warren, "Community Organizing for Education Reform," in *Public Engagement for Public Education*, ed. John Rogers and Marion Orr (Palo Alto: Stanford University Press, 2010).

4. For another single-case account of a community organizing effort to improve education, see Celina Su, *Streetwise for Book Smarts: Grassroots Organizing and Education Reform in the Bronx* (Ithaca: Cornell University Press, 2009).

5. LSNA organizers and parent leaders have presented at national conferences sponsored by organizations such as the American Educational Research Association, the Annenberg Institute for School Reform, and the National Community Organizing and School Reform Project. Arne Duncan, then CEO of the Chicago Public Schools, cited LSNA's community learning center at Monroe Elementary School as a citywide model when he launched an initiative to expand community schools in Chicago. Prior to this study, LSNA has been featured as a successful case in the following reports and articles: Suzanne Blanc et al., "Case Study: Logan Square Neighborhood Association," Strong Neighborhoods, Strong Schools, The Indicators Project on Education Organizing, Cross City Campaign for Urban School Reform, Chicago, 2002; Suzanne Blanc, Matthew Goldwasser, and Joanna Brown, "From the Ground Up: The Logan Square Neighborhood Association's Approach to Building Community Capacity, report, Research for Action, Philadelphia, 2003; Eva Gold, Elaine Simon, and Chris Brown, "Successful Community Organizing for School Reform," report, Cross City Campaign for Urban School Reform, Chicago, 2002; Mark R. Warren, "Communities and Schools: A New View of Urban Education Reform," *Harvard*

Educational Review 75, no. 2 (2005); Mark R. Warren, Soo Hong, Carolyn Rubin, and Phitsamay Uy, "Beyond the Bake Sale: A Community Approach to Parent Engagement in Schools," *Teachers College Record* 111, no. 9 (2009).

Chapter 1

1. Henry T. Trueba and Concha Delgado-Gaitan, eds., *School and Society: Learning Content through Culture* (New York: Praeger, 1988); Annette Lareau and Erin McNamara Horvat, "Moments of Social Inclusion and Exclusion: Race, Class, and Cultural Capital in Family-School Relationships," *Sociology of Education* 72, no. 1 (1999); Sara Lawrence-Lightfoot, *Worlds Apart: Relationships Between Families and Schools* (New York: Basic Books, 1978); Guadalupe Valdés, *Con Respeto: Bridging the Distances Between Culturally Diverse Families and Schools; An Ethnographic Portrait* (New York: Teachers College Press, 1996); Angela Valenzuela, *Subtractive Schooling: U.S.-Mexican Youth and the Politics of Caring* (Albany: State University of New York Press, 1999).

2. Lawrence-Lightfoot, *Worlds Apart*.

3. Ibid., 20.

4. Willard Waller, in a classic study, presents the school as a "social organism" immersed in the contexts of communities and broader social forces. Waller proposes that teachers and parents are more likely to view each other as "natural enemies," because of their distinct interests, expectations, and stances toward children. See Willard Waller, *The Sociology of Teaching* (New York: John Wiley & Sons, 1932).

5. For a rich discussion of the social and political forces that shape the relationships between parents and teachers, see Debra Miretzky, "The Comunication Requirements of Democratic Schools: Parent-Teacher Perspectives on Their Relationships," *Teachers College Record* 106, no. 4 (2004).

6. Vivian Gunn Morris and Satomi Izumi Taylor, "Alleviating Barriers to Family Involvement in Education: The Role of Teacher Education," *Teaching and Teacher Education* 14, no. 2 (1998).

7. Waller, *The Sociology of Teaching*, 59.

8. Sara Lawrence-Lightfoot, *The Essential Conversation: What Parents and Teachers Can Learn from Each Other* (New York: Random House, 2003), 8.

9. Ibid.

10. Herbert Gans, *The Urban Villagers: Group and Class in the Life of Italian-Americans* (New York: Free Press, 1962).

11. Valenzuela, *Subtractive Schooling*.

12. Joyce L. Epstein, *School, Family, and Community Partnerships: Preparing Educators and Improving Schools* (Boulder, CO: Westview Press, 2001).

13. For a discussion of these barriers to broad parent participation, see Michelle Fine, "[Ap]parent Involvement: Reflections on Parents, Power, and Urban Public Schools," *Teachers College Record* 94, no. 4 (1993).

14. James Comer, *School Power: Implications of an Intervention Project* (New York: Free Press, 1980); Concha Delgado-Gaitan, "Involving Parents in the Schools: A Process of Empowerment," *American Journal of Education* 100, no. 1 (1991); Sara Lawrence-Lightfoot, "Toward Conflict and Resolution: Relationships Between Families and Schools," *Theory into Practice* 20, no. 2 (1981).

15. Mark R. Warren et al., "Beyond the Bake Sale: A Community-Based Relational Approach to Parent Engagement in Schools," *Teachers College Record* 111, no. 9 (2009); Angela Calabrese Barton et al., "Ecologies of Parental Engagement in Urban Education," *Educational Researcher* 3, no. 4 (2004).

16. For studies that discuss a range of parent involvement practices and activities, see Kathleen V. Hoover-Dempsey and Howard M. Sandler, "Why Do Parents Become Involved in Their Children's Education?" *Review of Educational Research* 67, no. 1 (1997); Joyce L. Epstein, "Parents' Reactions to Teacher Practices of Parent Involvement," *Elementary School Journal* 86, no. 3 (1986); Joyce L. Epstein, "Effects on Student Achievement of Teachers' Practices of Parent Involvement," *Advances in Reading/Language Research* 5 (1991); Joyce L. Epstein, "School/Family/Community Partnerships: Caring for the Children We Share," *Phi Delta Kappan* 76, no. 9 (1995); Joyce L. Epstein, "Building Bridges of Home, School, and Community: The Importance of Design," *Journal of Education for Students Placed at Risk* 6, no. 1–2 (2001); Joyce L. Epstein and Susan L. Dauber, "School Programs and Teacher Practices of Parent Involvement in Inner-City Elementary and Middle Schools," *Elementary School Journal* 91, no. 3 (1991).

17. Warren et al., "Beyond the Bake Sale."

18. Annette Lareau, *Home Advantage: Social Class and Parental Intervention in Elementary Education* (New York: Falmer, 1989).

19. For a fuller discussion of how parent education programs can often view families from a deficit viewpoint, see Valdés, *Con Respeto.*

20. Jeannie Oakes and Martin Lipton, "Struggling for Educational Equity in Diverse Communities: School Reform As Social Movement," *Journal of Educational Change* 3, no. 3–4 (2002); Jeannie Oakes et al., *Becoming Good American Schools: The Struggle for Civic Virtue in Education Reform* (San Francisco: Jossey-Bass, 2000); Mark R. Warren, "Communities and Schools: A New View of Urban Education Reform," *Harvard Educational Review* 75, no. 2 (2005); Warren et al., "Beyond the Bake Sale."

21. Fine, "[Ap]parent Involvement."

22. For recently published and forthcoming cross-case examinations of education organizing efforts that involve parents, see Kavitha Mediratta, Seema Shah, and

Sara McAlister, *Community Organizing for Stronger Schools: Stategies and Successes* (Cambridge, MA: Harvard Education Press, 2009); Jeannie Oakes, John Rogers, and Martin Lipton, *Learning Power: Organizing for Education and Justice* (New York: Teachers College Press, 2006); Mark R. Warren, Karen L. Mapp, and the Community Organizing and School Reform Project, *A Match on Dry Grass: Community Organizing As a Catalyst for School Reform* (New York: Oxford University Press, 2011).

23. Anne T. Henderson et al., *Beyond the Bake Sale: The Essential Guide to Family-School Partnerships* (New York: New Press, 2007); Anne T. Henderson and Karen L. Mapp, "A New Wave of Evidence: The Impact of School, Family, and Community Connections on Student Achievement," report, National Center for Family and Community Connections with Schools, Austin, 2002.

24. Dennis Shirley, *Community Organizing for Urban School Reform* (Austin: University of Texas Press, 1997).

25. Two years after the publication of Shirley's *Community Organizing for Urban School Reform*, Marion Orr produced a compelling account of a long and contentious political struggle to develop civic capacity and improve schools in Maryland. For a detailed analysis, see Marion Orr, *Black Social Capital: The Politics of School Reform in Baltimore, 1986–1998* (Lawrence: University Press of Kansas, 1999).

26. M. Elena Lopez, "Transforming Schools Through Community Organizing: A Research Review," report, Harvard Family Research Project, Cambridge, MA, 2003; Mark R. Warren, "Community Organizing for Education Reform," in *Public Engagement for Public Education*, ed. John Rogers and Marion Orr (Palo Alto: Stanford University Press, 2010).

27. For more discussion of the different types of power and how they are strategically used in community organizing efforts, see Ernie Cortes, "Reweaving the Fabric: The Iron Rule and the IAF Strategy for Power and Politics," in *Interwoven Destinies: Cities and the Nation*, ed. Henry Cisneros (New York: Norton, 1993); Bernard Loomer, "Two Conceptions of Power," *Process Studies* 6, no. 1 (1976).

28. Eva Gold, Elaine Simon, and Chris Brown, "Successful Community Organizing for School Reform," report, Cross City Campaign for Urban School Reform, Chicago, 2002.

29. For more extensive discussion of this process, see Mark R. Warren, *Dry Bones Rattling: Community Building to Revitalize American Democracy* (Princeton, NJ: Princeton University Press, 2001).

30. Data collected from this study of LSNA was also included in the Community Organizing and School Reform Project, led by Mark Warren and Karen Mapp. Warren and Mapp, *A Match on Dry Grass*, explores the results of six community organizing groups working on school reform issues: LSNA in Chicago; Southern Echo in the Mississippi Delta; OneLA in Los Angeles; People Acting in Community Together (PACT) in San Jose; Northwest Bronx Community and Clergy Coalition

in New York City, and Padres y Jovenes Unidos in Denver. One year of the LSNA study was funded by the Community Organizing and School Reform Project. I am grateful to Mark Warren, Karen Mapp, and the research team for the opportunity to collaborate on this important study.

31. Warren, Mapp, and the Community Organizing and School Reform Project, *A Match on Dry Grass*.

32. For a more detailed discussion of the multiple spheres of experience (microsystem, mesosystem, exosystem, macrosystem, and chronosystem), see Urie Bronfenbrenner, *Two Worlds of Childhood: U.S. and U.S.S.R.* (New York: Russell Sage Foundation, 1970); Urie Bronfenbrenner, *The Ecology of Human Development: Experiments by Nature and Design* (Cambridge, MA: Harvard University Press, 1979); Urie Bronfenbrenner, "Ecology of the Family As a Context for Human Development: Research Perspectives," *Developmental Psychology* 22, no. 6 (1986).

33. Lawrence Cremin, *Public Education* (New York: Basic Books, 1976).

34. Elements of this model comparison are informed by an earlier research collaboration: Warren et al., "Beyond the Bake Sale."

35. Rudy Crew, *Only Connect: The Way to Save Our Schools* (New York: Farrar, Straus and Giroux, 2007).

36. Arne Duncan was interviewed for this study in April 2008 while he served as the CEO of the Chicago Public Schools. In that role, he was familiar with LSNA's work in Logan Square schools.

37. Warren, Mapp, and the Community Organizing and School Reform Project, *A Match on Dry Grass*.

38. Henderson et al., *Beyond the Bake Sale*; Warren, Mapp, and The Community Organizing and School Reform Project, *A Match on Dry Grass*; Henderson and Mapp, "A New Wave of Evidence."

39. Seth Kreisberg, *Transforming Power: Domination, Empowerment, and Education* (Albany: State University of New York Press, 1992); Bernard Loomer, "Two Conceptions of Power," *Criterion* 15, no. 1 (1976); Warren, *Dry Bones Rattling*.

Chapter 2

1. Felix M. Padilla, "The Quest for Community: Puerto Ricans in Chicago," in *In the Barrios: Latinos and the Underclass Debate*, ed. Joan Moore and Raquel Pinderhughes (New York: Russell Sage Foundation, 1993).

2. Suzanne Blanc, Matthew Goldwasser, and Joanna Brown, "From the Ground Up: The Logan Square Neighborhood Association's Approach to Building Community Capacity," report, Research for Action, Philadelphia, 2003.

3. Local Initiatives Support Corporation, "Logan Square: A Place to Stay, a Place to Grow," report, Local Initiatives Support Corporation, Chicago, May 2005.

4. John McCarron, "Economic Forces Collide in Logan Square," *New Communities Program*, May 11, 2004.

5. Suzanne Blanc et al., "Case Study: Logan Square Neighborhood Association," report, Strong Neighborhoods, Strong Schools, the Indicators Project on Education Organizing, Cross City Campaign for Urban School Reform, Chicago, 2002.

6. Secretary Bennett's comments were made at an education forum in Washington, DC, and in reference to the release of high school students' scores on the American College Test. Half of Chicago's sixty-four high schools were ranked in the bottom 1 percent of schools that gave the test. Secretary Bennett called Chicago public schools among the worst in the nation and urged parents to send their children to private schools. "Schools in Chicago Are Called the Worst by Education Chief," *New York Times*, November 8, 1987.

7. The momentum for this policy change is disputed among those who have studied Chicago school reform—between those who credit business and civic leaders for the policy change and those who credit a grassroots movement of parent and community activists. For more discussion on this topic, see Julia Wrigley, "Chicago School Reform: Business Control or Open Democracy?" *Teachers College Record* 99, no. 1 (1997); Michael B. Katz, Michelle Fine, and Elaine Simon, "Poking Around: Outsiders View Chicago School Reform," *Teachers College Record* 99, no. 1 (1997); Dorothy Shipps, "The Invisible Hand: Big Business and Chicago School Reform," *Teachers College Record* 99, no. 1 (1997).

8. Donald R. Moore, "Changing the Ground Rules," *Shelterforce of the National Housing Institute* (July–August 2001).

9. In an effort to institutionalize parent and community involvement, each LSC includes the school principal and two teacher representatives as well as six parents and two community members who are elected by adults living in the school attendance area. High school LSCs also consist of a student representative.

10. Details of the 1995 Holistic Plan are based on a press release for LSNA's 32nd Annual Congress, May 1994, and are found in Blanc, Goldwasser, and Brown, "From the Ground Up."

Chapter 3
1. As a participant and an observer during the 2006–2007 school year, I observed the development of one group of parent mentors at Funston Elementary School. For the two years that followed, I periodically interviewed participants and observed parent and school interactions at the school, still remaining connected to parents and parent leaders but in a more limited fashion. Parents who were formally interviewed for this study are identified by their real names. Parents whose words are quoted from training sessions, informal conversations, and other school events are identified by pseudonyms. While these parents understood my role as researcher in the setting, I did not have individual conversations with them about the research

study guidelines or informed consent. Unless they were formally interviewed, I also use pseudonyms for the school staff members I met and interacted with in this study. The teachers who opened their classrooms to me for observations of parent mentors are given pseudonyms as well, despite being formally interviewed and taken through the research guidelines, in an attempt to present the complexity of their classrooms without passing public judgment on their classroom practices. (As I explained in the introduction, all pseudonyms are indicated by italics the first time they are used and appear in regular typeface thereafter.)

2. While I followed four new parent mentors during the 2006–2007 year, I present the experiences of two parents (Graciela and Isabel) in this chapter to offer more depth in their experiences. The data from all four participants, however, is used in other chapters. I use pseudonyms for the two mothers I present in this study, in an effort to encourage their willingness to reflect openly on their experience as parent mentors and to keep their comments about the school, the classroom within which they work, and their relationships with parents and teachers confidential.

Chapter 4
1. Mark R. Warren et al., "Beyond the Bake Sale: A Community-Based Relational Approach to Parent Engagement in Schools," *Teachers College Record* 111, no. 9 (2009).

2. Karen L. Mapp and Soo Hong, "Debunking the Myth of the Hard-to-Reach Parent," in *The Handbook on School-Family Partnerships for Promoting Student Competence*, ed. Sandra L. Christenson and Amy L. Reschly (New York: Routledge, 2010).

Chapter 5
1. Annette Lareau, *Home Advantage: Social Class and Parental Intervention in Elementary Education* (New York: Falmer, 1989); Karen L. Mapp and Soo Hong, "Debunking the Myth of the Hard-to-Reach Parent," in *The Handbook of School-Family Partnerships*, ed. Sandra L. Christenson and Amy L. Reschly (New York: Routledge, 2010); Mark R. Warren et al., "Beyond the Bake Sale: A Community-Based Relational Approach to Parent Engagement in Schools," *Teachers College Record* 111, no. 9 (2009); Mark R. Warren, "Communities and Schools: A New View of Urban Education Reform," *Harvard Educational Review* 75, no. 2 (2005).

2. Mapp and Hong, "Debunking the Myth of the Hard-to-Reach Parent"; Warren, "Communities and Schools"; Warren et al., "Beyond the Bake Sale."

3. Concha Delgado-Gaitan, *The Power of Community: Mobilizing for Family and Schooling* (Lanham, MD: Rowman & Littlefield, 2001).

Conclusion
1. Sara Lawrence-Lightfoot, *Worlds Apart: Relationships Between Families and Schools* (New York: Basic Books, 1978), 203.

2. Ibid., 204.

3. Barton et al., "Ecologies of Parental Engagement in Urban Education." While the currently presented framework shares the ecological concerns and common terminology with Barton et al.'s concept of the ecologies of parent engagement, all facets of the current framework are derived from the current study.

4. Barton et al., "Ecologies of Parental Engagement in Urban Education," 3.

5. John B. Diamond and Kimberley Gomez, "African American Parents' Educational Orientations: The Importance of Social Class and Parents' Perceptions of Schools," *Education and Urban Society* 36, no. 4 (2004).

6. Karen L. Mapp, "Having Their Say: Parents Describe Why and How They Are Engaged in Their Children's Learning," *School Community Journal* 13, no. 1 (2003).

7. Lawrence-Lightfoot, *Worlds Apart*, 201.

8. Barton et al., "Ecologies of Parental Engagement in Urban Education," 7.

9. Michelle Fine, "[Ap]parent Involvement: Reflections on Parents, Power, and Urban Public Schools," *Teachers College Record* 94, no. 4 (1993).

10. Rudy Crew, *Only Connect: The Way to Save Our Schools* (New York: Farrar, Straus and Giroux, 2007), 155.

11. Anthony Bryk and Barbara Schneider, *Trust in Schools* (New York: Russell Sage Foundation Press, 2002).

12. See also Elizabeth Graue, "Theorizing and Describing Preservice Teachers' Images of Families and Schooling," *Teachers College Record* 107, no. 1 (2005).

13. Bryk and Schneider, *Trust in Schools*.

14. Xavier de Souza Briggs, "Bridging Networks, Social Capital, and Racial Segregation in America" (John F. Kennedy School of Government, Faculty Research Working Papers Series, Harvard University, Cambridge, MA, 2002); Robert D. Putnam, "*E Pluribus Unum*: Diversity and Community in the Twenty-First Century, the 2006 Johan Skytte Prize Lecture," *Scandinavian Political Studies* 30, no. 2 (2007).

15. For a more extensive discussion of the need for and role of cultural brokers, particularly in immigrant school communities, see Concha Delgado-Gaitan, *The Power of Community: Mobilizing for Family and Schooling* (Lanham, MD: Rowman & Littlefield, 2001).

16. John Dewey, *The Public and Its Problems* (New York: Holt, 1927).

17. For more discussion on the creation of a public to transform civic participation, see Archon Fung, "Creating Deliberative Publics: Governance After Devolution and Democratic Centralism," *The Good Society* 11, no. 1 (2002), 155.

18. Mark R. Warren et al., "Beyond the Bake Sale: A Community-Based Relational Approach to Parent Engagement in Schools," *Teachers College Record* 111, no. 9 (2009).

19. Logan Square Neighborhood Association, "A Community-Centered, Holistic Approach to Immigrant Families in Public Schools" (testimony presented at the Illinois New Americans Policy Council Meeting, Chicago, April 27, 2006).

20. According to annual school data on the Illinois Standards Achievement Test, reading and mathematics scores in third, fourth, fifth, and sixth grades increased between the 2003–2004 and 2009–2010 school years. During that period, the percentage of students meeting or exceeding state standards increased in all areas: from 32.1 to 42.4 percent in third-grade reading; from 59 to 62.4 percent in third-grade mathematics; from 37 to 46.2 percent in fifth-grade reading; and from 45.5 to 77.7 percent in fifth-grade mathematics. Data from Illinois State Board of Education, "Data Analysis and Progress Reporting," available at http://www.isbe.state.il.us/research/report_card.htm.

21. Barack Obama, "Why Organize? Problems and Promise in the Inner City," in *After Alinsky: Community Organizing in Illinois*, ed. Peg Knoepfle (Springfield: Illinois Issues, University of Illinois at Springfield, 1990).

Appendix

1. Martin Buber, *I and Thou*, 2nd ed. (New York: Scribner, 1958), 44.

2. Alfred Schutz, *The Phenomenology of the Social World*, trans. George Walsh and Fredrick Lehnert (Chicago: Northwestern University Press, 1967).

3. Michael Jackson, *Paths Toward a Clearing: Radical Empiricism and Ethnographic Inquiry* (Bloomington: Indiana University Press, 1989), 34–35.

4. Corrine Glesne, *Becoming Qualitative Researchers: An Introduction*, 2nd ed. (New York: Longman, 1999), 96–97.

5. Irving Seidman, *Interviewing As Qualitative Research*, 2nd ed. (New York: Teachers College Press, 1998).

6. Joseph A. Maxwell, *Qualitative Research Design: An Interactive Approach*, Applied Social Research Method Series (Thousand Oaks, CA: Sage, 1996), 66.

7. Glesne, *Becoming Qualitative Researchers*.

8. Jean M. Bartunek and Meryl Reis Louis, *Insider/Outsider Team Research*, Qualitative Research Methods Series (Thousand Oaks, CA: Sage, 1996).

9. Michéle Foster, "The Power to Know One Thing Is Never the Power to Know All Things: Methodological Notes on Two Studies of Black American Teachers," in *Power and Method: Political Activism and Educational Research*, ed. Andrew Gitlin (New York: Routledge, 1994).

10. William Henry Schubert, "Students As Action Researchers: Historical Precedent and Contradiction," *Curriculum and Teaching* 10, no. 2 (1995), cited in Stephen L. Payne, "Challenges for Research Ethics and Moral Knowledge Construction in the Applied Social Sciences," *Journal of Business Ethics* 26, no. 4 (2000), 10.

11. Sara Lawrence-Lightfoot and Jessica Hoffmann Davis, *The Art and Science of Portraiture* (San Francisco: Jossey-Bass, 1997).

12. R. K. Yin, *Case Study Research: Design and Methods*, 3rd ed. Anonymous (Thousand Oaks: Sage Publications, 2003); Louis M. Smith, "An Evolving Logic of Participant Observation, Educational Ethnography, and Other Case Studies," *Review of Research in Education* 6 (1978).

13. Sharan B. Merriam, *Qualitative Research and Case Study Applications in Education*, 2nd rev. ed. A Joint Publication in the Jossey-Bass Education Series and the Jossey-Bass Higher Education Series (San Francisco: Jossey-Bass, 1998); James R. Sanders, "Case Study Methodology: A Critique," in *Case Study Methodology in Educational Evaluation*, ed. W. W. Welsh (Minneapolis: Minnesota Research and Evaluation Center, 1981).

14. Sanders, "Case Study Methodology: A Critique," 44.

15. Richard B. Addison, "A Grounded Hermeneutic Editing Approach," in *Doing Qualitative Research*, ed. Benjamin F. Crabtree and William Lloyd Miller (New York: Sage, 1999); Yvonna S. Lincoln and Egon G. Guba, *Naturalistic Inquiry* (Beverly Hills, CA: Sage, 1985).

16. Yin, *Case Study Research: Design and Methods*.

17. This decision to alter the methodology was possible largely through the research grants and projects that allowed me to deepen and extend the study with more frequent data-collection trips that spanned two years of study in Chicago. More extensive time in the field was made possible through the various grants mentioned in the acknowledgments section of this book.

18. Margaret Diane LeCompte and Judith Preissle, *Ethnography and Qualitative Design in Educational Research*, 2nd ed. (San Diego: Academic Press, 1993).

19. David M. Fetterman, *Ethnography: Step by Step*, 2nd ed. (Thousand Oaks, CA: Sage Publications, 1998).

20. Lawrence-Lightfoot and Davis, *The Art and Science of Portraiture*.

21. Clifford Geertz, *The Interpretation of Cultures* (New York: Basic Books, 1973).

22. Lawrence-Lightfoot and Davis, *The Art and Science of Portraiture*, xv.

ABOUT THE AUTHOR

Soo Hong is assistant professor of education at Wellesley College. She studies the role of community organizing in school reform and the relationships between families, schools, and communities more broadly. A former elementary and middle school teacher, Hong is interested in the ways that research can be applied to the everyday questions and dilemmas of schools and communities.

INDEX

tradition of limited parent engagement, *continued*
  basis of conflict between teachers and
    parents, 13–14
  challenge of parent engagement, 29
  change in from past to present, 11–12
  changing the uneven power distribution
    between parents and schools, 20–21
  components of effective parent involvement,
    18
  core processes in building an ecological
    view, 30–31, 188–194
  dominance of white middle-class parents as
    participants, 18–19
  effective inclusion strategy elements, 20
  levels of transformation, 29–30
  new focus on relationship building, 21–22
  parents' view that schools separate students
    from their social networks, 15–16
  prevalence of adversarial or nonexistent
    relationships between parents and
    schools, 16–17, 20
  school culture's role in parent engagement,
    27
  schools seen as part of the interactions
    between all student environments,
    24–25
  traditional versus ecological model, 25–26

V

Vacco, Angela, 87
Valenzuela, Angela, 15
Valle, Miguel de, 198

W

Waller, Willard, 14
Warren, Mark, 22, 29, 202
Wolcott, Muriel, 85–86

Y

Yanun, Susan Adler, 42, 147, 152